Professionals and Careers in Computer Science and Technology

Professionals and Careers in Computer Science and Technology

Edited by

Adele Kuzmiakova

ARCLER PRESS

www.arclerpress.com

Professionals and Careers in Computer Science and Technology

Adele Kuzmiakova

Arcler Press
224 Shoreacres Road
Burlington, ON L7L 2H2
Canada
www.arclerpress.com
Email: orders@arclereducation.com

ISBN: 978-1-77407-744-3 (Hardcover)

ABOUT THE EDITOR

Adele Kuzmiakova is a computational engineer focusing on solving problems in machine learning, deep learning, and computer vision. Adele attended Cornell University in New York, United States for her undergraduate studies. She studied engineering with a focus on applied math. While at Cornell, she developed close relationships with professors, which enabled her to get involved in academic research to get hands-on experience with solving computational problems. She was also selected to be Accel Roundtable on Entrepreneurship Education (REE) Fellow at Stanford University and spent 3 months working on entrepreneurship projects to get a taste of entrepreneurship and high-growth ventures in engineering and life sciences. The program culminated in giving a presentation on the startup technology and was judged by Stanford faculty and entrepreneurship experts in Silicon Valley. After graduating from Cornell, Adele worked as a data scientist at Swiss Federal Institute of Technology in Lausanne, Switzerland where she focused on developing algorithms and graphical models to analyze chemical pathways in the atmosphere. Adele also pursued graduate studies at Stanford University in the United States where she entered as a recipient of American Association of University Women International Fellowship. The Fellowship enabled her to focus on tackling important research problems in machine learning and computer vision. Some research problems she worked on at Stanford include detecting air pollution from outdoor public webcam images. Specifically, she modified and set up a variety of pre-trained architectures, such as DehazeNet, VGG, and ResNet, on public webcam images to evaluate their ability to predict air quality based on the degree of haze on pictures. Other deep learning problems Adele worked on include investigating the promise of second-order optimizers in deep learning and using neural networks to predict sequences of data in energy consumption. Adele also places an emphasis on continual education and served as a Student Leader in PyTorch scholarship challenge organized by Udacity. Her roles as the Student Leader were helping students debug their code to train neural networks with PyTorch and providing mentorship on technical and career aspects. Her hobbies include skiing, playing tennis, cooking, and meeting new people.

TABLE OF CONTENTS

LIST OF FIGURES

LIST OF ABBREVIATIONS

AI	artificial intelligence
CS	computer science
DDR	digital depositories receipts
DSS	decision support systems
EDRMS	electronic documents and record management systems
ESS	executive support system
GDPR	general-data protection regulation
HBS	Harvard Business School
IT	information technology
KDD	knowledge discovery database
KMS	knowledge management systems
LAN	local area network
MaaS	mobility-as-service
MIS	management information system
ML	machine learning
NRC	National Research Council
SaMD	software-as-medical-device
SIGIS	Stratagems of Inclusivity: Gender and Information Society
SP	service provider
SWIFT	supporting women in it
TPS	transaction processing systems
UAS	unmanned aerial structures

PREFACE

With current digital advancements, computer science and technology are growing to become very popular career fields. The internet has opened up new frontiers of work that were unimaginable before, with more still yet to come. Unlike in the past when most work was done manually by humans, nowadays most organizations prefer digitizing their operations in order to reduce costs and improve efficiency. Moreover, computers are making it possible for people to work from wherever they are no matter the location. They have managed to break down the distance barrier and truly made the world a global village., as it's often said by experts.

In this volume, we are going to look at the socioeconomic impact of computer technology in the modern society. Over the recent few years, this field has been growing at a very fast pacest leading to phenomenal breakthroughs in areas such as business, education, retail, and health, which all rely in some form of technology in one way or another. Technologies such as Blockchain and Artificial Intelligence (AI) in particular have revolutionized the way that we conduct our day-to-day activities. Blockchain inspired the creation of cryptocurrency, which is a form of digital currency that's unregulated by the formal banking system. On the other hand, AI is bringing a human aspect to computers by making them capable of reading human mind and emotions.

The volume is divided into 10 chapters that discuss different aspects of computers science and technology professions and careers. Chapter 1 talks about new careers and professions that are being spurred by technology, Chapter 2 delves into competence in computing, Chapter 3 delves into regulation of technology, Chapter 4 explores computer knowledge supervision, Chapter 5 explores the impact of ICT in society, Chapter 6 investigates ethical standards to be maintained in computing practice, Chapter 7 delves into gender disparities in computer science as well as technology professions, Chapter 8 explores computer science and IT professional associations, Chapter 9 investigates staff matters in IT and computer science careers and Chapter 10 discusses mentoring, training, and counseling of people in IT.

Readers are taken through these topics in a comprehensive and detailed manner to, so that they can gain a clear understanding of the status of computer technology now and where it i's going in the future. For instance, with the invention of smartphones and tablets, technology has been made more portable and accessible to everyone around the world even those in remote areas. Information can be shared at the touch of a button from anywhere and it will reach others in a different location instantly. This uninterrupted flow of information has the potential to open up otherwise backward areas to development, thanks to the rapid transfer of knowledge.

Despite these benefits, authorities in the technology sector are still concerned about imposing regulations in the field, so that innovation adheres to ethical and moral codes that ensure safety of users. Without such policies, it may be difficult to put a check on the direction that technology takes and this can have harmful rather than helpful effects to society. By the end of the piece, readers should be able to understand the impact of computer science to everyday life, the opportunities that technology provides and emerging issues in the industry.

CHAPTER

1

Emerging Jobs in Computer Science and Technology

CONTENTS

1.1. INTRODUCTION

Computer science and technology has opened up many job opportunities to the students who study this subject. This has led to more students studying computer science as they are guaranteed to acquire employment after their study. Computer science (CS) and technology has more than one hundred job opportunities and more job opportunities are being discovered every day in this field. Aside from this, most jobs employers employ people who have computer skills. The following are some of the jobs that are available in the CS and technology fields.

1.2. DIGITAL MARKETING

Digital marketing is a job area that combines the use of internet and marketing. Several companies are taking up digital marketing to keep up with the digital work. It enables them to connect to a larger market. With this revolutionization, many people have been able to gain employment opportunities with several individuals engaging online marketing. This more so applies to the youth. They are given the required training and after acquiring some experience, they are able to carry out online marketing though well-established companies opt to hire individuals with some years of experience.

Digital marketing combines both aspects of technology and CS. This enables the devices to be connected to the internet. It uses technology to facilitate the marketing. Gadgets, such as phones, tablets, and computers, can be used in digital marketing. The advantages of using such is that it can be carried out at the convenience of the individual. They can work at any time and any place with no challenges (Nash, and Sofer, 2012).

1.2.1. Ways in Which Digital Marketing Is Carried Out

Search engine optimization: This entails the individual creating a higher ranking of the company's website so that when an individual uses a search engine, the company website will easily pop up. Since many companies want this, individuals who offer such services are high in demand, making it an emerging job opportunity. The individuals may choose to work on the content that is within the blog or website or work on the off-page activity of the website.Content marketing: Content marketing involves the creation of content in order to market the given brand. That is in order to create more awareness on the given brand. These types of marketers have a variety of tools at their disposal. For instance, they can use blogs to market the brand. This involves them writing articles on the given company or brand. The articles give off more information about the brand and help customers know what they are getting. They can also use infographics which is basically website but it focuses more on the visual aspect. They can also use e-books which have more of lengthy content on the given topic. The advantage of using e-books for marketing is that it gives an opportunity for feedback from the buyer.

Social media marketing: Here, individuals use available social media platforms to market the company products. Social media marketing is a good approach as several individuals use social media, making it a good employment opportunity. Examples of social media platforms include Facebook, Twitter, Instagram, Pinterest, and snapchat among others. Several companies have hired individuals with higher following in such platforms to market their products (Nash, and Sofer, 2012).

Among the ways that digital marketing has been used in creating employment is through the use of pay per click. This basically involves people being paid to view ads. The ads are most at times linked to the company's website. This includes the paid ads on social media platforms such as Facebook and Twitter. The ads may include videos, animations or even images. They increase the public engagement in the company's interactive platforms. The pay per click involves the buyer or customer being paid in order to view the ad. In relation to this is the affiliate marketing. This type of marketing is different from the pay per click in that the individual receives a commission when they promote other individuals' products. This can be demonstrated when a platform like YouTube air clips of a product such as Grammarly.

Native advertising: This is similar to affiliate marketing but the only difference is that the content is not paid for in order to be marketed. This is available in platforms such as Facebook.

Marketing automation: Marketing automation refers to the use of software that improve marketing operations by automating it. An individual may gain an employment opportunity as a developer of such software though it will require them to have much knowledge on CS. Marketing automation involves the emails where by it automatically sends information to the subscribers on the programmed time. It also includes social media posting where the automation facilitates the posting of information at a scheduled time (Nash, and Sofer, 2012).

Email marketing: This is where individuals are paid in order to communicate and interact with the consumers. As they interact, they can promote content and also inform the audience on the different events being held. It includes blog subscription newsletters which are emails sent to the consumer once they purchase or download a package.Inbound marketing: This involves attracting, delighting, and engaging buyers every step of the way. These marketers are involved at every stage of the buying process or journey. They employ various aspects of digital marketing to ensure that the process runs smoothly (Nash, and Sofer, 2012).For some individuals, they opt to specialize in the different fields of marketing in order to be at an upper hand in getting employment. For instance, some of them become content marketing specialists. They specialize in creating the content that will be used in marketing of the products. They also decide on the marketing strategy that will be incorporated during the marketing process. Others specialize in social media management. These individuals control the social media platforms of the company. They get to decide which content is worthy to be posted and which one is not.There many other fields under digital marketing that have not been mentioned. The growing use of technology in the various aspect of human life has made digital market to be an ever-growing employment opportunity even though it was recently developed (Nash and Sofer, 2012).

1.3. DRONE PILOTING

The use of drones has become the latest trend. The use of drones was developed as a way in which people are able to capture their most precious moments. Drones are among the latest advancements in technology.

Figure 1.1. Drones incorporate both computer science and technology into their structure.

Source: https://ppmag.com/news/aerial-milestone-dji-phantom-4-pro.

Drones use several elements to ensure that they run smoothly. First, they should have a camera or a video which takes a record of the events taking place. They contain also a memory card. The memory card is used in storing the recorded videos or pictures. They also use aeronautical principles to facilitate its flight (Freedman, 2011).

The use of drones has become more popular. The drone pilots are the ones who control the drones so that they can capture the events that are required. The reason for the name drone piloting and not drone control is because for one to become a drone pilot, they need to have knowledge and skills on aeronautics. As aeronautics is majorly involved in the aviation industry, it bought about the name drone piloting.

Drone piloting is among the emerging job employment opportunities in relation to technology and CS. This is because it has been incorporated into other carriers making it to be on high demand. Some of the carriers that have incorporated drones include farming. The drones used in agriculture are known as agricultural drones. They have been very useful in farming organizations.

For instance, some of these drones are used in spraying the farms, where they will spray the chemicals at the set time. They are also advantageous as they give farmers an opportunity to have an overview of the farm. They provide a view of the farmland from a higher ground. It has been useful in increasing crop production as well as monitoring crop growth. These drones are used in large farms that will use more than two or three drones. This has contributed to the demand for drone engineers (Freedman, 2011).

Drones have also been used in cinematography and photography. They have been used as an alternative for the use of helicopter in getting shots. They are actually a much easier and safer way of obtaining such shots. The biggest advantage is that it is much cheaper compared to using helicopters. Using of drones has enabled filmmakers to get higher shots such as the sky which they incorporate into their films. The drones are also used when performing stunts. It is a much safer option for the producers more so those who produce action movies. It is a very good tool when one wants to capture aerial photographs. It facilitates aerial cinematography.

Drones have also been used in sports. There are a variety of sports that are incorporating use of drones in their systems. Sports such as pro-golf and action sports require aerial views for the sports to be broadcasted because if the sport is broadcasted from the ground, not much content will be covered and it also poses a danger to the team broadcasting the sport. The drones are set to capture both live and taped footage though the live broadcast requires one to be highly skilled in order to achieve the live footage. The drones incorporated in sports like in cinematography, are slowly replacing the helicopters all for the same reasons. They are much cheaper, safer, and more convenient compared to helicopters. The footage obtained from the drones have also been used by coaches in carrying out player and team analysis. This creates the need for the drone pilots.

They have also been incorporated into the teaching sector and higher learning. Drones have been used in predetermining the areas of study before the students come to survey the area as a project among other educational aspects. Teaching has also been applied in the point of view of training students on use of drones. The extensive uses of drones in the various carriers have been a major factor contributing to the increasing demand for drone pilots (Freedman, 2011).

There are several factors that would encourage one to become a drone pilot. This includes its flexibility and independence. Many people are taking up drone piloting as an employment opportunity as it allows them to become self-employed. Being self-employed makes them to be more financially stable and allows flexibility while working this way they can work as drone pilots and do another job on the side. The other advantage of taking up drone piloting is that more and more carriers are taking up the use of drone technology. This shows the individual that more employment opportunities will open up as a result of drone technology. For instance, drone technology can be incorporated into real estate when taking pictures of the property for the purpose of marketing.

Since the use of drone technology is recent in the market, it gives individuals more time to carry out jobs involving use of drones before they become automated and get replaced.

The automation of the drones will mean that the drones will be in a position to carry out various tasks on their own. But the drone pilots can relax as there are more years before the automation is done.

The use of drone technology also enables individuals to work with the latest technology. They get to work with artificial intelligence (AI), computer vision as well as robotics. Drone technology is among the best emerging jobs in technology (Freedman, 2011).

1.4. APP DEVELOPER

App development is also among the emerging jobs brought about by CS and technology. App development involves coming up with apps that will meet the needs of the consumer. It is a job opportunity that is emerging because several people are getting to use the latest gadgets in. for example in the current day, almost everybody possesses a smartphone. This employment opportunity is more beneficial for individuals who have knowledge in CS. They need to apply them various principles of CS in order to develop the apps. Technology is involved in the aspect that the applications will be developed for use of the electrical gadgets.

The area of app development is quite large. There are various jobs that can be obtained from app development. This includes the mobile app development. In mobile app development, the individual only specializes in making mobile apps that will be used in the mobile devices such as the personal digital assistants or the mobile phones among others. In most cases, these apps are usually pre-installed in the devices so that the user does not have to undergo the installation process. This means that most of these mobile app developers have a close relationship with the manufactures. But for other applications, they are installed according to the needs of the user and are installed by themselves (Nash, and Sofer, 2012).

They develop the apps depending on the technology used in the device. For some of them, they are involved in the creative process in that depending on the need they will be required to come up with the technology that will be used. App development is not entirely restricted to the mobile phones. They can also develop applications for the other gadgets such as laptops. The applications that run in mobile phones are not the same one that run in the computers. The ones in the computers are more complex and will use up much of the phones' storage.In app development, some individuals choose to specialize in the creation of the software. This is referred to as application software development. Their work is to come up with the software that will suit the gadget in questions. Most of them have attained training in CS and they know how to apply the skills they acquired. They know the factors they should consider when they want to create a software. This includes the hardware specifications, the size of the screen as well the configuration. The configurations are useful in ensuring that the application will get a good chance for installation as it faces competition from other applications.

There are many reasons why an individual should take up jobs in the app development. For one it is flexible. Many people make their own money creating their own apps. This ensures that they work according to their own pace and can also take up other jobs to add more income. It also allows the individuals to be self-employed. It is a good business opportunity more so for the youth (Nash, and Sofer, 2012).

1.5. COMPUTER SCIENCE LECTURER

It is important for every lesson to have a teacher and therefore there is need for CS to have a lecturer. A lecturer is an individual whose main duty is to pass information and knowledge to their students in a classroom. Lecturers who teach CS are well equipped with CS skills that they can easily pass to their students in the classroom easily. These lecturers are required to have the gift of teaching such that they can pass information to students easily and they can easily interact with the students in the classrooms. Since CS is introduced fully in all major universities in the world being a major cause, the need for more lecturers has increased and the job opportunity has risen. CS is also taught in schools that are of lower level than the universities such as the elementary schools and there is still need for CS teachers who can teach the children at this level. Most CS lecturers are well paid, which is similar to the other lecturers in the teaching profession. The CS and technology lecturers are required to have a bachelor's degree in education in the sector of CS. They should aver the knowledge on how to use computers and they should be qualified in the field of teaching. Applying for a CS and technology job is very easy and can even be done online through the net. The main duty of a CS teacher is they give the students the ability to know how a computer functions, understand the hardware's and software's and give them the basic computer skills so that they can be successful in the field of computer. Just like the other lecturers, CS lecturer should follow all the lecturers' behavioral requirements such as they should not engage in any wanting relationship with their students, they should follow the appropriate dressing, they should be open to the students' suggestions and they should treat every student fairly and they should attend to all classes on time and in the appropriate dressing. Acquiring a CS and technology job when one has the necessary requirements is very easy. Aside from the normal CS lecturer, there is a special breed of CS lecturer who teach students who have special need. An example is the computer teachers who teach the disabled children. These teachers should have the skills and knowledge of using a special computer that is designed for the special kids. Their wage is normally higher than that of a normal CS lecturer (Goldberg, 2002).

The growth rate of compare science lecturers' job is currently at three to four percent and it is growing continually with the coming up of new schools and institutions that teach CS. Also, by adding CS as a core subject in most schools and institutions it has led to the increase in CS and technology lecturers' job.

1.6. SOFTWARE ENGINEERING

Software engineering are individuals who develop computer software applications that are required for the hardware to be relevant. They have the same obligations as computer programmers. These software engineers use scientific and mathematical skills to come up with these computer programs and software. Software engineering is an important part in CS and technology because it leads to the development of software that the computer needs to function. Computer software is a set of instructions that guide the computer on what to do and how to do it therefore a computer cannot operate without the software. Software engineering treats the approach to making the software as a formal process like in traditional engineering.

The origin of software engineering is analyzing the needs of the users. Software engineering work hand in hand with the computer programmers such that the computer programmers write the codes the software engineers need. They then create the software, test it, and maintain it. However, writing the program is still the responsibility of computer programmers. This is because computer programmers have more programming skills that the software engineers. The type of software that the software engineers design includes computer and mobile games, software operating systems and network control systems. The software designed by the computer scientists can be installed into the computer hardware that enables the functioning of the computer hardware. The installation of the computer software is very easy (Goldberg, 2002).

Figure 1.2. A software engineer at work.

Source: https://www.youtube.com/watch?v=b1rwGfyLUG0.

The process of making a computer software is a long process that require a lot of skills. Software engineers need to be organized and set on what they want to make. In case of any malfunction in any part of the system, the software will not work as it is supposed to. Software engineers use software tools to develop their programs. The process of software engineering involves a lot of paperwork such that paperwork is more than the coding process itself. Software engineers are required to make a lot of righting before they come up with the computer program. The paperwork enables the software engineers to be more organized and to ensure the success of the computer software. The paperwork involved in software engineering is close to 70% of the whole process while the coding takes the remaining 30% (Niver, 2015).

Software engineers face a lot of trouble when they are designing the their programs. When manufacturers want to invents things, such as an aircraft, they expect software programmers to invent the programmers for these technologies being invented to work appropriately. This requires that the software engineers to take place and work thoroughly to ensure that they invent the needed software that will be workable and that will not faulty because faulty programmers can lead severe accidents that can be a national disaster. The process of software engineering is also very difficult and tiresome. It requires a lot of skills that should be put down together and the work is tiresome because of the workload as it requires a lot of paperwork. Software engineers work day and night tirelessly so as to see the end of their project. In the invention of some computer software a lot of care and thoroughness is required because when the software goes wrong it may lead to the loss of lives and therefore software engineers are pressured to ensure that their software have no flaws.

For one to be a computer software developer they need to have the knowledge on CS, software engineering, mathematical or computer information systems. CS gives software engineers the necessary skills to develop a certain software and it also equips them with the knowledge on computers and how they work. The knowledge on software engineering is mainly obtained in higher level of education and an individual cannot study software engineering if they do not have CS knowledge therefore, they work hand in hand. Mathematical or computer information system is also important specially in the calculation sector and the sector of determining the codes to be used during coding. Programmers need the programming language for them to code. The programming languages include Java, C#, Python, PHP swift and Javascript. For one to code they need they have the computer language knowledge because coding is done in the computer languages because the computer can only understand this language. The most commonly used computer language in the process of coding is the Java since it is easy and simple to use (Nash, and Sofer, 2012).

Software engineers and computer programmers differ in the following ways; Software engineers work as a team together so as to come up with the software but programming involves very little teamwork and most of the time the individual is working alone solitarily. Software engineering involves the whole process of coming up of the software but computer programming involves only a single part of the process and hence in the process of developing a software most work is the software engineers work. The software engineer works hand in hand with other engineers to create useable software programs.

Software engineering is a well-paying job and it is very marketable since new technology is being invented daily and it requires a software to be made so as to ensure the workability of the technology. Software engineering is also involved in the process of software update where the software engineers create an update of the software such that the software works better than it did before. Students who learn software engineering can easily find employment in a variety of areas and sectoers (Nash, and Sofer, 2012).

1.7. VIDEO GAME DEVELOPER

A video game developer is an individual who designs video games. Most individuals who develop video games have excelled in technology, have CS knowledge, know how to develop a software, are very creative such that they can invent new things that have never been seen, they are entertaining or fun, unique, and they have thinking skills. For those people who want to become video game developers they must have thought about their career early in their education so that they can acquire the necessary skills early enough so that they have the required level of education to obtain a degree. For instance, it is very hard for an individual who did not learn CS in his elementary school to be a video game developer hence he may fail to access his degree. Students who do not keep this in mind may lack jobs because no employers can employ an individual who does not have the required skills that they need. A video game developer must also have programing skills and CS skills (Goldberg, 2002).

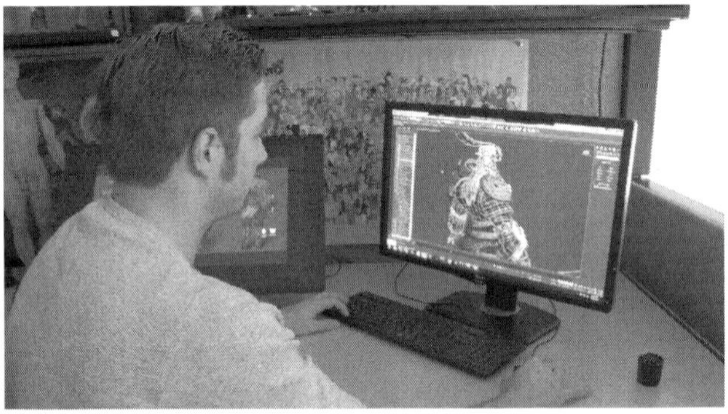

Figure 1.3. A video game developer at work.

Source: https://www.youtube.com/watch?v=3SH3CPJhthE.

Aside from designing games, individuals who have graduated with video game designing can also make webpages and can also create artistic work for televisions and movies. The work of video game designers is to develop game apps and software that are installed in computers, mobile phones, and websites. The games are normally a fun recreational activity that mainly target the youth and the children. Also, some adults may get involved in playing video games. Unlike in the olden times when games were mainly physical and involved outdoor activities, video games have made it easier for one to enjoy playing a game when they are indoors at the comfort of their homes. It does not involve a lot of physical activity which may pose as a disadvantage since children may lack exercises but it has enabled these children to prevent being idle and indulging in unwanted behaviors latter on. Most video games that are invented are normally easy to play, user friendly and they are enjoyable. There are game designs that are supposed to be met and therefore video game designers work with the gaming companies to ensure that the required status is met. These gaming companies also assist the video game to make its way to the market and hence they help advertise the games. These gaming companies include game loft, Ubisoft, and Nintendo.

The responsibilities of the video game designers include they are required to develop the theme of the game such that they know what the game will involve for example is it a cooking game or is it a racing game. They are also required to set the setting of the game for example if the game is a cooking game then most definitely its setting must be in a kitchen. They should also form the characters of the game for instance if it's a racing game then the game needs racers and these characters are given different names, traits, strengths, and stories. Aside from this they also determine the rules of the game such that the game has to have rules that the player must follow to avoid losing. Candidates can also make obstacles in the game to make the game more interesting and enjoyable. Video game designers may look at the market to determine the type of game that they will design according to the requirements of the players. The video games include Cora racing games, dressing games, cooking games and many other interesting games (Goldberg, 2002).

The major skills that video game designers require include: technological and analytical skills. Technological skills are needed because for one to invent a video game they have to have technological skills so that they may understand the technology they are using to make the video games. In case a video game designer does not have these skills, they cannot form video games hence they are requiring to first undergo training to acquire the skills

They also require creativity skills which are the skills that a person has that he can invent new technologies and new things that were not there before. For one to invent a game they need to be creative enough so as to come up with the process and storyline of the game itself. Research skills are also necessary because the video game designers have to research so that they can know what kind of games the people enjoy playing the more. They can carry out their research by asking the players directly or observing the people who play the games and taking note of the games they play more. The video game designers also have problem-solving skills since a lot of problems may arise when they are coming up with the video game software and hence, they require the problem-solving skills so that they can came up with the required solutions for these problems. Time management is also a necessary skill that the video game designers require. Because video game designs mainly work with deadlines that they have to meet. They therefore have to be fast and keep time so that they are done with their project before the decline is due. Video game designers also have teamwork skills since they have to work as a team so that they can develop a program. Teamwork also makes work way easier for the individuals since they work together. Lastly, video game developers have to have the skill that enables them to pay attention to any detail because a small mistake in the software will cause the whole program to be nonfunctional. They therefore work together as a team to ensure that the project has no errors at all (Goldberg, 2002).

The salary of game developers is quite high and it is therefore a course that is very marketable. As long as one has the required creativity to invent a game then they cannot fail to secure a job. Many students should therefore take up this core since it is rewarding.

1.8. COMPUTER SYSTEM ANALYSIS

Computer system is the hardware and software parts of a computer. Therefore, computer system analysis is the process of checking for problems within the computer system. This brings about the term computer system analysts. They are the people who carry out the troubleshooting of the computer systems to identify the possible errors. There are several jobs that are emerging with the use of computers in the current age. They include computer system analysis. In the present day and age, almost every household has a computer. Therefore, there will be a high demand for computer system analysts.

Figure 1.4. Showing computer system analysis.

Source: http://www.bluequills.ca/computer-systems-analysis/.

In the current business set up, computers are being used in the running of the workplace. They need personnel who are trained to manage their computer systems. They are required to update the computer system to make it current and always up-to-date. Their work is to also ensure that the system is efficient. The computer system analysts have to apply their knowledge of CS and critical thinking skills to design efficient systems. They therefore deal with the development and designing of computer, software, and hardware systems (Goldberg, 2002).

Many of the computer system analysts are hired permanently by a given company. As a result, they can design software and hardware according to company's internal requirements. The major work involved in computer system analysis is the resolving of issues that have been found within the systems. If the analysts developed the system on their own then it will be easy to identify and solve the problem but if another person developed the system, it might not be quite easy to identify and solve the issue.

Besides computer system analysis, there is a large variety of lucrative jobs. For instance, one can obtain a job as a teacher in computer system analysis. Here, an individual who has such skills can be hired in an institution of higher learning. As a result, they will get to train others on computer system analysis. For one to qualify to be such a teacher, they are required to have a master's degree in computer system analysis.

Others can get employment opportunities by creating online courses that offer an individual the ability to gain information on computer system analysis. If the course is certified by a given board of education, then the individual will be able to get a well-recognized certificate after completing the course. Some individuals choose to specialize in the given field. For instance, some of them opt to do computer system design or architecture depending on their areas of interests.The advantage of computer system analysis as an emerging job opportunity is that it allows individuals to carry out private practice. This is beneficial as it will allow flexibility. The computer system analysis jobs are very high on demand in the market (Goldberg, 2002).

1.9. VIRTUAL REALITY DEVELOPER

Virtual reality is a combination of both technology and CS. Virtual reality entails a program that, when used by a user, creates a simulation of a real-life event. In most cases, it is used in the gaming world to develop games that entail virtual reality. This is an emerging job because several people are embracing the concept of virtual reality. It is the same concept that is used in virtual simulation. For one to be a virtual developer, they are required to have skills on CS.

The CS knowledge is necessary to create the virtual world. It enables the user to borrow certain concepts from the real world to incorporate it in to the application. There are many job opportunities available in virtual developing. For instance, one can work at a gaming company where the individual gets to develop games for commercial purposes. In such companies, there is typically a group of individuals with much of experience in developing games. They further use their skills to develop games on virtual reality. For this job, it requires much of group work in order to develop quality games.

Figure 1.5. Showing a virtual reality game.

Source: https://medium.com/@gracejack989/virtual-reality-games-glasses-and-headset-a1a91e29166c.

There is also an option to develop the technological equipment used in developing such games. Such tool applies the concept of night vision goggles. The tools are fitted with the virtual reality programs. For some of the virtual game's developers, some of them are paid to be testers. Testers in the sense that they are played to test the games that have been developed. Their opinions are used to evaluate whether the game is fit to be released for the public use. It can also be used in determining the future prediction on the games in terms of the income expected from marketing the games (Freedman, 2011).

The advantage of a virtual reality developer is that a person can enter into many different CS sub-fields. They can start small businesses in virtual reality development. If they choose, they can work with a group of friends to start their own virtual developing companies. This will bring enormous flexibility. In virtual reality developing, they are able to work on their areas of interests.

Virtual reality development uses virtual simulations. Here individuals get to work in areas that employ the use of virtual simulations. For instance, organizations such as NASA employ the use of virtual reality. It is also used in various training companies for individuals who want to join the army. This enables them to know what to do when they are faced with different challenges. It improves their critical thinking abilities. The virtual reality development is a good emerging job opportunity more so for creative and innovative individuals (Freedman, 2011).

1.10. ROBOT MANUFACTURING AND TRAINING

A robot is a technology invented that can do most functions that a human being can perform. It has the memory of a human being but it is made by man. It has led to many people losing their jobs since it is cheaper than a human being and it performs the roles of a human being. Many employers therefore prefer having a robot than having a human being. Also, a robot does not get exhausted therefore they are cheaper and more efficient.

In the current world, there is a growing use of technology and CS. This has brought about the use of robots. Robots have been created to make the lives of human beings much easier. They are used in the daily lives of human beings. This is having created a large employment opportunity for a majority of individuals. Individuals can work in the creation of such robots

They are required to have knowledge in CS and technology. CS is used in programming these robots. The robots that have been created so far relay on the use of commands. The commands are instilled in the robots through programming.

The individuals program the robots to carry out a variety of tasks and depending on the requirements of a company or organization, the robot may be programmed to carry a specific task.

There are a variety of jobs in the area of manufacturing of the robots. One can engage in the programming aspect. Others can be used in the developing of technology used in creation abs assembly of the body parts of the robots. Others can be involved in the area of checking whether the parts of the robots' body are fully functional.

There is also a job opportunity in the running of the machines used in the assembly of the robots' body parts. There are a variety of job opportunities in the area of the creation of the robots. It is a really emerging job opportunity more so now that the scientists are looking into creating robots that use AI. So many projects have been undertaken in order to produce such types of robots who will be able to facilitate research more so when looking into the chance of carrying out space travel (Freedman, 2011).

Before the robots are released to be commercially sold and used among people, they have to be trained.

This has become an emerging job opportunity. The robots are programmed to fulfill a specific task. For them to be able to effectively carry out what they have been programmed to do they required to be trained in order to do so. This creates a job opportunity on its own. Individuals may offer services to manufacturing companies as trainers for the robots.

They are first given a set of instructions on what they are expected to do as they train the robots. At first, as they train the robots, they will first give the robot some instructions which they expect the robot to carry out. This will form a basis on which the trainers will be able to choose an appropriate method of training the robots. At some point, the trainers will have to guide the robots on what they should do

Afterwards, the robots will be required to do the given task on their own. After the robots are fully trained, they are then ready to be released and sold to various individuals or organizations (Freedman, 2011).

1.11. COMPUTER OPERATIONS SUPERVISOR

A computer operations supervisor is an individual who works in an organization and his main duty is to ensure the computers are functioning appropriately and in case of any malfunction they are to fix it.

A computer just like any other machine, a computer is prawn to failure at a particular time such that it stops functioning and it therefore delays the progress of the organization.

The computer operations supervisor is therefore employed to carry out this duty such that when the computer fails, they fix them and incase a software fails they can be able to identify the problem.

Figure 1.6. A computer operator at work.

Source: https://www.123rf.com/stock-photo/computer_operator.html.

The skills that a computer operation supervisor need the most is problem-solving skills since their career revolves around solving problems of a computer that may arise. This skill they easily gain when they are learning CS since they learn about programming and coding and in the process, they endure a lot of problems that they need to solve them. Problem-solving skills also enable the computer operations supervisor to identify a problem before it arises. Aside from the problem-solving skills also help the computer operation supervisor can solve their own problems even in their personal lives.

Another duty that a computer operations supervisor has is to supervise the operations of the computer so that they can identify a problem that may arise. In an organization identifying a problem before it arises is a key factor to prevent many risks that may arise. The computer operations manager therefore has a duty to observe how the computers are working so that he can ensure they are working in the right way such that they ensure that they do not fail in the process when they are being used. Computer operations supervisor are therefore important in any organization (Freedman, 2011).

Another major duty that a computer operation supervisor has is to teach computer operators. Many individuals may be employed in an organization that lacks the computer skills and does not know how to operate a computer. Only a computer operation analyst knows these details on how to handle the computers. The analyst is a valuable asset for the company because he/she may offer classes to train other employees.

Lastly, the computer operations analyst handles computer maintenance schedules. When a new computer is brought into an organization, the computer operations supervisor ensures it is installed appropriately and functioning correctly. They therefore handle the computer maintenance schedule and know when exactly the computer needs maintenance. When the time is due, they work on the computer and check for any malfunctions that may be present then they fix it and reinstall the computer back. This ensures the computer has a long-life span (Freedman, 2011).

1.12. COMPUTER HARDWARE ENGINEER

Computer hardware are the parts of a computer that are visible to users that they can touch and see. The work of a computer hardware engineer is to design, develop, and test the hardware of a computer. Computer hardware include the keyboard, mouse, circuit boards, routers, and the memory devices. Computer hardware engineers need to have the knowledge 0f CS for them to design this hardware because they cannot develop a mouse without knowing and having the knowledge of how this hardware operates and therefore no computer hardware engineer lacks the knowledge of CS.

Figure 1.7. Computer hardware engineer developing a hardware.

Source: https://www.livescience.com/48326-computer-engineering.html.

The skill that a computer hardware engineer needs is creativity. Creativity is the ability of a person to come up with a new idea that was not initially there. In order for computer hardware engineer to make a new hardware, they need to be creative enough to know how the hardware will look like and how it will function (Goldberg, 2002).

Another skill that the computer hardware engineer requires is technical expertise. This refers to the ability to ascertain how the computer technology looks like and how it works. It is simply the underlying expertise and experience. Computer hardware engineers should have extensive experience in order to manufacture, design, and develop computer hardware. Having the expertise will help computer hardware engineers enormously to become confident in what they do.

Aside from this, computer hardware engineers also check on the workability of the hardware they invent. They test to see what could be going on in case of a technical problem. A computer hardware engineer can collaborate with a computer operator supervisor since they have the knowledge of what they invented. Computer hardware engineers can also be self-employed. Some of the computer hardware that are being invented in the recent days have high technology that are more advanced than those that were being invented before. They include the MiFi that is a technology that is assisting in the current world (Goldberg, 2002).

The typical wages of a computer hardware engineer range up to $115,120 and experience a continuous growth of 5% since May 2017. The compensation is very lucrative and it stimulated a lot of interest in studying CS. However, students still need to preserve in their study until they fully understand the material and get the academic result that they need.

1.13. DATABASE ADMINISTRATOR

A database administrator works with computers and technology to safeguard and organize a company's data. Any organization own a lot of important data needed for future reference. Database managers work with the computers and technology to store this data safely. The data stored may include payrolls and financial numbers that should be confidential. They ensure the data is well organized such that it can easily be retrieved and it will be orderly so that information will be easily understood.

A database administrator works at organizations that have many databases, such as insurance companies. Most database administrators spend most of their day behind a computer caring out their normal duties (Goldberg, 2002).

Storing data on a computer is better than storing it traditionally. The advantages of storing information on a computer include long availability and durability. Data stored in a computer can be retrieved in tens or even hundreds years in future. Information and data stored on a computer is also safe and cannot fall into a third hand easily because using a computer one can easily secure their data using a password.

The skills that a database administrator needs to have include organization such that a database administrator is organized in what that are doing. A work of a database administrator is very easy and enjoyable as it involves the database administrators organizing any data that comes in using the computers. Though it is tiresome as information streams in all the time and it needs to be stored, they still get a high wedge. Database administrator is ranked highly and has been able to acquire top five in the best technology jobs. A database administrator earns up to $116,060 per month which is a good sum of money to encourage more people to take up this course. The payment rate is still growing with the passing years (Goldberg, 2002).

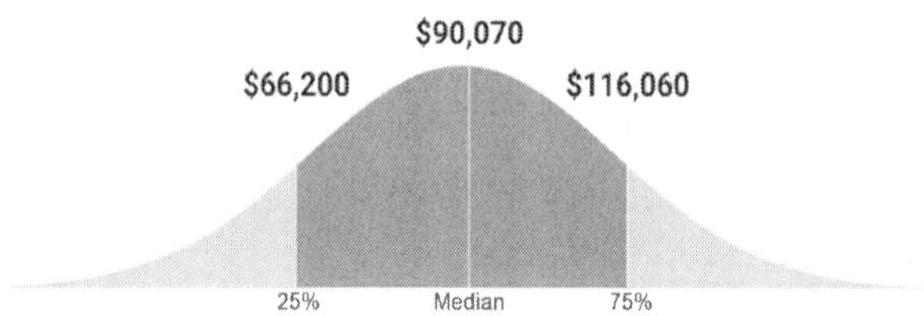

Figure 1.8. The amount of money a database administrator earns on the lower and upper side.

Source: https://money.usnews.com/careers/best-jobs/database-administrator.

1.14. CYBER SECURITY

With the recent use of technology, many users and company members have easy access to important data. This access to information enables other individuals to take advantage of others, for example by bullying or blackmailing them. They can access individual medical records among other information. On the other hand, the rise of such problems contributed to job growth in cyber security. Cyber security deals with programs that assist individuals to determine whether their information has been accessed by another party. People who would like to work in areas such as cybersecurity still need to have an in-depth knowledge on networking. The main goal is to identify the security protocols that are followed when accessing the internet (Freedman, 2011).

They also must have knowledge on ethical hacking. With such knowledge they are able know different ways of creating solutions to combat cyber-crimes. With a combination of such knowledge they are able to create such programs and applications that protects the users' data. The frequent cases of cyber-crimes have led to the need for such applications. This is the major reason that has led to the need for more individuals to create cyber-security applications.

Another way in which individuals can gain employment is through the creation of online courses. For a majority of individuals, they do not have much funds to enable them gain knowledge on cyber-security. With such need for education, some individuals have taken it upon themselves to avail such knowledge to a variety of users. They do so by creating online classes. For them to make this possible, they need to have knowledge on CS. If not, they work hand in hand with individuals who have knowledge on CS in order to create such classes (Freedman, 2011).

Their work will be to look for the content that will be used during the learning process of the individuals. This way they are able to gain earning from their programs. The major advantage is when the courses that they offer become fully certified by a board of education on higher learning. This will increase the number of users that access their sites. Here individuals are able to get a degree in cyber-security without them having to go through institutions of higher learning.

Individuals that develop cyber-security packages have a great advantage. For one they are on high demand more so in institutions that handle large amounts of data. Their work therefore is to ensure that the data in such institutions more so in hospitals, are safe. They can also venture into private practice whereby they can start their own companies that create awareness on cyber-security and create the programs an application (Freedman, 2011).

1.15. ARTIFICIAL INTELLIGENCE DEVELOPER

AI is being incorporated into the daily life of human beings. The most common examples of AI are the virtual assistants. They include Siri, Google Assistant, and Alexa. Such virtual assistants enable an efficient interaction between human being and the machines that they are interacting with. The use of such virtual assistants has been brought about by the use of technology in the everyday life of man. Such virtual assistants have come in handy more so for businessmen.

For one to develop these virtual assistants, they need to have knowledge on CS and technology. When it comes to developing of AI, there are a variety of job opportunities. For instance, one can work in the military. In the military today, it has become more advanced such that so many technological tools have been incorporated into it. It is more beneficial for individuals who have knowledge on CS and technology in the field of AI. Majority of the warfare tools have been generated and have incorporated the use of AI. Majority of individuals have been able to get employment opportunities in this field (Freedman, 2011).

One can also get employment as a machine learning (ML) researcher. ML researcher greatly apply the use of AI in order to full fill their work demands.

AI enables the individuals to closely monitor the machines. Also, the current machines being used today employ the concept of AI. For the AI developer, they get to be incorporated to into the research process. This will enable them to get a source of income as they assist during the research process. For most of such developers, the have a masters or PhD degree in AI.

The AI developer can also gain employment as a video game programmer. AI on its own borrows some key aspects of programming. It on its own basically entails programming because they need to program the machines to carry out a given task. This is why they are able to work as video game programmers. They are able to gain employment in gaming companies or even venture into private practice alongside individuals with gaming knowledge.

They mostly use programming languages such as Java and C++ in order to create such games.

Apart from video game developer, they can also get employment as a robotics programmer. Here they will be involved in the process of programming a robot to carry out given instructions or set instructions depending on the requirements. They can also work as data mining analysts. This more so tends towards the research aspect which tends to deal with numerous amounts of data. Most organizations require such people and therefore has created a high demand for the data mining analysts (Freedman, 2011).

The AI developer can also gain employment as a software engineer. These are but some of the jobs under AI developing.

1.16. NETWORK ENGINEERING

A network engineer is an individual with the necessary technological skills to ensure network remains in connection. Network is involved in making of calls, sending messages and keeping communication continuous between different parties. Network engineers are individuals who have the necessary skills to ensure that this network is not lost and that network is present in any part of the universe. In the olden days, communication involved passing of information through messengers who would deliver the message. This method was very ineffective as it was tiring and a lot of information was lost or distorted along the way.

Network engineers are also known as network architects. A network engineer has the duty to formulate a computer network. Formulating a computer network involves the making of the network. Network engineers come up and invent networks in areas where the network is not available. In most parts today, network is available but some parts like the interiors may lack network and therefore the network engineers are given this role. Network engineers require to have creativity skills so that they may create this network. Formulating a network is a complicate process that require a lot of skills and hence individuals may work as a team to come up with the network (WetFeet, 2009).

Network engineers also have the obligation to implement a network into an organization. After coming up with technological network there is need for network engineers to implement the network. Implementing the network is followed by executing itThe main goal of a network engineer is the ensure any business organization has the required network and infrastructure. Their pay is also very good and it has encouraged many individuals to take up the course. The work of a network engineer is very marketable and individuals who study network engineering cannot fail to get employed (WetFeet, 2009).

1.17. 5G SOLUTIONS ENGINEER

When network was first invented it was very slow and it took a long time before one could load or download a certain video from the internet and therefore there was need to come up with a faster means of network. This brought about the revolution of the 2G to the current 4G. in most places in the world they use the 4G network but in some parts, they still use the 3G internet. The 4G internet is very fast a video can be downloaded in the shortest time possible as compared to the 3G interment.

Due to the internet need and a need for a faster internet there is need for a faster network to be introduced and this has therefore brought about the need for the invention of a 5G network. The 5G network solutions engineer are therefore the individuals who take part in developing the 5G network which should be faster than the other networks and videos will be able to download way faster. An individual who wants to take part in 5G solution engineering must therefore undertake CS so that they may have the necessary CS skills.

1.18. TECH VLOGGER

A tech vlogger is an individual who uses technological devices to take videos of events. The upcoming of tech vloggers was mainly as a result of the coming YouTube that enabled many people to share their videos. Many vloggers visit events and take videos of these events then they upload the videos in their Youtube pagers. The more views they get can guarantee them to get a specific amount of earning that encourages more people to enter into vlogging. Vloggers need to have CS skills so that they can have the technological experience on how to use the technology and that they may know how to edit their videos using the computer software.

1.19. CLOUD ARCHITECT

A cloud architect is an individual who is behind the developing of the cloud and ensuring that the cloud functions as required. The cloud is where information is stored as a backup for footer reference. In case an individual loss their mobile phones, they can easily discover their photos and data through the cloud and therefore important data and information cannot be lost easily. The cloud also acts as an additional storage and therefore on needs not to worry about their mobile phones filling up fast as they can store the data on the cloud and free up their mobile phone storage.

In conclusion, CS is needed for most careers and therefore it is becoming a course that is not easily avoidable. In the next few years it will be used by most employers as a key factor on who they employ into their company. Therefore, most students are encouraged to take part in CS learning as they will be able to safeguard themselves employment more easily than those who don't have CS education. This is why most schools have ensured that they incorporate CS learning to their classes as a core subject that all the students must be taught and they cannot graduate without these skills and knowledge of this subject.

CHAPTER

Professionalism in Computer Science

2

CONTENTS

2.1. INTRODUCTION

There are many different tasks performed by computing professionals. Some of them include designing pipelines that are instructional for superscalar processors, making diagnosis timings of any problems in systems that are embedded, testing, and validating software systems, making recommendations of security policies for information systems in the medical sector, etc.

These professionals have an obligation to ensure that these tasks are performed conscientiously due to the fact that any decisions they make can affect how the computer systems perform and functions, which will then lead to a negative effect on the users of the system in a direct manner and even those who are concerned indirectly.

A major example includes having to work on a software that deals with controlling the transmission (which should be automatic) of an automobile.

This software should be able to ensure that the gasoline consumption is kept at a minimum and also make sure that the driver and any other passengers or pedestrians are safe. Just like civil engineers, the obligations that they have are quite similar to those that computing professionals have. Professionalism refers to the skills and the ability to work and perform tasks efficiently, all which professionals are expected to have.

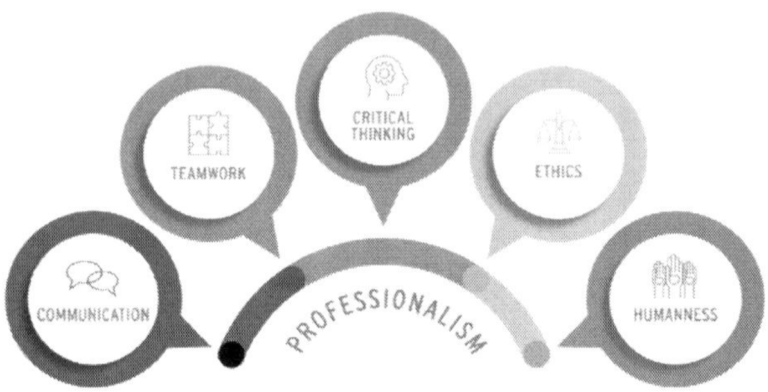

Figure 2.1. Five main principles of professionalism that are required of employees in any field of work.

Source: https://memp.pratt.duke.edu/professionalism-five-principles.

There is a specific way the professionals should carry themselves. They should be able to honor their work in a way that allows them to respect themselves and therefore also respect others. They are obligated to carry out their responsibilities of their professional work in a professional manner, and be able to build work relationships with the employers, clients, the public, and even other professionals. So as to be professional it is important for them to love their work. It is not possible to practice professionalism if you do not love what you are doing.

2.2. WHAT EXACTLY IS PROFESSIONALISM IN COMPUTER SCIENCE?

Professionals in computer science (CS) include software engineers, system analysts, designers of hardware, computer scientists, and database administrators.

There are certain professions that have specific characteristics and these are called strongly differentiated professions. These include those that have special rights as well as special responsibilities. Examples of these professions are lawyers.

These professions have specific characteristics including skills and knowledge that is specialized, research that is systemic, professional associations that are robust, and even a social good that has been well defined and is associated with the profession. These professions gain their knowledge through an education as well as practically gaining skills (Bott, 2005).

CS professionals are also taught in professional schools where they are able to gain the knowledge through education and also through the utilization of practical skills. Going to the schools helps them to learn certain values and practices that are referred to as professionalism. They are taught to have a great value for efficient work, to love their work, to have great people skills, etc.

Professionalism involves being able to have a great value for the expansion of knowledge by doing research that is considered systematic.

This is very important for computer scientists and computer professionals because they do not rely on apprenticeship and passing down of information from the past because they have to learn their daily developing aspects of technology.

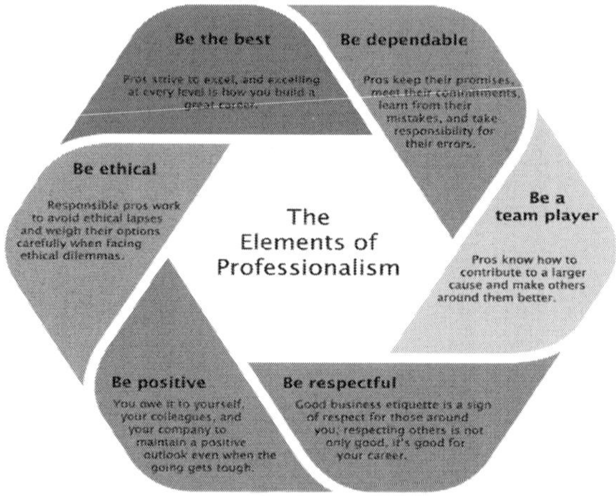

Figure 2.2. Professionalism requires one to have six elements illustrated above.

Source: https://safety4sea.com/cm-the-6-elements-of-professionalism-in-seafaring/.

Professionals are able to understand that professional knowledge is always advancing, and therefore they always engage in a continuous education through learning more about what they are doing, attending conferences, and even reading different articles on the matter. Computer professionals mostly have clients instead of customers and they know that this information on the client needs to be kept confidential. In addition to this, they need to make sure that they are able to meet the needs of the client.

Due to the fact that computer professionals have knowledge that is specialized, the clients are not able to make full evaluation of this service quality that they are given by the professionals. This means that only the other professionals in the same unit are able to come to an understanding on the quality of the work that the professional has provided. Computer professionals are accredited and licensed based on the quality of their educational program (Bott, 2005).

All in all, professionalism refers to the conduct of an individual at their workplace. This quality is important and it is noted by both clients and bosses. Lacking this quality can have a severe consequence in your career path. Professionalism can have a major effect on your chances of advancing or even being able to keep your job.

2.3. BASIC CHARACTERISTICS OF PROFESSIONALISM

There are many different personal behaviors and qualities that show the level of professionalism in a certain individual. These help in the demonstration of the commitment that person has to performing effectively in the job they are doing.These are a couple of characteristics that can make one person stand out and be acknowledged as having the quality of professionalism, and others that can evidently show the lack of professionalism. Below are some of these characteristics:

2.3.1. Dressing Appropriately

Professionals are expected to be neat all the time. This means meeting or even exceeding the requirements that are in the dress code of the company, as well as paying a lot of attention to how you appear when having meetings with your clients.Most of the people who work in the computer profession tend to have a loose dress code, especially those who Freelance and work for themselves. The CS environment mostly has no specific dress code; however, does that mean that you should wear whatever you want to wear just for the sake? Years of research have shown that what you wear and the image you show to your clients matters a lot. People will always judge you by how you appear.Our brains are able to look at the details of surface appearances and hastily make assessments on them. This can be very important especially if you are meeting a client for the first time. Despite the fact that you work for yourself, it is important to always make sure that the assessments made by your clients based in your appearance can be very important in determining whether you will get the job or not.

Figure 2.3. These are some of the examples of smart casual dressing. One does not have to wear full official clothing, but being presentable is very important.

Source: https://www.mentalfloss.com/article/78992/8-rules-dressing-appropriately-office.

It is hard to control the fact that people are mostly judged by their appearances. The only way to do so is to follow the stereotype and dress appropriately. In this world, despite the fact that you will be appreciated for your intelligence and your amazing skills in coding, dressing in an appropriate manner can steer you to a stronger work ethic. Most people in the computing field are advised to dress two levels above their positions. Not exactly how your boss would dress, but something more acceptable than shorts and a T-shirt.

If the computer specialist is working for a company or an organization, there is definitely a dress code. This should be followed to the latter. Dressing appropriately will most likely give you better opportunities in your job. This is a level of professionalism that is very important. The outward appearance has a huge effect on people, especially bosses and clients. When you dress appropriately, the management is able to notice the effort your putting in, and this will go very far. They could even just consider you for a higher job position because you look the part (Bott, 2005).

2.3.2. Being an Expert at What You Do

Being well knowledgeable in technology is a skill set that many different employers look for all over the world. In CS especially, there are very many different sections, and being knowledgeable in most of them can take you further up in the chain.

There are certain computer skills that can help in improving your level of professionalism. Being able to use these set of skills to make demonstration of your abilities to an employer can turn into a massive paycheck. This means that it is important to be knowledgeable on the many different careers that are involved with CS. Some of these include: web development, computer programming, developing software, creating applications, coding, etc. Depending in what exactly you are targeting, being knowledgeable in the main skills to an expert level can take you very far (Bott, 2005).

So as to stand out in the field of CS, it is important to continuously read in the different skills that can be a bonus in helping you during an interview. Professionalism involves being an expert in exactly what you choose to do. If you choose to program, you need to know everything about programming. You need to be skilled in Java, JavaScript, Python, and all the other programming languages.

Most employers look for someone who is able to solve problems as well as think in a computational manner while performing tasks. So as to achieve this, you have to be well equipped with all the information that you need to perform the job, which means being an expert in it (Weckertand Lucas, 2013).

Figure 2.4. Being an expert in what you do, gives you an advantage over other professionals. This is one of the main qualities of professionalism.

Source: https://www.forensisgroup.com/expert-witness/computer-science/.

Professionalism involves thinking about long-term needs as opposed to short-term fads. Due to ever-changing nature of this field, constant learning is a must. Constant learning can allow one to keep up with the different innovations that come up almost every other day. Technology is field that grows almost every day, and this quality expects one to be well aware of all the new advancements.

Being an expert in what you do means also having other skills, such as presentation skills. One should be able to write and present work that can be understood by both the bosses and the colleagues, in the case of a presentation in a workplace. One can end up being given a presentation to present to stakeholders or board members who are willing to fund a certain project you are working on.

If you have all the knowledge on the work you are presenting but no presentation skills, it will be hard to win over their hearts. Being able to explain your work in a manner that will be understood by everyone is a skill that can build on your professionalism. Effective communication and explanation are always a huge plus. Being able to achieve this is a sign of expertise in what you do (Bott, 2005).

There are also some skills that are not that common but can help in improving your level of professionalism. These are some of things that can draw employers to you:

- Being able to navigate codes – this is one of the most underrated skills that one can have. Being able to navigate codes so as to find your way around a certain project is a skill that all computer professionals should have. Being well knowledgeable in this skill can prevent one from getting lost in codebases. It may not seem that important, however, being able to make analyses and also picking up on the things that are happening in a code that exists is a major part of being an expert in programming.

- Having an online portfolio – being an expert in your field also involves having websites or even libraries that you can present to show your skill. This can be more beneficial if they are an open source, because this gives an opportunity to your employer to see the manner in which you code. Having portfolios can also help your employer see your discipline in finishing projects.

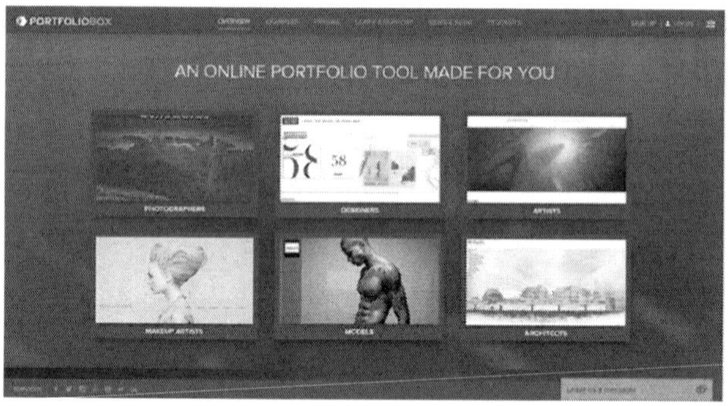

Figure 2.5. Online portfolios are able to show the work that you are able to do. A good coder is able to provide such work.

Source: https://www.mockplus.com/blog/post/free-online-portfolio-websites.

- Having a deployment strategy – there are many different programmers who are well equipped with the knowledge to create algorithms, data structures and even languages, however, they have no idea on the manner in which to deploy applications that are large-scale in the work place. Thinking about development and technical architecture in a manner that help in mapping to a deployment strategy is a skill that is not acquired by many programmers.

All these skills can be very helpful in showing your expertise in your sector and therefore showing professionalism.

All computer professionals should be well knowledgeable on all the skills that they need to be experts in their fields.

2.3.3. Behaving in a Moral and Ethical Manner

Ethics refers to certain practices and standards which are set for the influencing of the manner in which people behave and do things. It is not compulsory to follow these rules; however, it is a huge plus if you do. It benefits everyone. They do not show us what is right and what is wrong in accordance to the law, but what is right and wrong in the eyes if the society (Bott, 2005).

CS also has ethics that need to be followed so as to show your level of professionalism. They are a combination of moral standards that help in governing how computers are used. It involves the views that the society has in the use of computers, including both the software and the hardware. Some of the common issues of computer ethics include: intellectual property rights, concerns about privacy, and how they affect the society.

Figure 2.6. Computer ethics are the guidelines that help in governing how computers and information systems are used.

Source: http://cs.swan. ac.uk/~csbob/admin/ethics/.

2.3.4. Concerns About Privacy

Hacking – this involves unlawfully intruding a certain network or computer. Hackers tend to intrude through certain levels of security that are found in a network or the system if a computer, allowing them to gain access to other computers without authorization. Hacking can be very dangerous if it is done with malicious intent. It can lead to the violation of one's privacy, breaching security, gaining access to private information without authorization, alterations in the system operation, and even performing attacks that are malicious on the computer system. This is not acceptable as a computer professional.

There are times when one is legally allowed to hack and good examples include retrieving lost and important information that is lost (especially if one has forgotten or lost a password) or placing effective preventative measures to avoid breaches in the security system.

Malware – this is a malicious software to cause the impairment of a computer system. Some of the commonly used malware include viruses, worms, spyware, and trojan horses. Viruses have the ability to delete files from hard drives and spyware can aid in the collection of information from the computer. Malware has many downsides.

One can get a virus on their personal computer which can cause many different problems, including damaging your computer completely to the point where it cannot start. With a malware, your personal computer can become much slower.

In addition, it may lead to your applications not starting. Malware normally gets installed through pop up advertisement that show up on different sites.

These viruses can steal all the information on your laptop or a computer and some can even lead to your computer crashing and deleting all your data. When there are too many viruses in your computer, it is possible for applications to refuse to open. Computer professionals need to know how to deal with these issues and also not code them.

Protection of data – this is also known as data privacy. It involves being able to ensure that your data is safeguarded. This data is normally guarded while still considering the balance between the privacy eights of the individual and being able to authorize for this data to be used for the purpose of business.

Anonymity – This involves being able to keep the identity if a certain user masked, which is done using certain applications.

2.3.5. Intellectual Property Rights

Copyright – this is a right that guarantees that you, as an author, will be the sole person to publish, distribute, and use your content. No one else is able to employ or disseminate the content without your permission.

Figure 2.7. Copyrights are very important in ensuring that your work is not stolen. They allow for the owner to sue in such a situation.

Source: https://www.businessdailyafrica.com/lifestyle/pfinance/New-law-will-curb-abuse-of-online-products-copyright/4258410-5301228-view-asAMP-12cw99h/index.html.

Plagiarism – This concerns people who copy and publish the work of another person without making the appropriate citations. This is equivalent to stealing the work of another person and making it look like the work is yours. Plagiarizing work can make you, as a computer scientist, lose your professionalism. Once caught plagiarizing work, it will follow you for the rest of your career. Your bosses and colleagues end up losing any respect that they have for you. In addition to this, one can get major legal repercussions. This brings us back to the copyright issue. The laws that are stated in copyrights are absolute. It is not permitted for one to use the work of another person without providing citations and also references. The author has all the power to sue you. There are some other forms of plagiarism that can result in prison sentence. In order to avoid all this, programmers need to properly cite other people's work to maintain their professionalism.Cracking – This is a manner in which one can break into a computer system while bypassing security features. This involves being able to skip the steps that are required, such as registering and authenticating. Once one is caught doing this, the repercussions could be similar to plagiarizing. You can lose your professionalism.Licenses for software – This gives a person permission to utilize certain digital materials as long as they follow the agreement on the license. The ownership of the digital material remains with the owner who has the copyright. However, those who are using it have been given permission to do so based in the agreements that are stated in the software license.Computer scientists are expected to follow these rules and ethics so as to be acknowledged in terms of their professionalism. In fact, they should be the least likely to perform any of the above actions, unless the action is legally accounted for. Those who are not able to abide by the computer ethics, are also not considered to have professionalism which can prevent one from getting jobs or moving to senior positions that are more senior (Bott, 2005).

2.4. COMPUTATIONAL THINKING

In addition to all the aspects that have been mentioned above, computational thinking is one of the most important aspects of professionalism in CS. Most of the things one will be dealing with is solving problems, be they big or small. Considering the fact that most of the things in the workplace are now data-driven, computational thinking has become a major aspect in the proper functioning of any business. For those working in the CS sector, it is actually much more important than most of the other skills. It involves being able to make analyses of certain situations and being able to think through those problems in a manner similar to how a computer would think about them.In addition to being able to understand and think through these issues in a similar manner to a computer, computer scientists are also expected to come up with solutions using computers and programming languages. These skills are important in any industry, such as finance, insurance, or telecommunications. As a result, a computer scientist should be a quick adaptable learner to be able to design solutions using a variety of programming languages (Butterfield, 2016).

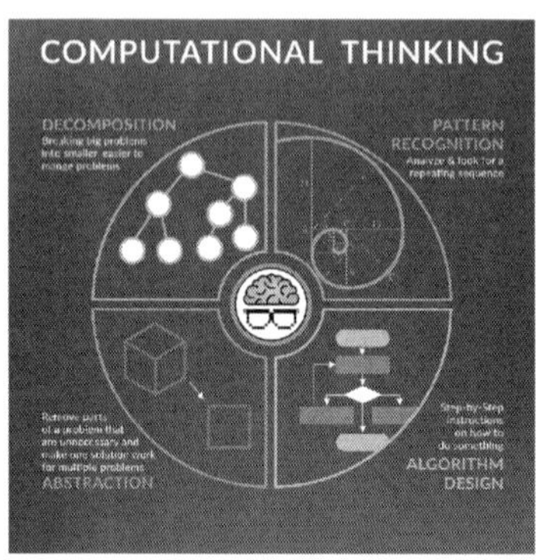

Figure 2.8. Above are the four main components of computational thinking. They are necessary if one is going to be able to notice and solve problems. It requires one to think just like a computer so as to come up with solutions for problems.

Source: https://medium.com/@sarahyam/how-can-we-use-computational-thinking-to-solve-business-problems-6e8e37913804.

Considering the fact that most businesses require computers on a daily basis, a computer scientist should be ready to take up any job that they are asked to do. This involves commercial businesses and even public services. Being able to plan and forecast certain issues is based on being aware of patterns of abstraction. In addition to this, a computer science professional needs one to be able to break down a problem into its main constituents using algorithmic thinking. All these skills are important in acquiring professionalism in computer-related jobs (Bott, 2005).

There are some advantages of computational thinking that all computer scientists should consider in order to build on their level of professionalism. Some of these are:

Thinking computationally promotes problem solving – using computational thinking has proven to be a method that is structured and designed. There are four main parts of computational thinking. The first one is decomposition. This involves the ability to break down complicated problems into parts that are much smaller and easier to manage. Secondly, there is pattern recognition. This requires one to look for similar aspects among and within the problems that they want to solve. The third part is abstraction. In this section, one is supposed to focus on the crucial data only, and ignore that which is not relevant. The final part are the algorithms. This requires the computer scientist to develop a solution the system should follow so as to avoid recurrence of the problem. Employees need to acquire these algorithmic skills and be able to do them without any problems. This will aid in providing a scope of their professionalism to their employers, thus providing more and more opportunities.

Using computational thinking to innovate – innovators always work at creating new things and they do this by taking amazing ideas and enhancing them so as to apply them for new and more improved purposes. Abstraction has proven to be the process within computational thinking that has helped in the process of thinking of new strategies. This involves being knowledgeable on making proper determinations on the factors that needs to be extracted from a certain system or problem so as to come up with solutions. This means having to think about the major factors in different ways, so as to find out those that are relevant and those that are not, allowing one to eliminate irrelevant factors from the equation. This skill then allows one to use their skills, tools, and resources available to them to come up with new solutions and instructions that are innovative. By doing this, one has the upper hand in the workplace, and this is a show of professionalism.

Thinking computationally is a skill that has been researched on and tested – computational thinking was initially introduced to us in the 1980s by Seymour Papert. It was proven to be effective globally by Jeanette Wing. Her research stated that the designs of algorithms, CS, and technology create important jobs in our society as of today including in science, controlling traffic, and even online shopping. After this research, many important leaders in the world today were able to identify computational thinking as an essential skill . Having computational thinking skills can be very important to computer scientists. There are many different companies that train staff in computational thinking, such as Google and Microsoft. It is an essential skill and can be a major advantage in obtaining jobs as a computer scientist (Bott, 2005).

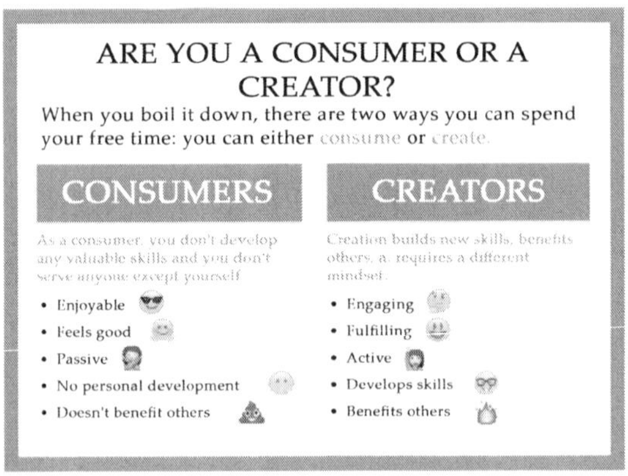

Figure 2.9. Above are some of the differences between being a consumer and being a creator. Computational thinking can promote innovation which is proving to be more advantageous according to the above image.

Source: https://www.slideshare.net/alykhangulamali/are-you-a-consumer-or-a-creator.

Computational thinking allows one to move from consuming to creating – in comparison to humans, computers are really good at what they do, especially in performing jobs that are repetitive, boring, and tiring, in an efficient and accurate manner. However, for computers to perform these functions, they have to have gotten instructions from someone telling them what to do and how to perform the function. This is what is referred to as algorithmic design in computational thinking. An algorithm is referred to as a set of instructions that the computer can use to perform tasks. This is similar to recipes that I used in cooking and equations that I used in mathematics. In CS it is referred to as coding. Computer scientists should be well knowledgeable on algorithmic designs, as it is a logical part of the process of computational thinking, that allows them to perform the creation of algorithms using programming languages such as python, which in turn allow machines and computers to perform functions that they previously could not have performed. Being able to do this in an effective, efficient, and accurate manner can add onto your level professionalism (Bott, 2005).

Computational thinking has proven to be very important for one to perform jobs in this specific market. There are many concepts in CS that cannot be performed without the knowledge of computational thinking. This skill can be used in any area and it can be very advantageous in providing more opportunities. These skills should be applied every day in the lives of computer scientists so as to add onto their level of professionalism.

2.5. RESPONSIBILITIES

As a part of professionalism, all computing professionals have responsibilities that they perform to their clients and users, their employers, to other professionals, and even to the public (Bott, 2005). Below is a discussion of each of these aspects.

2.5.1. Responsibilities to Their Clients and Users

It does not matter if a computing professional is working as a consultant for a specific person or as an employee in a certain organization, there are certain obligations that this professional is expected to perform. He or she is expected to ensure competent performance of tasks that have been assigned, according to the professional standards. Not only do these professional standards include attention to excellence technically, but also do they deal with the manner in which computers socially affect users, the public and operators.

It is important for the computing professional to be candid when it comes to making assessments of the capabilities and risks of certain computer systems. This means being able to honestly and accurately report all findings that are relevant. Not only does the professional have to consider the client's specifications while designing a new computer system, but also how this system has an influence on the life quality of others. An example of this includes designing an information system for a clinic that is able to provide quick access by the medical staff, and at the same time protect the medical records of the patient from access that is not authorized. In this situation, there might be a conflict between providing quick access and ensuring that the patient's privacy is not invited (Butterfield, 2016).

Figure 2.10. Clients are entitled to many different things. Above are some of the examples of client rights.

Source: https://firststepnc.com/client-rights-committee.

There is a lot of freedom in making decisions on the different specifications of a computer system that is enjoyed by computer professionals. All they have to do is meet the minimum requirements that are needed for the performance of the computer which are: reliability, speed, and functionality, all within the set budget. Other than that, they are able to make many other different decisions, such as better response time or better graphics.

It is important for computing professionals to identify potential biases when choosing their computer designs. This is because these choices have an effect on the value of competition. An example includes designing a search engine for a retailer that is online to make a display of the items that are most expensive first, which may benefit the retailer who is trying to maximize his/her profits. This option however may not be beneficial to the client who is trying to keep costs at a minimum.

Some of these choices are hard to make, seeing as even the computer programs that are moderately large are still quite complicated and prone to errors. In addition to all this, the development of technology is making software even more complex than it is right now. This means that it is reasonable to conclude that all computer programs have errors in them. Even after vetting and finding out that a computer program has no errors at all, it is quite hard to prove how correct it is (Butterfield, 2016).

Figure 2.11. Professionals are supposed to respect the wishes of their clients without breaking any ethical laws. They should also ensure that their clients' needs are met.

Source: https://www.asyr.ca/get-started/client-rights-responsibilities/.

Due to this reality, it's becoming more and more difficult for responsible software engineers to provide software that will not end up failing the user. But how can this be changed? Most software fail due to errors that are designed into the original programs. As an aspect of professionalism, computing professionals should take responsibility for software that may fail by exercising due diligence in the creation of the software and also being as honest as possible on the faults that are known and those that are not known in the software. This is very important especially in software that are created for safety critical systems and failures in this software can be a threat to people's lives (Butterfield, 2016).

Being honest about errors gives the consumers an opportunity to make better informed decisions before they purchase the software. It involves honesty from software developers: they are expected to explain any risks that may occur when using their software, including possibilities of any unforeseen errors. This forthcoming behavior has helped motivate computing professionals to be honest and even to continue in their search for methods that can discover faults in software and measure any risks. Being able to achieve this can help in improving your level of professionalism.

2.5.2. Responsibilities to Their Employers

Most CS professionals work at organizations. Relationships with managers and other employees are normally contractual. This means that the computing professional makes a promise to perform jobs for the employer in exchange for receiving salary and benefits. These computer scientists normally have the employer's proprietary information and they are expected to keep this information secret. Not only do they have to keep that secret confidential, but they should also work at honoring all the other forms of intellectual property that the employer owns. This means that the computer scientist is not able to make profits from selling things from the employer's business independently or even using intellectual property such as any of the software that he or she has developed with the resources of the employer.

Loyalty is an aspect that is expected from each employee when it comes to the work ethic. To be more specific, computing professionals need to be aware of the different conflicts of interest that may potentially happen, whereby the employee might owe loyalty to different parties apart from the employer. This conflict of interest occurs when the computer scientist is asked to make a decision that may interfere with corporate or personal interests. For example, ordering computing equipment from a vendor with whom the professional has a previous relationship may provide a biased reaction. The employer may think that the employee is making a biased judgment even when the equipment that he or she has ordered may be of the best quality. This means that the employer would not trust the decision of the employee. In such a situation, employees need to show professionalism. A computer scientist who has a high level of professionalism would eliminate himself or herself from the situation and ask a different professional who is as qualified to make the decision (Butterfield, 2016).

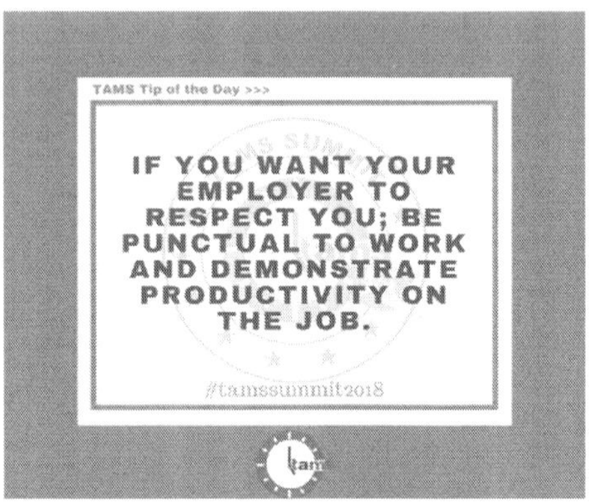

Figure 2.12. Professionals are expected to show the utmost respect to their employers, but at the same time they should not break the moral code to keep them happy.

Source: https://www.nairaland.com/4516486/how-earn-respect-employer.

There are many professionals in the computing industry that have managerial duties and there are others who are mainly managers. Having managerial roles can make the responsibilities of computing professionals complicated due to the fact that managers have responsibilities to do with administration and an interest with the organization they are working for. Being able to acknowledge this relationship between you as the professional and your employer, can show a great deal of professionalism and can also help one grow in the business (Weckertand Lucas, 2013).

2.5.3. Responsibilities to Your Fellow Professionals

This refers to a type of respect called collegiality, which is expected in an interaction between two professionals in the same field. Despite the fact that everyone deserves to be respected, this is normally a bit different. For example, if in one computer scientist used an idea from a different computer scientist, it is important that the first computer scientist gives credit to the second one. This is similar to authors who normally give credit to other authors that they have gotten their ideas from, by properly providing citations. Without acknowledging this, it could be considered as a plagiarism.

Plagiarism has always been considered unethical due to its representation of theft of someone's work and representing those ideas in the plagiarist's own words. Due to the fact that non-technical customers may not able to efficiently make evaluations as to who the original author is, the professionals know that they need to give their work to other professionals to evaluate for plagiarism. This is normally referred to as a peer review and normally happens in both research and practice.

Research findings are typically presented during specific computer conferences. Before the information on the research findings is presented at the specific conferences or published in journals, this information has to undergo review by peer researchers who are well knowledgeable on the matters that are being presented (Weckert and Lucas, 2013).

Due to the fact that professionals in the computing sector work together, they are required to ensure observation of professional standards. These practice standards are normally formed by other people who are in this profession or in related organizations.

For example, the convention for names of variables in certain codes is a major practice standard. By following the standards of coding, the professional who developed the software is able to run the modified code quickly.

There are many times in which professional standards should be utilized in an appropriate manner. However, sometimes controversies occur. This can be seen in the problems that arise when the Institute of Electrical and Electronics Engineers and the Association for Computing Machinery are attempting to provide a standardization of a body of knowledge for the engineering of software, so as to ensure that the licensing of software engineers is possible (Weckert and Lucas, 2013).

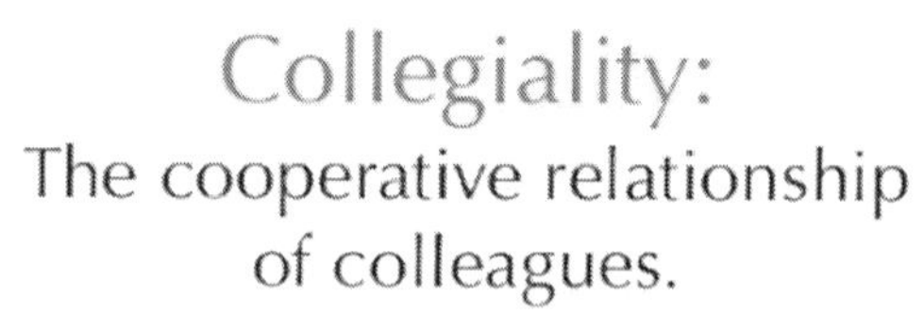

Figure 2.13. Collegiality is important in building teamwork amongst professionals. It also allows for professionals to grow together as they are well aware about the importance of collaboration.

Source: http://hypnoticthoughts.com/collegiality-series-kerrilee-pietroski/.

Computing professionals who are in most senior positions have the job of mentoring professionals in the same field who are in the junior positions. Despite the fact that all professionals have a high level of education, those in the junior positions still require mentorship so as to gain additional experience and also learn more in the field, and this will help them in developing professional judgment. This requires for a tutelage of the junior professional by the senior professional.

In the engineering field, for one to receive a Professional Engineer license, the junior engineer is required to work while being supervised by an engineer who is already licensed for a minimum of 4 years. All in all, it is important for all professionals to help each other in continuous learning as well as development professionally, which is still a necessity for one to maintain a license. Computing professionals are also able to contribute to the field by becoming peer review volunteers. Most of the peer reviews are done by reviewers and editors who have volunteered and even the activities that are conducted in the association are normally done by a group of volunteers (Bott, 2005).

2.5.4. Responsibilities to the Public

Despite the fact that no one should ever plan to endanger another person, there are special obligations that engineers have to make sure that the objects they produce are safe. Professionals in the computing field also have this obligation, to ensure that the public is safe and also in improving the quality of life for the people who are using computers and information systems.

So as to meet this obligation, it is important for professionals in the computing field to create awareness to the public when it comes to the understanding of computing. The computing profession as a whole has the major responsibilities of ensuring that the public is well educated on these matters. Different computing professionals will be able to meet this responsibility in their own different ways. For example, a computing professional can speak in front of his/her church, and talk about the advantages of purchasing computing equipment and also give advice on good and bad options. A different computing professional could write an article and send it to the editor of a certain magazine or newspaper, on the different issues concerning the use of the internet (Bott, 2005).

Figure 2.14. The public needs to be aware of the positive and negative effects of technological products.

Source: https://www.ictworks.org/12-challenges-facing-computer-education-kenyan-schools/amp/.

It is necessary for professionals in the computing field to give contributions using their knowledge in these technical matters, during discussions that involve public policies, especially those that are related to computing. There are many different people who are making considerations on measures that have been deemed controversial, such as installing of software that help in filtering the web on computers that can be accessed publicly, e.g., in libraries. Professionals in the computing field are able to give their opinion in this decision-making discussions by providing technical facts. There are many controversies related to technology that are talking about how computers are socially impacting the world as of today (Bott, 2005).

When a professional is put in a precarious position, they should alert other professionals in the similar field about a serious threat to the safety of the public.

There was once an issue, where computer engineers alerted other professionals against their employer when they were developing the Bay Area Rapid Transit in the United States.

They were able to note some errors in how the software and electronics has been designed for the control system if the automatic train. These errors caused harm to the public. They tried to fight for what they believed but the employers were not having it. In the end, they decided to release the information to the newspapers, through one of the members in the board of directors.

The professionals were however fired for not being loyal to their employers. Later on, an accident occurred and this was able to prove that their concerns were valid. The professionals were able to proclaim that they were obligated to ensure that the public is safe, in accordance with the code of ethics (Bott, 2005).

2.6. MORALS

Professionalism requires one to be morally upright. There are some imperatives that should not be second guessed.

2.6.1. Contributing to Society's Well-Being

Professionals in every field have an obligation to ensure the protection of the fundamental human rights as well as to make sure that all diversity of cultures are respected.

This is the main principle when it comes to the quality of life. Professionals in the computing field always aim at ensuring that negative consequences that are involved with computing systems, are kept at a minimum, including any factors that may threaten the safety and health of the public (Weckert and Lucas, 2013).

Figure 2.15. Professionals need to make sure that society's well-being is catered for, for example by creating medical software.

Source: https://www.123rf.com/photo_38514714_social-network-social-media-business-people-support-concept.Html.

When these professionals are making designs or implementations of systems, they are expected to make sure that the products are utilized in a manner that is socially responsible, meet the needs of the public, and not have a negative effect to the public's well-being. Not only should they be able to provide a social environment that is safe, but also a natural environment that is safe. Well-being includes both of them. This means that professionals in the computing field have to be alert when designing and developing these systems and also make sure that the public is aware of any damages that may occur to the environment, both locally or globally (Weckert and Lucas, 2013).

2.6.2. Ensure That No Harm Occurs to Others

In computational terms, harm may mean physical injury or undesirable consequences such as losing information, losing property, damage of property, or even negative effects on the environment. This means that professionals in the computing field are prohibited from utilizing technology in a manner that will cause harm to: the public, the users, the employer, the employees, and even the environment.

Some of the actions that may cause harm include destroying or modifying programs and files intentionally which can cause one to lose resources or even using human resources unnecessarily. It is also important to note that actions that intend well including ensuring that you have accomplished duties that have been assigned to you, can also lead to unexpected harm. In this situation, the professional is expected to that the negative consequence is undone or mitigate to the maximum extent. So as to avoid unexpected harm, the professional can make careful considerations of the impacts that may potentially occur when designing and implementing these systems.

In order to lower any chance of causing indirect harm to others, professionals in the computing field are required to lower the number of malfunctions that may occur, by making sure that they follow the standards that are generally accepted for the testing and designing of systems. In addition, it is also important to ensure that they have made assessments of the social consequences of the designed system, so as to make projections of any potential harm that could be caused to others. If the features if the system are not well presented to the supervisors, users, and coworkers, any resulting injury will be the responsibility of the professional (Weckert and Lucas, 2013).

Figure 2.16. Computer professionals should not use their skills to take advantage of other people, such as by installing malware into public or private computers.

Source: https://amp.economist.com/leaders/2017/04/08/how-to-manage-the-computer-security-threat.

The professional in the computing field is expected to report any indications of dangers in the system that may end up resulting in damage, socially or personally. If the employers are not willing to mitigate these issues, the professional is expected to alert the public so as to ensure that the problem is corrected or even ensure reduction of the risk.

Despite the fact that it is important to report any dangers, providing reports of violation that are misguided can be very harmful to the professional. Before making any reports on any suspicions the professional may have, it is important to fully assess all the relevant aspects of the incident. All in all, one has to provide a credible assessment of risk and responsibility. This can be achieved by seeking advice from other professionals in the same field (Weckert and Lucas, 2013).

2.6.3. Being Trustworthy and Honest

If one wants to be trusted, one needs to be honest. You cannot have one without the other. It is not possible for an organization to function effectively without trust. An honest professional in the computing field should not provide claims that are false or deceptive, in a deliberate manner, about the design of a system, or the system itself. However, they should be able to provide an honest review of all the limitations and problems in the pertinent system.

Computer professionals are also expected to be truthful about their own qualifications, as well as all the circumstances that may cause conflicts of interest. There are some volunteer organizations such as Association for Computing Machinery, where joining them could place one in a situation where his or her actions are interpreted as a way of representing a larger group of professionals.

2.6.4. Being Fair and Taking Action to Avoid Discrimination

This imperative is governed by values such as tolerance, equality, respect for others, and even the principles of equal justice. There are many different forms of discrimination including discrimination on the basis of religion, sex, age, race, national origin, disability, etc. and thus is a major violation of the policies that are provided to professionals in the computing field. Discrimination should never be tolerated. Using or misusing information and technology can result in inequities between various groups of people (Butterfield, 2016).

Figure 2.17. Discrimination is completely unacceptable. Everyone should be accepted as they are and not judged based on their social, economic, financial or religious status.

Source: https://i-sight.com/resources/discrimination-in-the-workplace-guide/.

Fair communities allow the people within it to have equal opportunities in the participation of, or benefits from the use of computer resources no matter what race they are, sex they are, age, whether they are disabled, their national origin, religion, etc. This however does not mean that using computer resources in a manner that is not authorize will be justified, nor does it mean that it is providing an adequate basis for one to violate other ethical matters in the codes.

2.6.5. Honoring Property Right Including Patents and Copyrights

In most circumstances, violating the terms of license agreements, patent, copyrights, and even trade secrets is against the law. This is still applicable in situations where the software is not fully protected, and this is a violation that is contrary to professionalism. One should only make a copy of a software once they are given a proper authorization. Duplicating materials without authorization is not condoned.

2.6.6. Giving Proper Credit for Intellectual Property

Professionals in the computing field are expected to ensure protection of the integrity of intellectual property. It is more specific to state that one is not allowed to take credit for another professional's ideas or work, even if the ideas or work has not been fully protected using copyright or patents.

2.6.7. Respecting Other People's Privacy

The technology that is used to compute and communicate allows for one to collect and exchange personal information on a large scale. This means that the probability of having the violation of individual and group privacy is highly increased. Professionals in the computing field I left with the responsibility of maintaining integrity and privacy of information describing individuals. This involves being able to take precautions to make sure that data is accurate, as well as being able to protect it from people who are not authorized or accidental disclosure to individuals who are not appropriately to gain that information. In addition to this, there should be creation of procedures that give individuals the permission to review and correct inaccuracies in records.

All in all, this means that there should be collection of the necessary amount of information, data should be clearly defined and not be used for different reasons without the permission of the individual (Butterfield, 2016).

Figure 2.18. Although professionals in the computing field gain access to a lot if information, they should respect user privacy.

Source: https://uogmcm12.wordpress.com/2013/05/24/respect-the-others-privacy/amp/.

These are unspoken rules, which apply to all forms of communication: be it electronic or physical. Data monitoring should be prohibited, without user approval or authorization.

Information on a specific individual that is being observed during the normal functions that are carried out during system operation and maintenance need to be treated with a high level of confidentiality,

Except in a situation where it is evident that the law has been violated, regulations of the organization, or the code. In such a situation, the information including the content or nature of it, can only be shown to those who are authorized.

2.6.8. Honoring Confidentiality

Issues to do with confidentiality of information are an extension of honesty, especially when one has explicitly promised to honor confidentiality, or implicitly, when information that is private and is not in direct relation to how one performs their duties, becomes available.

Unless the law or other principles of the code require one to provide certain information, the professional is expected to respect the confidentiality to users, employers, clients, and other employees. This is a major ethical concern.

2.7. BASIC PROFESSIONAL RESPONSIBILITIES

2.7.1. Striving to Achieve Effectiveness, Dignity, and the Highest Quality if Products and Processes

The most important obligation of a professional is excellence. The professional in the computing field is expected to strive for the achievement of quality and also be well aware of the major negative consequences that may occur due to systems that are poor in quality.

2.7.2. Acquiring and Maintaining Professional Competence

Only individuals who are able to take responsibility for being able to acquire and maintain professional competence may be deemed excellent. Professionals are required to play a role in ensuring that standards are set for the expected levels of competence, and they should also work to make sure that those standards are achieved.

There are a couple of ways in which one can upgrade technical knowledge and competence: studying independently, getting time to attend courses, seminars, or conferences; and being a part of professional organizations.

2.7.3. Knowing and Respecting the Laws That Exist Pertaining to Professional Work

Professionals are expected to obey the laws that exist whether they are national, international, state, local or provincial, unless there is a specific reason based on ethics that prevents them from doing so.

They also have to obey the procedures and policies that are set in the organizations they either participate or work in. It is however important to balance compliance with the fact that some of the laws and rules may not be moral or appropriate and, therefore, they should be challenged.

It is considered ethical to violate a regulation or a law that does not have enough moral basis or when it is causing conflicts with a different law which is considered more important.

The professional however must take responsibility for their actions and consequences if they ever decide to violate a rule or law due to viewing it as unethical or even for other reasons (Butterfield, 2016).

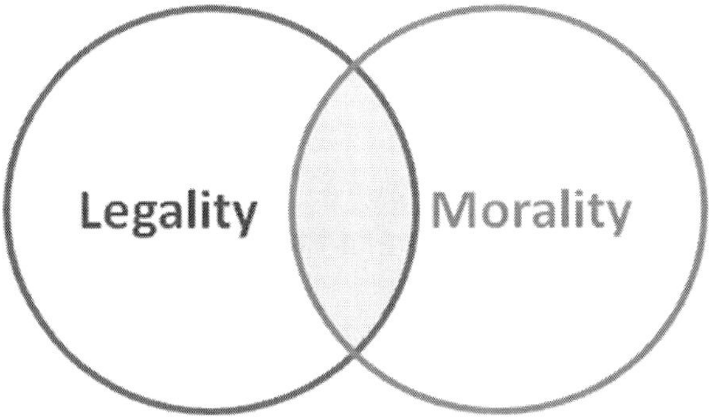

Figure 2.19. There is a fine line between legality and morality. Professionalism requires one to know when it is acceptable to break a law due to moral values.

Source: https://godplaysdice.com/2018/05/04/if-its-not-illegal/.

2.7.4. Accepting and Providing Appropriate Professional Reviews

In the computing profession, work that is of high quality and professional, all depends on critiquing and reviewing in a professional manner. It is important to use peer reviews when it is appropriate to do so, so as to provide reviews that are appropriate and professional. One can also review the work of others.

CHAPTER

3

Regulating Technology

CONTENTS

3.1. INTRODUCTION

As new technologies continue to impact on fresh business and service trends, it's essential for governments to quickly create, modify, and implement regulations. The pressing issue is ways of protecting citizens and ensuring fair markets, whereas allowing innovation and business to grow. Encompassing technological improvements are inspiring various changes in the modern regulatory environment, presenting significant difficulties for regulators who seek to maintain some balance between providing innovation, protecting customers, and addressing the possible unintended outcomes of disruption.

Figure 3.1. Artificial intelligence is one of the emerging technologies that requires standard laws.

Source: https://www.information-age.com/answer-regulating-ai-123486185/.

Modern-day technologies, such as machine learning (ML), artificial intelligence (AI), big data analysis, distributed ledger innovation, and IoT or Internet of Things are generating new methods for customers to network with each other and disrupt conventional business models. This is an era when machines train themselves to acquire new knowledge, autonomous cars communicate with each other, and smart devices react to and foresee consumer needs.

In retrospect, regulatory stakeholders are faced with certain challenges, such as what is the best ways to protect citizens to ensure fair markets, while permitting these new technologies and companies to thrive. The hypothesis is that regulations may be crafted gradually and deliberately but then stay in place unaffected for long periods.

While new business systems and services continue to emerge, such as ridesharing agencies and initial coin offers, state agencies are facing challenges with forming or revising regulations. Besides, they should do this while operating within legacy frameworks. If we look at history, when regulations on cars—particularly laws meant to safeguard pedestrians and motorists—delayed progresses in automobile technology by decades, we realize we don't want to face the same trials. As a result, regulators need to balance their duty towards protecting citizens with ensuring progress in new technologies.

3.2. PRESENT STATUS OF REGULATION

The initial phase in the pre-regulatory stage should include a detailed review and comprehension of relevant existing regulations, checking out those which may be blocking invention, are obsolete, or even duplicative. Present state refers to the entire ecosystem of regulation which may apply: from vertical solution or sector modulation, for instance, for car businesses to convergent directives where multiple departments are entailed; to lateral regulation like employment or licensing of businesses.

Oftentimes, a retrospective analysis propels regulators to assess whether substitutes to regulation or amendments to present rules might sufficiently address the supposed problem. Europe formed a task force for challenging obsolete legislation and protocols in the emergence of unsettling business models (Zwanenberg, Ely, and Smith, 2013).

3.3. IDEAL PERIOD TO ENFORCE REGULATIONS

Technology regulators must be careful to avoid both the too quick and exceedingly slow problem. Various principles such as adaptive regulation or regulatory sandboxes can be applied for answering the question "when," by both drawing regulators nearer to the technological advancements while also moving to a more responsive regulatory model.

Additionally, policymakers have various reasons behind technology regulation. However, generally, they are seeking to protect citizens, encourage competition, and adapt externalities. Besides, in fields varying from cryptocurrencies to self-running vehicles, there are various regulatory models emerging across the spectrum. Think about regulations relating to unmanned aerial structures (UAS), for instance, or drones.

Considering the fast pace in which new technologies are emerging and business models rising, it is a great thing that for regulations to remain relevant they must be revised regularly within every few years or so. There are different ways to affect these automatic reviews; which vary from supervisory sun-setting with regular review to procedures, such as the EU's

Regulation Fitness and Performance service, which performs retrospective assessments to check for laws which are outdated or require some revision (Zwanenberg, Ely, and Smith, 2013).

3.4. REGULATORY SYSTEMS FOR NEW TECHNOLOGIES

3.4.1. Adaptive Regulation

This refers to a responsive and iterative methodology to technology regulation. Oftentimes, quick change, shifting business structures, and experimentation are the main hallmarks of innovation-driven businesses—though are rarely the standard in regulation.

Usually, regulators impose fresh rules and policies in reply to market trends or new legislation. Afterward, they may spend several months or years creating rules and developing an initial draft for general review. Lastly, they review these comments—besides there could be multiple others—and modify the anticipated draft accordingly (Reins, 2019).

The challenge with this procedure is twofold. For starters, regulators usually don't realize how companies and consumers may react to fresh regulations; besides, the guidelines are rarely reviewed once implemented.

Adaptive methodologies to regulation, contrarily, depend more on testing and error and co-development of rules and standards; besides they have quicker feedback loops.

Increased rapid feedback loops permit regulators to assess policies against established standards, adding inputs into revising procedures. Technology regulatory institutions have various tools which can be applied to seek the necessary feedback: establishing policy labs, generating supervisory sandboxes, crowdsourcing policymaking, as well as availing representation to industries in the governance procedure through self-regulation and private standard-forming bodies.

Soft law refers to mechanisms or systems that create substantive prospects which are not directly enforceable—provide another device for shifting to other adaptive regulation. Contrary to hard law tools like treaties and decrees, soft law may consist of informal guidance, support for industry self-regulation, good-practice guidance, principles of conduct, and affiliate certification and accreditation (Reins, 2019).

Though not legally tying, soft law implements have various benefits over formal regulation, especially in the field of emerging technologies. These systems allow regulators to adjust quickly to variations in innovation and business models, plus to address matters as they come up without stifling technology. Besides, through high engagement with concerned stakeholders, they can help regulators to understand the hindrances of the technology including its possible impacts.

One means regulators can use soft law is by defining the scope of matters to be addressed, including asking the business sector to create its own unique standards and principles of conduct as a result. Technology regulators must develop comprehensive codes so that industry players can develop strong standards for conformity. Regulators may then certify the standards created by private industry (Reins, 2019).

3.5. CASE POINT: FINLAND UPDATES ITS TRANSPORT TECHNOLOGY REGULATION

Recently, the Finnish government recognized the need for reforming their transport policies to conform with their mobility-as-service (MaaS) upgrade, which considers transport as an integrated network of different services. Officials say that citizens must consider the transport network as one entity, without any borders plus with the capacity to share information on payments, location, and tickets digitally.

As such, the country decided deemed it fit not to revise any separate policies on taxis, roads, and public transport, or transportation of goods but rather create a fresh integrated transportation code. Officials decided to do away with the old laws and develop a new transport decree that integrates all transport systems into a single set of legislation, in order to be innovation-neutral, and to build the same smooth playing field for various transport modes. The goal is to deregulate present transport infrastructure while creating the fundamentals for MaaS technology.

3.5.1. Regulatory Sandboxes

Here, the goal is to test out new approaches through forming sandboxes and accelerators. A highly popular trend for regulation agencies is the formation of accelerators or "sandboxes," allowing for partnerships with private firms and businesspersons to experiment with emerging technologies in fields that promote innovation. The goal of a regulator is to become a partner bringing safe and effectual technologies to customers and individuals (Boothby, 2018). Judging by their name, accelerators are established to fast-track innovation. They typically entail partnerships with private firms, academic bodies, and other agencies which can offer guidance in certain areas. Alternatively, Sandboxes are controlled settings which permit technology developers to test items, services, or fresh business models without needing to follow any standard regulations.

In Canada, for example, the country's Securities Administrators introduced a regulatory sandbox which provides time-constrained relaxation from various regulatory requirements set on startups. The goal of this program is facilitating the capacity of those companies to use advanced products, services, and systems all across Canada, whereas ensuring suitable investor protection (Boothby, 2018).

Recently, a company known as Impak Finance was the first business ever to lawfully raise $1 million through a crypto currency crowd sale system in the Americas. Being a part of CSA sandbox, it got exempted from registration as a securities dealer and availing a prospectus. The company shall be allowed to stay in the sandbox position for two years.

In the meantime, the U.S. is steering a sandbox operation for UAS (UAS). The Federal Aviation Transportation Department has selected 10 public-private collaborations to test UAS. These pilot programs shall test the safety maneuvers of drones in different conditions presently forbidden. They include flying above people, past the sight line, and even at night. Rather than directives from the authorities, this system takes another approach by allowing interested groups to test their drones in any way they are contented with.

The Sandbox approach is intended to assist regulators to clearly understand fresh technologies and work mutually with industry stakeholders to create suitable rules and guidelines for emergent products, services, and corporate models. However, Sandboxes are not without some detractors who believe regulators may get too near to the startups (Boothby, 2018).

Having this in mind, some scholars suggest that the better metaphor would be that of the greenhouse. It is a representation for the environment where small plants are placed in sun and surrounded by transparent walls, allowing for a unique growth environment. Such an environment allows the crops to grow and thrive. Similarly, some companies may fail, while others will mature and flourish. However, there is, always complete transparency and nourishing environment.

3.5.2. Outcome-Based Regulation

Here, the focus is on results and overall performance instead of form. Conventionally, regulations have seemed to be prescriptive plus focusing only on inputs. But when the regulatory focus moves from inputs onto outcomes, the way state intervenes in the markets may change. The shift may create operational proficiencies for regulators and increased freedom for developers.

Basically, outcome-based regulation describes necessary outcomes or objectives instead of describing the way that they should be realized. This method of regulation provides businesses and people more freedom to select their unique way of conforming with the law (Boothby, 2018).

Emphasizing on performance and results allows governments to form regulations (or other, easier mechanisms like guidelines) which focus on the constructive effects regulators are seeking to promote (or the negative outcomes they want to prevent).

Typically, emerging technologies' actual potential may be harnessed just when they are merged together, like using blockchain technology to protect data formed by autonomous cars, or using a mix of ML and natural language procedures to define medication through a chatbot. For these connections to occur, innovators require room to invent. Outcome-focused regulation may provide the freedom needed to experiment.

3.6. REAL-WORD EXAMPLE

Australia's new policies for autonomous cars is a great case study of outcome-based regulation. The country has established performance-based regulations for autonomous cars. These guidelines are better to legislation since they permit for flexibility, quick amendments and updates, if necessary. The document goes ahead to say that protocols for automated cars must be "proportionate, outcome-based, and frequently reviewed.

Transport executives, nevertheless, believe various issues must be checked before making self-driving cars a fact on the road. Focus should be on verifying that the regulatory system stays flexible enough to cover evolving technologies when they enter the market, but still prioritizing public safety.

Likewise, industry players are assessing performance-based principles. Institutions such as Australia's Automobile Association recommend that criteria for programmed vehicles must be performance-focused plus technology-agnostic, plus that the accountable parties and procedures for certifying car modifications where technology is involved must be clearly defined and unambiguous.

3.6.1. Risk-Weighted Regulation

In this approach, you move from a one-size for all regulation framework to a more data-driven, partitioned approach. Market speed is crucial for businesses, particularly startups having business models which are based on emergent technologies. Speed to market may also make virtual solutions and products more effectual. While in use, they typically collect information on their operators (Reins, 2019).

Through the help of modern analytics plus, in most cases, AI, the information may then be examined to detect fresh patterns and trends, or data that may make the item more precise, safe, effectual, and tailored for the need. Due to this iterative aspect, the quicker safe and effective items are introduced to market, the greater the impact.

Among the ways to quicken the acceptance of business models centered on emerging technologies shall be drawing motivation from the pre-check structures for airline travel applied in many nations. They function by using available data to endorse low-risk flyers, who can then enjoy less scrutiny and inspection. Another similar method may be applied to help fast-track the approvals of fresh business models. This would allow certain businesses to pass through a streamlined yet predictable approval procedure, based on their availing access to vital information.

However, a data-based, risk-oriented system shouldn't be only limited to pre-acceptance. It may be stretched to include a dynamic, regulation approach, reliant on actual data flows existing between firms and their regulators. Currently, many regulatory agencies, ranging from the European Commission to U.S. Securities and Exchange Commission have instituted such data flows within the industry (Reins, 2019).

The emergent data can then be examined and compared against the regulations or anticipated outcomes, in order to determine whether a company complies. Companies in compliance shall be marked as safe, but if not, then data systems may create a group of action objects to achieve the standard, or, for the case of serious violations, provide reprimands or fines like exclusion from the safety list.

Additionally, regulators can apply open-data to support their own information or for autonomous inspection. For the case of virtual health software, regulators may monitor products using publicly available information on software bugs or error reports, client responses, software revisions, app store data, social media, as well as GitHub.

When the data streams are integrated, it means this aspect of the regulatory procedure can be automated. Implementation may become dynamic, besides reviewing and assessment may be constructed into the system.

Take the case of Boston City in the U.S. Their typical food safety procedures, which depended on random choices of restaurants for additional scrutiny, required improvement. The municipality's data portal lists public information on restaurant meal safety inspections and various other attributes of city life (Reins, 2019).

In order to effectively detect restaurants that require regulatory attention, the metropolis partnered with Yelp as well as Harvard Business

School (HBS) to promote an open competition for developing an algorithm that may predict health policy violations. Well over 700 contestants contributed, applying restaurant inspection information and Yelp reviews gathered over the years.

Although participants examined the reviews, checking for common words as well as phrases, economists from Harvard examined the proposals against the metropolis's original inspection reports.

The result was that the successful algorithm could enhance inspectors' capacity to detect violations by a ratio of between 30 – 50%.

Yet another type of risk-based analysis may reduce the high entry rates of regulatory certification. Scientists from the Data Innovation Center recommend advancing to a "cloud-based model of regulation," whereby scalability is established within the regulatory model.

Case in point, if a firm's product or services are aimed towards just a few users, they may receive much lower checks considering its possible adverse impacts may be limited.

It's only after the firm grows and begins selling its items more widely that it may encounter a more detailed investigation (Reins, 2019).

3.7. THE FDA'S PRE-CERTIFICATION PROCESS

Figure 3.2. Regulating tech companies can help prevent malpractices.

Sources: https://mitsloan. mit. edu/ideas-made-to-matter/will-regulating-big-tech-stifle-innovation.

FDA already applies risk-based methods that balance possible risks with patient advantages. Being part of the Digital Health Invention Action Plan, FDA formulated a Pre-Cert pilot course for qualified digital health developers which showcase a culture of value and organizational excellence depending on the goal criteria—for instance, succeeding in software formulation, development, and testing. Basically, the pilot seeks to check first the software development process or virtual health technology developer, rather than the product itself (Boothby, 2018).The principle behind this is allowing the FDA to fast-track the time for marketing lower-risk health items, while focusing most resources on those which pose a greater possible risk to patients. Pre-certified developers may market lower-risk products without extra FDA evaluation, or with a more basic premarket review.

However, precertification is only one aspect of the model. FDA seeks to assess the activity of these firms continuously, using real-life information. Scorecards and related Pre-Cert levels may move up or down depending on performance as well as the effectiveness data. In case the scores drop below an identified threshold, the company may lose some benefits, like expedited assessments for less-risky items or suitability for Pre-Certification standing until it can rectify any product concerns through a fresh assessment (Boothby, 2018).

3.7.1. Collaborative Regulation

Collaborative regulation allows for aligning of regulation nationwide and internationally, through engaging a wider set of participants across the technology ecosystem. A recent universal survey consisting of around 250 professionals and stakeholders of financial institutions revealed that regulatory deviation—inconsistent policies across various nations—may cost financial establishments anywhere between 5 to 10% of their yearly income. The patchwork of global financial regulations additionally cost the international economy roughly $780 billion yearly.As the virtual economy grows, with fresh business models, products, technologies, and services, technology supervisors around the globe can benefit from mutual approaches like co-regulation, global coordination and self-regulation. From multi-stakeholder meetings which produce solid policy regulation and voluntary benchmarks, firms, and regulators including other interested parties may be involved in the process.This ecosystem method—whereby multiple regulators from diverse countries cooperate with each other including those being regulated—may promote innovation while protecting clients from possible fraud or safety issues. In this method, private, standard-setting groups and self-regulatory companies also have significant roles to play with regards to enabling partnership between developers and regulators (Boothby, 2018).

The Fintech field has revealed signs of regulatory integration. For instance, Singapore has ratified 16 agreements with modules in 15 different nations. These contracts include data exchanges with different nations' regulators, plus regulated companies, referrals of companies seeking to enter a regulation partner's country, and guidance for businesses on the guidelines of countries they want to enter. These agreements may lead to common frameworks and procedures across nations.International and local institutions are capable of playing a major role in expediting these cross-border contracts. For instance, Asia-Pacific Economic Cooperation allows for cross-border information flow among its key members via a set of policies and guidelines developed to form cross-border privacy security while avoiding obstacles to information flows. Companies agree to abide by the privacy guidelines; independent organs meanwhile monitor and take the companies liable for privacy breaches.

3.8. INTERNET REGULATION AND MULTI-PLAYER INVOLVEMENT

In some cases, regulators may benefit from working with businesses, inventors, and other stakeholders to define policies for developing technologies. For instance, the web's decentralized, international structure posed a risk of defying regulatory logic and required a fresh framework to handle its evolving nature.

Back in 1997, after the Clinton regime considered different regulatory systems to web governance, they released a group of principles known as 'The structure for international electronic commerce' for determining the creation of virtual communication technologies. Generally, the framework outlined various principles to determine the state's management of cyberspace and anticipate aggressive regulatory activities. Such as, where state involvement is required, its objective should be supporting and enforcing a predictable, stable, and straightforward legal atmosphere for business (Byrne and Pitt, 2012). It's also advisable that governments must avoid unnecessary limitations on electronic commerce, plus recognize the web's unique qualities. Besides, electronic commerce via the internet needs to be facilitated internationally. Factored together, these protocols create a de facto regulation structure which sidesteps the conventional process for promulgating fresh policies in favor of a co-regulation system and multi-stakeholder activities. These systems may help encourage constructive communication among different players who may otherwise be less willing to compromise.

3.9. CHALLENGES TO CURRENT REGULATION POLICIES

Researchers have identified various challenges to emergent technologies existing in traditional regulatory models, varying from coordination issues to regulation policies to the mere volume of outdated policies. These challenges can be grouped into either technological or business-focused ones.

3.9.1. Business Challenges

The pressing problem in business is whether regulators are able to keep pace with Fintech. Oftentimes, drone regulators tussle to stay abreast with the quickly growing technology, or regulators find it difficult to keep track of healthcare technology invention.

Current regulatory systems are typically slow to adjust to shifting societal and economic conditions, besides regulatory agencies normally are risk-averse. Swift adaptation to evolving technology, thus, poses significant risks—and, consequently, to the technology sectors, where change happens at a quick rate.In case the volume and rate of virtual transformation continues remaining how it is, then the present regulatory system may not work. The space between technological innovations and the techniques meant to adjust them—often known as the "pacing issue"—is only getting wider.

There's some disengagement between the pace, iterative progression and universal connected nature of virtual health innovations and the existing regulation structures and processes. The present regulatory approach isn't capable of supporting the fast-paced nature of development.

Generally, the pacing matter has gained fresh urgency because of the speed in which modern technologies are scaling. Virtual products, solutions, and businesses may become very big, very quick. The policy system often takes anywhere between 5 to 20 years, while a unicorn startup may grow into a firm with universal reach in just a few months. Case in point, Airbnb moved from 21,000 flight arrivals back in 2009 up to 80 million by 2016.

In the meantime, municipalities, and states are continuing to determine how, and whether, they can standardize temporary rental markets. Some ride-hailing solutions have experienced with same hyper-growth as guidelines in the space endeavor to adapt. Strengthening regulation for emerging, high-visibility businesses brings new political as well as shareholder burdens. It's one thing when regulation reduces the rate of launch for new businesses or industries—plus another different matter if it inhibits their growth (Reins, 2019).

Financial companies are generally expected to attract around $46 billion in investments in 2020. However, this shall depend, partly, on regulation. From a particular survey, it was discovered that 53% of Asian fintech entrepreneurs cite tightening policies as among the leading setbacks to fintech, ranking next only to risk-management, besides 89% believe these policies will continue to get tighter.

Industry regulatory setbacks are usually doubled by the prevailing patchwork of regulations. Most national regulatory structures are complex and partitioned, with various answerable agencies practicing overlapping authority. The business friction coming from any particular redundancies or regulation patchworks rest at the core of modern trade agendas. Synchronizing with regulators across different borders is another possible setback. As from the late 80s, many companies and consortia have emerged to act as independent standards-development bodies which capture the special needs of developing technology sectors.

Disruptive types of technological changes usually cross traditional business boundaries. When products and services change, they may shift from one regulation type to another. For instance, in case a ride-hailing firm begins delivering food, then it might fall under the authority of health regulators.

But if it grows into helicopter service, then it may fall under the domain of aviation regulators. In case it uses autonomous cars for passengers, then it may be grouped under the authority of telecommunications regulators. In spite of facing challenging regulatory systems, ride-hailing businesses have grown quickly and have piled considerable pressure on conventional regulatory regimes.

Ensuring consistency in policies and regulation can be particularly challenging in data sharing businesses, which typically blurs lines between traders, facilitators, and customers (Reins, 2019).

The dynamic, interlinked nature of disruptive trade models also may make it hard to dispense liability for customer harm. For instance, in case a self-driving vehicle crashes, it may be challenging to determine who exactly is liable—whether it's the software developer, car manufacturer or owner.

The Swedish automaker, Volvo, anticipates liability to move from the motorist to the manufacturer.

They believe vehicle makers must assume liability for any technology in the car. Therefore, the company has acknowledged that in case of any malfunction affecting the [driving] mechanism when operating autonomously, they shall assume product liability.

Likewise, consider 3D-printed items. How can product liability regulation be used in such a situation? It's also puzzling to determine who's culpable if 3D-printed fittings fail, whether this should be the store which printed the product, the design supplier or printer manufacturer.

The anonymous and decentralized nature of digital currencies presents an especially difficult task for regulators. By June 2016, the Anonymous Autonomous Organization, a program using Ethereum's blockchain-based system, was robbed of $55,000,000 when a hacker exploited a defect in the code.

Even up until now the offender hasn't been identified and issues of liability still remain. Here we can see that some of the aspects that make technology attractive also can permit con artists and fraudsters to exploit the industry's general lack of maturity (Reins, 2019).

3.9.2. Technological Challenges

Figure 3.3. Technology must comply with quality standards present in the industry.

Source: https://www.123rf.com/photo_87274901_compliance-rules-law-regulation-policy-business-technology-concept-.html.

Modern-day technology is faced with a lawful, regulatory framework that's built upon the context of paper and words, up against an emerging global system that's digital, continual, 24/7, and established on bytes and bits. There's need to blend these two worlds.

The growing usage of smartphones, networked devices, and sensors have formed a massive virtual footprint in buyers' lives—something that may only accelerate heading into the future.

Coming from a regulatory viewpoint, one key question is who manages all this information—the operator or service provider (SP) who stores it.

If the SP owns the data, then what obligation should they have towards storing and protecting it? Besides, to what degree can information be shared with other third-parties? Without any particular universal agreement on information protection, regulators all over the globe are taking diverse positions on these matters (Reins, 2019).Close to 30% of all countries around the globe don't have any data protection regulations.

For those that do, typically they have conflicting policies. The EU's Data Protection Regulator, for example, preserves the edict of privacy, availing strict regulations over cross-border information transmissions and providing citizens the privilege to stay anonymous.

In a recent study, it was found that 82% of Europeans claim they intend to apply their new privileges to see, restrict, or erase their online information. The American approach, in comparison, focuses on sector-based policies (like health care, retail, and financial) including state laws.

One evolving sector influenced by data laws is virtual health and medicine. A major progress in digital health innovation is Software-as-Medical-Device (SaMD), which is capable of diagnosing medical disorders, propose treatments, and determine clinical management systems.

SaMD permits patients to contribute more actively towards their specific healthcare needs. Regulatory agencies normally have structured SaMD in quite a similar way as conventional medical devices like heart stents. However, as the FDA points out, this method isn't "suitable for the quicker, iterative design, creation, and kind of validation applied for software-derived medical technologies.

Some technology products continue to remain untouched by their respective device makers even upon launch into the market. But, there are software developers who regularly make changes to their items remotely, following release. These changes might be based on security, feature upgrades, or enhancements based on the information gathered from users. Though current regulatory endeavors stress on vetting before items are launched (Reins, 2019).

Another crucial regulatory test in the digital field is cybersecurity. Experts agree that malicious online activity has increased, becoming bolder and complex, more original, and global. Online security is especially crucial in fields like fintech, virtual health, digital system, and intelligent transport modules. The financial solutions sector was breached around 130 million times in 2017, whereas cyber-attacks in the payment field alone rose by 452% since 2015.

In the virtual health sector, SaMDs constantly collect and review information on medical photos, physiological position, lab outcomes, and more, creating potentially serious issues regarding the security of patient data. Self-directed vehicles may be susceptible to cyberattacks as well. The question is what precautions manufacturers of autonomous cars must take to guarantee that malicious hackers don't force cars to crash, or adjust signals to trigger traffic jams in the cities.

In a 2017 poll, 71% of respondents responded that there needed to be national guidelines on AI in the U.S., besides 67% called for global regulations modulating AI technology. However, AI in its different forms poses various tests to conventional regulation.

Among these issues is the "black-box" problem. Nowadays algorithms make measurements of strategic decisions, ranging from accepting loans to measuring heart-attack risk.

Considering the significance of algorithms for customers and companies, it's vital to comprehend them and make the best decisions based on available data.

However, algorithms usually are strictly held by the companies that formed them or are very complex such that even their inventors can't describe how they function.

This is referred to as "black-box", which means it is the lack of ability to see what is found or detected by an algorithm. To counter this, some professionals in the sector have suggested the use of algorithms in a way that is open to public inspection (Reins, 2019).

Some regulations aren't made public due to nondisclosure treaties with the businesses that developed them.

This is likely to be changed, nevertheless, at least in regions like the EU. In 2018, there are laws that went into effect wanting companies to explain exactly how algorithms through the use of personal information of clients operate and make decisions.

Algorithms are regularly being used to make crucial financial, credit, contracting, and legal decisions. Hypothetically, this may lead to balanced and fair decisions.

Though there are algorithms which have been discovered to have integral biases. Plus, while in some nations regulations plainly proscribe discrimination in various areas, gray zones exist and frequently the fundamental algorithms are opaque.

With this system, clients may basically get or not obtain those things which they require based on scores which they don't understand, plus sometimes may not even know are there (Reins, 2019).

3.10. STATUS OF TECHNOLOGY REGULATION

Recently, Google's top policy head called for "collective rules" globally in regards to technology regulation, this coming amid continuing debate around the globe concerning how to make proper legislation for the web economy. While a one-size for everyone approach towards regulation may not work, stakeholders still welcome some form of "convergence" that will set the rules straight internationally.

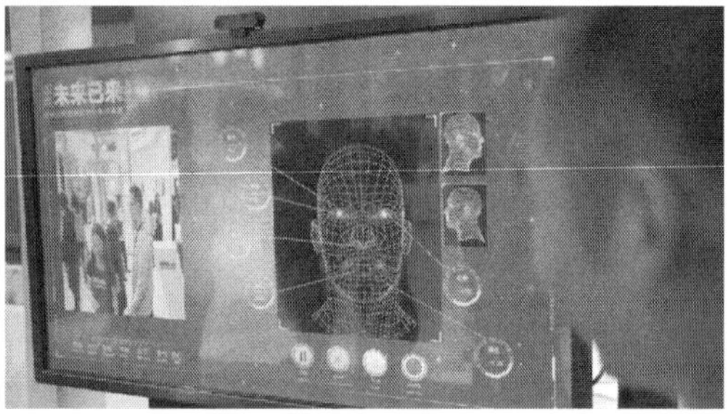

Figure 3.4. Facial recognition is a security-based technology that can be used by data companies.

Source: https://www.aljazeera.com/news/2019/08/eu-seeks-regulation-facial-recognition-technology-190822164833919.html.

There needs to be coordination and great levels of collaboration for this to work, besides it's going to be very critical in ensuring safety for tech users. All around the world, governments are seeking to determine how they can manage technology in all aspects, including data, taxation, and privacy (Reins, 2019).

Presently, the largest set of laws is the General-Data Protection Regulation (GDPR), governing all businesses that operate in 28 EU member states. Though other nations have gone their individual ways also. In America, for instance, California State is seeking to introduce its unique privacy rules in without any federal regulation. Equally, China has its exclusive rules especially around suppression of content.

There's increasing consensus toward imposing rules by policymakers, partly due to the criticism against huge technology firms that many see as having advanced largely because of unchecked practices in the last few years. Among the most famous incidents that increased awareness concerning data privacy needs were, the Cambridge-Analytica and Facebook scandals whereby millions of users' social network profiles were reaped for data.

In America, where legislation may be fragmented because of various state-level rules, stakeholders may call for a federal system. Apart from Google, other key participants in the technology sector, such as Apple, have also confirmed that they support federal privacy laws (Reins, 2019).

3.10.1. Rethinking Tech Regulation

As concern mounts regarding the risks that people face from driverless vehicles, AI, and social media, it is progressively becoming common to hear proposals for regulation, not just from legislators but even corporate titans who are shaping the future of innovation. What's still lacking is the urgency for revamping the future of policy and it's an issue.

The current regulatory tools, such as digitally terms and conditions which we all largely accept, plus the complex regulations which government bureaucracies establish, aren't up to the duty. They aren't quick enough, shrewd enough, or responsible enough to accomplish what we wish them to accomplish, whether it's improved privacy, data safety, or personal confidentiality. Besides, they may be too costly for most individuals to depend on (Zwanenberg, Ely, and Smith, 2013).

Case in point, it might be too soon to tell, however if the rush of new "approve" boxes on websites in reaction to the EU's GDPR is anything to go by, the actual impact on operator privacy and control would be too small since people still don't understand what they're assenting to. It shall also be expensive for individual users to monitor and legally challenge what companies are really doing with their information. Among the key reasons why regulatory frameworks are becoming so impractical is because there hasn't been sufficient funding, energy, and time for reviewing the way that people develop regulation since industries have to come up with fresh technologies.

People continue relying on existing tools to manage their businesses and communities, but given the fast pace of technology these may soon become obsolete. The goal is to create the necessary systems for coping with and managing emerging socioeconomic challenges brought about by technology. Regulation stakeholders should harness the same creativeness and motivation that built Facebook or other big techs to create the regulatory structures of the digital era, recompensing business and nonprofit inventors who may emerge with superior regulatory tools. This can be called "super-regulation" since it puts governments away from the work of legislating on ground-level particulars, and into the role of ensuring that a new viable market of private controllers works in the public's interest (Reins, 2019).

Consider the duty of regulating emerging gig-based e-businesses like Uber. States want to guarantee the safety of everyone who uses the service, including fairness for everyone who labors towards it. Though under present methods of regulation, there is need for a whole set of new regulatory principles covering labor privileges, information security or car safety standards as concerns this technology. Moreover, some standards may morph from one country to another, creating problems for inventors, and significant challenges for operators and workers. This movement towards a greater role for private firms in the shaping of regulatory systems is already underway, prompted by the double pressures of digitization and universality.

The private regulators shall be supported to invest in creating better ways for achieving the needed results. For the case of highly-demand driving services such as Uber, this may see supervisors contributing to ML innovation in order to confidently anticipate any accident risks, or innovation delivered across the driver's smartphone to gauge speed and other driving activities directly (Reins, 2019).Low-cost online dispute resolution systems, probably tied to blockchain, may be applied to ensure that drivers get paid as agreed.

The shift towards a greater role for private firms and companies in the development of regulatory structures is already underway, spurred by modernization. The advocates of this change are often eventually regulated businesses themselves—seeking to define a practically reliable playing-field where both them and contestants meet. This endeavor sees companies such as Microsoft, for instance, directing efforts to form universal standards for cybersecurity and anonymity, plus Google submitting to AI safety standards.

Businesses are also writing most of the regulations determining their own practices through their individual terms of service—that's in theory the result of "settlement" with their staffs and clienteles but which actually are under nearly complete corporate administration. The pressures of having many of the policies written down by private companies which are nearer to what's happening, at incredibly high rate, on the ground as well as in the cloud won't go away (Reins, 2019).

Conventional bureaucracy-driven regulation is just going to drop further behind or become more irrelevant, which is why it's essential that people create a controlled industry for private regulators. In this way, technology users can gain the best of all scenarios: the objectives of regulation are largely set by government agencies however the regulation technology, referring to the detailed way that those objectives are met, plus driven into a market system whereby 3rd parties better serve all factors related.

Private regulators must keep governments satisfied so that they can keep their licensure regulation. Besides, they must keep their regulatory clienteles happy by building easier, less expensive and more elastic ways of effecting regulatory controls. The quicker we move past the idea that traditional regulation is capable of handling the trials of our advanced new technologies, the greater. The call for regulation is needless unless people determine how to takes advantage of the influence of markets, as well as new approaches to state responsibility, to practice.

3.10.2. Europe's Effective Tech Regulation Measures

Studies show that almost half of all tech proposals globally originate from the EU. The continent has arisen as a frontrunner in regulating technology businesses, offering nearly 200 new rules within the initial half of 2019 alone, based on an all-encompassing universal survey. The assessment, done by a law firm called Hogan Lovells, established that well over 450 active legislative applications across 16 nations including France, Germany, China, Japan, Russia, South Africa, Mexico, the UK, the UAE, and the US.

Discussions varied from antitrust, technology tax and material regulation to information access and requests to subdivide tech firms. These proposals were suggested by organs such as governments, industry organs and NGOs. Generally, almost half of the suggestions made came from Europe, which may either be from the EU body or within specific member states, thereby making the area a trendsetter in matters regulation.

America accounted for roughly 28% of regulatory proposals, while China came in near the bottom with only 3% of tracked tech regulation. The data is significant since the initial mover in technology control usually has the capacity to influence other regions and international organs like G7 and OECD. Worldwide, antitrust enforcement ranked among the most renowned category, consisting of 26% of the total proposals made.

Among the most impressive things concerning competition, policy is the tools which antitrust agencies, such as Competition and Markets Authority possess. Sometimes, they can enforce severe penalties so it allows regulators to operate at the capacity of these large companies. Germany is regarded as an aggressive or super active country when it comes to matters of antitrust. The country recently introduced a draft law which proposes that for starters in the world's history, a firm will be regarded as dominant in case it has accessibility to information that's greater to others' information sets (Reins, 2019).

In the meantime, big U.S. technology businesses face several different federal and state-run investigations concerning their corporate influence in the US, probes have been launched targeting Facebook, Amazon, Google, and other large techs to find out whether they've unfairly repressed competition, thereby harming users in the process.

There's greater anticipation for antitrust enforcement as well as regulatory activities concerning digital platforms, big data, and algorithms, which is clearly not restricted to Big Tech, though may affect any business that's active in digital space.

Another field of regulatory concern lies with content control, particularly aspects like copyright, fighting hate speech online, and manipulating elections. In France, Singapore, and Germany, laws have also been enacted to combat fake news and hate language which are becoming quite common today. Currently, the UK is also working towards formulating a draft law concerning online dangers that may impose a risk of care on technology businesses. This may inspire them to police data more carefully on their platforms plus accept liability for any unlawful content (Reins, 2019).

3.11. MODERN REGULATION PRACTICES

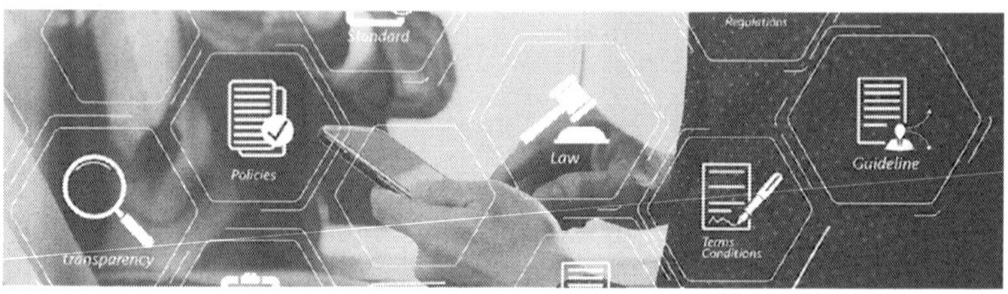

Figure 3.5. Tech regulation often gives businesses a level playing field in the market.

Source: https://www.bdo.com/digital/insights/grc/layered-security-protecting-your-organization.

Today's collection of privacy laws as well as industry self-regulation don't have transparency or coherence, plus may not go far enough towards protecting clients and competition. Within the last decade, technology giants have arisen to become some of the largest firms in the world, meanwhile working with minimal formal, structured state oversight. Though this lack of proper oversight may come at some cost.

One way that state authorities may put technology businesses on a standard playing field among each other, plus with contestants in regulated sectors, would be introducing a regulator who can check the tech sector in their country. Having a regulation system with nationwide principles and well-defined policies of engagement shall also reduce the price of innovation, whereas holding businesses accountable for managing abuses of their technologies, varying from criminal actions like hiring of terrorists to socially dangerous acts such as distributing user data and enabling the spread of false news (Byrne and Pitt, 2012).

In order for a countrywide tech regulator to become effective, they must adopt guidelines and new supervisory approaches capable of remaining ahead of the possible threats presented by emerging technological changes. The first nation to establish the best methods to regulate the wider tech industry may become the focal center for the next phase of the globe's digital revolution.

Borrowing on lessons coming from other regulated businesses, several ideas can be proposed on how to achieve this with large tech. To properly regulate technology, governments must first determine the proper regulatory range for the industry.

Outlining what is within the controlled perimeter is essential in determining how to participate with both controlled and unregulated zones. This also offers clarity for private users of tech and businesses on what's protected plus what's not captured.

There are certain overarching objectives which technology regulators should have. First, there is need to safeguard people and society from mistreatment; promoting responsible invention and robust competition; plus establishing understandable and reliable strictures for data privacy as well as monetization. The regulatory goals must be strengthened by metrics which shall allow agencies to judge whether tech firms are complying with countrywide statutes. In case they don't comply, then the agency must be empowered to perform a specific set of disciplinary actions to promote appropriate behaviors like cease-and-desist directives, comply-or-explain demands, fines, and lawful sanctions (Byrne and Pitt, 2012).

Additionally, innovations emerging from tech companies including the risks accompanying them are changing so quickly that it is quite easy for controllers to fall back. Standards-based regulatory systems capable of adjusting to technical and social change may help regulators to get at the fore and remain there.

While standards may be revised for new risks, still regulatory changes and laws need broad public consultation. Through a standards-based method, regulators can introduce fresh guidelines to inspire sensible innovation or, alternatively, quickly hold tech firms accountable when unexpected risks arise. Same as conduct standards found in financial solutions and energy sectors, standards-based regulatory systems can quickly adjust to gray zones of regulatory compliance. The process is most significant in the field of AI ethics. Stakeholders should also rank activity depending on the level of risk. Innovation companies regularly introduce new applications, unique software, and hardware internationally, besides there's a real risk that even when cash-strapped states implement new guidelines, they may not afford sufficient staffing to appropriately enforce them (Reins, 2019).

Therefore, regulators must apply a risk-based technique to prioritize the businesses and activities which place the most individuals at risk, plus rank the scale of potential threats. The amount of supervisory intrusiveness must be proportionate to the dimension of the potential threats which companies pose. Large companies may need devoted in-house supervisory staffs, whereas much smaller teams may oversee mainly programmed data-driven information from startups. This makes sure that startups aren't unethically disadvantaged because of high rates of regulatory compliance.

Yet another regulation strategy is making supervision virtual by default for companies. Likewise, machine-executable regulations, assimilated data networks, and application coding interfaces for recording must be included among the standard operative model from the first day, in order to decrease the compliance, cost for businesses while improving the efficiency of risk management. Through substituting quarterly filings with technology platforms which allow regulators to draw information tied to key risk pointers from businesses' systems directly, regulators shall be in a position to monitor firms more adeptly.

These methods are being introduced in major fiscal services markets, such as those in the United States, United Kingdom, and Singapore. There are various initial signs that programmed supervisory technologies are decreasing the rate of compliance for technology firms, including the rate of regulation for supervisors. They're also improving the efficacy of risk management through limiting human data-entry flaws. Moreover, initiatives such as the Global Fiscal Innovation Network of supervision agencies globally, which allows firms to test fresh supervisory technologies and solutions in the financial industry across jurisdictions, must be simulated for the tech sector globally.

Furthermore, regulators can contribute significantly in preventing potential flaws from materializing by establishing controlled partnerships for working with tech companies, in order to detect and address newly forming risks with fresh regulations as fast and competently as possible. Of great importance is having a standing body for facilitating engagement that is fully staffed and able to perform research and analysis, it ensures that data is shared and fresh threats are addressed (Reins, 2019).These partnerships are present in other industries already. For instance, the Joint Currency Laundering Intelligence Unit established by banks, regulation agencies, and the UK government trades and evaluates information tied to money laundering, including other wider fiscal threats. The activities tech giants practice today inspires not just worldwide growth but also possible threats. States must contribute in rekindling public trust in technology firms by instituting national regulators which can combat abuses, meanwhile allowing for technological advances since these firms' technologies affect the very fabric of our daily lives, besides practical action can make some significant difference to millions of tech users. This shall require well-organized, countrywide regulatory regimes which can hold technology firms accountable while promoting innovation and better competition (Boothby, 2018).

3.11.1. Blockchain Regulation Considerations

The invention of blockchain is regarded as the most crucial and revolutionizing technology. Considering the quick growth of blockchain, particularly following the launch and widespread adoption of Bitcoin, the technology has gained considerable attention over the last few years.

Nevertheless, blockchain still has a long way to go before being released for mass adoption because of different viewpoints of regulators.

Due to some negative effects and potential criminal features of Bitcoin, countries should implement their own rules for managing blockchain, bitcoin as well as other cryptocurrencies.

3.11.2. Implementation Measures

Any new technology requires time for new regulations to be implemented, particularly in the fintech industry where regulators are tasked with coordinating and ensuring industry steadiness. Blockchain, a promising technology that is providing progressive applications in business, isn't an exception.

Following the launch and adoption of Bitcoin, it has gained exponential impact in the last few years, inspiring many platforms, startups, applications, programs, and research. After the invention of blockchain, the growth and triumph of cryptocurrencies have gathered more momentum. In fact, currently there are well over 1,100 cryptocurrencies officially trading in the finance market. Because of the immense attention and possible growth of blockchain as well as cryptocurrencies, the authorities are working towards fulfilling blockchain regulation in America.

Blockchain innovation is regarded as a trustless innovation which means that a transaction is verified, reviewed, and imposed without the existence of a reliable third party or major institution because of its decentralization Furthermore, blockchain has no borders plus leads to an inexpensive, faster infrastructure for substituting units of value. Even though there are various opinions concerning blockchain and cryptocurrencies, U.S. controllers must develop a greater understanding of blockchain innovation's impact potential, since they continue participating in its regulation.

3.11.3. Diverse Judgments and Protocols

Because of blockchain's benefits in fintech like improved transaction security and lessened risk of manipulation, the new innovation is among the biggest regulatory setbacks for regulators. Still, some regulators are concerned about blockchain's influence on financial stability as well as market integrity, meaning they must quickly evaluate how to expertly regulate this innovation with regards to the issue of instability.

Up to when the regulators determine a coherent reaction to blockchain innovation, each regulatory agency can move autonomously and inconsistently to implement their own interpretation. Besides, blockchain and cryptocurrencies like Bitcoin and Ethereum must be supervised by its unique applications.

For instance, the American Internal Revenue Service or IRS requires that cryptocurrency traders should reveal their uniqueness and cryptocurrency transactions must be taxed in the same way as property transactions. Furthermore, the U.S. Treasury's Fiscal Crimes Enforcement Network, also known as FinCEN, provided a "directive that a digital precious metals trade using blockchain innovation was subject to regulatory cash transmission regulations (Boothby, 2018).

Contrarily, the American Commodity Futures Trading Agency considers cryptocurrencies as commodities which are within their jurisdiction. The commission identified that "lack of market standards up to date is due to the point that blockchain innovation is still rising and their execution shall be incremental."

Furthermore, the American Securities Exchange Commission or SEC, which has been vigorously exploring potential systems of blockchains for fiscal services businesses in the open securities market, made convictions that cryptocurrencies should be under their influence. Besides, the SEC has been on the forefront of early blockchain adoption pertaining to securities hosted on its blockchain platform.

In the US the authorities don't have any constitutional pre-emptive power to manage blockchain to the restriction of states, meaning that the states can remain free to present their own policies and regulations. For instance, at least 8 U.S. States have handled bills approving or promoting the usage of Bitcoin as well as blockchain system in 2017 (Boothby, 2018).

3.12. CANADA'S TECHNOLOGY RULES AND POLICY

Figure 3.6. Technology is the gateway to a more productive and dynamic future.

Source: https://canada.businesschief.com/technology/1114/Technology:-The-Future-of-Business-in-Canada.

The overall attitude of Canada's government (as well as regulatory agencies) towards cryptocurrencies has for the large part been a mixture of care and encouragement. There must be caution in regards to protecting stakeholders and the public, plus encouragement in terms of supporting new technology. Case in point, just recently in 2015, Standing Senate Commission on Banking, Trade and Commerce delivered a report called, "Online Currency: You Can't Turn This Coin," where the committee agreed that a balanced regulation system is required in the online currency sector.

For once, the committee is aware that the state bears responsibility for protecting customers and rooting out unlawful activity. Furthermore, it's imperative that government activities don't repress innovation in online currencies and its related technologies which are within the early and subtle stage of development. Following completion of research, the commission is of the viewpoint that the opportunities availed by online currencies, technologies, and companies outweigh the setbacks (Boothby, 2018).

Experts are confident that execution of the agreed recommendations shall have positive consequences for customers, merchants, virtual currency-related companies, and Canada's fiscal services sector among others. They also look forward towards a timely government participation designed to make the most of the prospects and control the challenges that face digital currencies sector. The Canadian government is also experimenting a lot with the blockchain system, showing prospects of a brighter future in terms of mainstream adoption of technology.

Currently, the National Research Council (NRC) is testing blockchain for purposes of publishing research grant as well as funding data in real-time. For taxation reasons, cryptocurrencies are handled as commodities, and not as cash. Under securities regulations, a good number of "tokens" and cryptocurrencies are categorized as securities. While cryptocurrencies aren't considered as legal cash in Canada, it's still being widely used across the country (Boothby, 2018).

Borrowing from Section 8 of Canada's Currency Act, a legal tender is any currency that's issued by Royal Canadian Mint with permission from the Royal Canadian Minting Act, including notes supplied by Bank of Canada. While cryptocurrency hasn't yet been authorized as legal tender, still there's progress considering that Bank of Canada recently tested the Digital Depositories Receipts (DDR) to act as the virtual representation of Canadian money in 2017. The technology is a means of transferring central bank cash through a distributed ledger innovation platform. Typically, DDRs are provided as online tokens on the blockchain system, and function as a central bank reserve claim.

The government also launched "CADcoin" so as to better comprehend the possible effects of blockchain innovation on Fiscal Market Infrastructure." This was a joint project between public and private businesses, piloted Payments Canada and Bank of Canada with assistance from banks and companies. Mutually, they developed and tested a sealed, simulated payment structure to better comprehend the possibility of blockchain to enhance or substitute FMI. This project marked the very first DLT experiment whereby a central bank affiliated with private monetary institutions.

There were two stages of the "CADcoin" project. The first phase was established on an Ethereum system. Ethereum operates using Proof-of-Work or "PoW" accord protocol to systematically settle transactions. In phase two, the Corda platform was developed. During this test, the Canadian Bank acted as a notary, gaining access to the whole ledger and validating the transactions. Furthermore, Bank of Canada considered lawful settlement finality.

The project was also designed such that the exchange of DDR corresponded to a complete and irrevocable exchange of the fundamental claim on central banking deposits. Even though using DDR needs considerable Bank of Canada participation in a system which many hope shall be decentralized, still it provides certainty concerning lawful settlement finality seldom found in blockchains.

For Canada, cryptocurrencies are mainly regulated under the securities policies as part of securities' controllers mandate to safeguard the public. Securities laws within the country are also ratified on a provincial as well as territorial basis instead of federally. Regulation trends in the country, across all territories and provinces have mostly been harmonized (Boothby, 2018).

Moreover, the Canadian Securities Administration (the "CSA"), an informal agency, represents every province and territory sanctioned securities controllers in Canada. The trial for determining if a transaction comprises of an investment contract, hence a security, for reasons of Canadian securities policies was instituted by the Canadian Supreme Court, denoting from the U.S. jurisprudence. In case the cryptocurrency holds a particular value during the period of its disposition, which is in surplus of its tax rate, then it would be crucial to determine if the holder must report these excesses as representative of capital account, or if the proceeds must be recorded as business income.

CHAPTER

Computer Knowledge Management

4

CONTENTS

4.1. INTRODUCTION

This field refers to any kind of system of IT that is used in storing and retrieving any knowledge that was stored from different sources that were hidden to improve the computer knowledge management system. This is any information that helps people in any company or organization to easily share ideas, access or even improve their knowledge and information in business.

It involves the proper understanding of how and where the forms of Knowledge Management (KM) can be found in creating a good environment for proper learning, sharing, and knowledge building, and hence creating the accurate knowledge materials to the right personnel at the correct time.

It should, in turn, provide the right tools, people, knowledge, structures, and culture to improve the value and the use of the new knowledge built. The main purpose of knowledge management of computers is building values and meeting strategic and tactical needs, it comprises of initiative, processes, strategies, and systems that can hold and improve the storage, assessment, sharing, refinement, and creation (Wallace, 2007).

4.2. THREE TOPMOST KNOWLEDGE MANAGEMENT EXAMPLES

The first example is Evernote, which has a very simple organized procedure. For example, their search bar is in the front center and very visible. Their help center has a list of top articles as well as a more detailed way of acquiring information from other resources if the need arises.

The second example is Canva, which values customer interactions on their website because they know this is the greatest success. With the customers having a big say on Canvas, the company can grow their business to greater heights.

The canvas knowledge management provides' a sidebar with simple titles and well-organized methods centered around creating designs, account basics and its use for work.

The third example is Instacart, which has a simple web layout suitable for people who aren't advanced in technology. They have a clear search bar and answers to the most popular customer questions, such as how Instacart works, etc.

4.3. ELEMENTS OF KNOWLEDGE MANAGEMENT

There are four elements of knowledge management: people, process, content or Information technology (IT) and strategy. Despite the industry or organization size people are needed to sponsor and support knowledge sharing, being the most important in knowledge management people who are either in the inside or outside tend to build, organize, transfer, apply knowledge hence having meaning to the humans only. Clear processes are needed to define and measure knowledge flows.

They are also four pillars of knowledge management and this is leadership, technology, learning, and proper organization. They are also tools used in knowledge management and these are customer relation procedures, learning management systems and knowledge basis. The organizational level is assisted by 4-dimensional knowledge sharing and these are individual, social, managerial, and cultural dimensions. Computer knowledge management helps businesses to tackle common business mistakes and also improving their benefits due to the availability of leading experts and also to leading practices.

Therefore, knowledge is the proper or inside understanding of something or someone such as the small factors, descriptions, and skills. There are also factors that make this computer knowledge management system fail, e.g., lack of proper support in managing and technical support when installing and using it, seeing that the technology is knowledge management solution on its own, lack of proper content management, not understanding the pros and cons of each particular system, lacking of proper content management and lack of proper understanding of what each firm needs. We usually consider elements such as quality, innovation, personnel, finances, and resources but they are still other important ones like knowledge by understanding the different skills and information (Wallace, 2007).

There are two types of knowledge management and this include:

- External knowledge management systems (KMS) this specific on the client, their preferences and their habits, the brands of the completion and the whole market outside. But also includes the distributes, their suppliers and the third agent who normally play a big part in the production chain.
- Internal knowledge here we focus more on the information that takes place inside the company and not anywhere else, hence it is its heritage and in turn creating unique.

4.4. FACTORS THAT PLAY A BIG ROLE IN COMPUTER KNOWLEDGE MANAGEMENT

They are two important factors that play a big role in computer knowledge management:

- Skills and talents are very important to the companies or organization and to efficiently which require time and resources to transmit them to new minds during training;
- Information is faster because it is transmitted by the user computer system and if it is well designed it can gather outside information;
- In a company set up, managers or bosses meet various challenges especially in the field of computer knowledge management;
- Encouraging a team to have teamwork and be able to share their ideas and proper sharing of data can be difficult at times;
- Knowledge contribution cannot be measured hence it depends on shared purpose rather than its efforts or resorts;
- Security is another one if proper levels of security are not installed or permissions to ensure the correct information is shared through the right channels or the intended persons;
- Managers should ensure the information stored is up to date by ensuring they install reminders and monitors to remind them to regularly update their stored data;
- Data or information that is provided by various groups should be easy to interpret for another group by installing proper standard procedures;
- By keeping up to date with the ever-changing technology which in turn opens new doors to different opportunities;
- By not overloading the user with unnecessary information proper meta-data should be installed to reduce unnecessary data that doesn't help the users;
- By proper rewarding for clients which can be tough at times but very necessary as it creates a strong community who supports you but also this encourages new clients to join;
- Determining who is the right person to head the institution can be very difficult but with the right breakdown of work in a community one can easily pick out the best candidates for the desired positions and this works best is a community was set up before; and

- Many people have a lot of tension when it comes to sharing leadership and they need to feel so match attached that they need to approve various things.

Proper knowledge management greatly reduces the cost of inefficiency by making company knowledge easily available, accessible, and accurate.

This scope of the field comes with its benefits also and they include:

- When information is easily accessible it reduces the number of hours or minutes trying to find it creating it;
- It also helps in getting information and answers faster;
- When information about past mistakes is easily accessible mistakes done in the future will be highly reduced as one can learn and know how to hand them;
- By sharing lessons learned or even researches that were previously done it will greatly help when coming to decision making;
- Proper documentation and shared processes ensure that everyone is following the right procedures and is on the same page, unlike telephone conversations which can easily be distorted; and
- Proper services to employees and customers by solving their issues quickly and within a short time, enable the customers to stay happy and very productive enabling them to able to invest more and purchase from these companies.

It not only creates positive outcomes in the business field, but the goal of knowledge management should also be creating positive outcomes among its employees and their customers (Wallace, 2007).For any business or organization to succeed or survive with the changing trends it depends on how better it fits in the business environment and by the use of computer knowledge management a lot has changed. To understand knowledge management better one should differentiate between knowledge and information like for instance information comprises facts and data that solve the problems while knowledge is all about truth and beliefs, concepts, and know-how. Information relates to description or definition while knowledge comprises of strategy, practice, method or approach. With proper IT infrastructures like E-mails, documents, data warehousing, workflow software all support in knowledge management. IT is an important facilitator for improving an organization.Knowledge management processes are different ways of creating, acquiring, and using knowledge. This is usually human information that normally exists as to their thoughts. This is very broad because it commonly exists and is applied in intensive business processes, training, and events. Knowledge management can also include the study of various fields like business administration, information systems, management, library, and other fields of knowledge in science (Wallace, 2007). Has 3 dimensions which sustain competitive advantage that help in an organizations' development and planning that create more value to it and this are,

- The strategic dimension which gives more insight into the concept of knowledge and management in an institution strategy;
- Managing dimension gives more insight into the institutional knowledge assessment and management; and
- Operation dimension sheds light on the creation and usage of knowledge and intellectual assets.

4.5. PROCESSES OF KNOWLEDGE MANAGEMENT

They are 4 processes of knowledge management;

First, we have the knowledge generation due to the great number of information and data that is created in companies daily it's important for the organization to create a plan whereby the new found knowledge is stored so that it can be used in the future to solve arising issues. If the companies cannot meet the knowledge requirements that are needed to they can source or develop from their internal knowledge or external knowledge.Second is knowledge codification where proper documentation and decoding of knowledge for learning, utilization, both external and internal will be very easy. Data and information are collected and later analyzed to turn them into useful knowledge that will be used later.The third is the knowledge application with proper documentation and storage of knowledge proper goals within the company can be achieved.Fourth is a very dynamic knowledge transfer and it can be used in learning and sharing. Individual knowledge has no big impact as collective knowledge so sharing within an organization is highly recommended.Proper knowledge management implantation can significantly reduce common challenges, minimize the risks and in turn maximize the profits below are some of the ways;

- Creating knowledge management program objectives and for one to identify the proper program objectives, recognize, and document the business problems that need resolutions and the business drivers who will enable the smooth running of the business. In addition, it should be documented in short-term and long-term objectives; short –term objectives should ensure that the program is running on the right track while long-term objectives will help to communicate and build the bigger picture.

- Preparing for successful implementation of new knowledge within an organization to reduce resistance knowledge management champions should be recruited to encourage positive sharing of ideas within the staff and the embrace of the new knowledge management system.
- Laying out of the high-level process as a foundation will help with the effective implantation of the knowledge management process.
- Determining and prioritizing the technology needs a market place for knowledge management solutions is very big and diverse and it's good to know the primary providers, understand the cost and benefit of each type of technology and finding a way to use each solution that would help to reach the desired objectives. By finding out what employees are using and what their challenges are, and ways of gaining more insight on the important issues.
- Accessing current state after laying down the proper program objectives, preparing for cultural changes, defined a high-level process and fully determined and prioritized the technology needs, assessing knowledge management within the organization will be very easy. Assessment should cover the five most important knowledge management points, e.g., people, processes, technology, structure, and culture. A good report should be able to detect the gap between current and desired states and give the best recommendations for closing the gap.
- Building a knowledge management implantation road map – having solid information about the shortcomings of a particular organization and with the proper strategy, the roadmap will yield some short-term objectives which will help boost the long-term objectives effectively. As time progresses the roadmap should constantly be updated according to the changing economic conditions and the business drivers.
- Implementation requires adequate funding and resources to enable the smooth running of a new knowledge management process. Then put in actions the objectives of the road map to work but always ensure that the short-term goals are met in order not to lose focus or the supporters.

Always measure and improve the knowledge management program, keep old records, and compare them with new records that way it will easily tell you if there is an improvement or not and what achievements or milestones that have been attained (Wallace, 2007).

The use of knowledge management takes a lot of time and resources to be implemented however if properly supervised the outcome can be great and the risks can be greatly reduced by taking a different approach that has promising benefits at each step. Companies or institutions that have invested well in knowledge management have in the end gotten good results at the end.

Knowledge includes the techniques and tools used to gather, integrate the information. We have a few different models and which can later be analyzed into two categories and the first is a forbidden subject to the IT scope and while the second is about organization development and insists on the structure and corporate culture to facilitate the interaction between the different individuals. It consists of four different stages of knowledge management and they are acquisition, creation, reuse, and sharing (Nonaka, 2005).

Acquisition knowledge is an external knowledge source which is the most important integral part when it comes to the acquisition of the information. This type of knowledge comes in many forms such as knowledge obtained from suppliers, customers, partners, external experts, and even competitors.

Knowledge creation is the heart of the organization because it creates new ideas available. The line between the act of knowing and possessing are considered to be the most important movers when it comes to the creation of new knowledge and hence knowledge sharing and creation go together.

4.6. KNOWLEDGE REUSES

There are three main roles in the reuse of knowledge and these are as follows;

- Creator of knowledge who is the original producer;
- Intermediary who indexes knowledge packs it, and prepares it so it can be adequately stored, retrieved when needed to and shared again; and
- Knowledge consumer who is known to be the recipient and after on the user of the knowledge in question.

All of the functions can either be performed by different people or be performed by the same individual. As far as tacit knowledge is concerned, the role of an intermediary belongs to the expert himself or herself, as he or she is the one that must present knowledge through practice and socialization. The functions imply that someone has to produce knowledge in the first place which is further going to be made available to all who require that particular knowledge (Nonaka, 2005).Knowledge sharing is the most important as various knowledge management issues depend on it. It is all about providing the right knowledge available at the right time to the right people.Knowledge management is not only about the information created it is also about the people who have been recruited, trained, developed, and promoted within the organization. It also doesn't involve the implementations of a software system it involves understanding the business needs, culture, and personnel at work.

For the knowledge management initiative to be successful, they required five steps should be followed;

- By understanding the key business drivers to improve the bottom line either they should increase the revenue and reduce the cost. If the initiative of the business is not defined before it is implemented the organization won't adopt it in its system.
- By getting executive sponsorship it can be the biggest difference between success and failure and the best sponsor is the main key driver of the business
- Analyzing the knowledge – the most common downfall of knowledge management is to attempt to collect and distributing the information in the organization. The amount of cost used to collect and categorize the data information tends to be very costly at times. If not done effectively it might be impossible to access the data and employees will not be able to access the useful information. There is no point at collecting all the organization knowledge what is important is to identify the knowledge that greatly affects the business drivers and collect only that. Particular types of knowledge such as project statues update should be shared in real-time, also they are other types of knowledge such as the best practices learned from implantation that need to be shared across an institution.

- Providing rewards and recognition to make knowledge management successful in an institution is recommended. Visible recognition in an organization may have a big impact.
- Implementing in phases by breaking the process in small manageable phases will greatly help the people in the organization to get used to change, Each phase should yield important lessons and new ideas that should be used in the next phase. The benefits of knowledge management can be very promising but initiating it can be tricky.

Computer knowledge management training should be constantly done because not everyone can be successfully trained. Examples of training methods include classroom courses, recorded webinars, and self-paced courses to allow everyone to know what is expected of them (Maier, 2007). These learning strategies are recommended by experts:

- The classroom course is the best method because it captures the full undivided attention of the individuals but this method can prove expensive if funds are not available.
- Webinars – these are courses which are easy to attend because it can be done through various ways, e.g. via conference calls. The participants meet in a meeting room where they can watch presentations and chat with other participants. The conference call can be recorded and the individual can listen in later at their own free time.
- Self-paced courses – these are interactive presentations and can include the web pages where students read and follow as they go. Students can bookmark their favorite pages and continue at any time they want.
- There are also different delivery methods:
- Web-based – this is done through a web browser either on the intranet or the internet.
- Client-based – is delivered as a downloaded application run on the client PC.
- Portable media-based – delivered as a CD/ DVD or the flash memory plugged in.

The training plan should include the following elements for each course: the delivery method of the course, the schedule, duration which it will last, the intended audience, the instructors/tutors, developer, compliance the context, and publicity.

Some of knowledge management benefits include:

- Improved organization agility;
- Better and faster decision making;
- Quicker problem-solving;
- Increased rate in innovation;
- Supported employee growth and development;
- Sharing of specialist expertise;
- Better communication; and
- Improved business processes.

With a good computer knowledge management system, it will be very easier to find and to reuse information across the business (Maier, 2007). This, in turn, will help in:

- The creation of better goods and products or services.
- The development of better strategies;
- Increasing the profit margins;
- Reusing existing skills and expertise;
- Increasing operational efficiency and staff productivity;
- Recognizing new incoming trends in the market and taking advantage before the competitors; and
- Creating the most out of the intellectual capital.

The most important key for knowledge management to thrive is to know its limitations and how to handle them and below are some of the most common challenges in this field;

- How to find new ways to create and record business knowledge;
- Resources and information can be hard to find;
- The process of motivating people to reuse, apply, share the information which they can refuse;
- The aligning of business strategy and knowledge management can be head in meeting the precise goals;
- Also choosing and implementing knowledge management technology can be hard; and
- In existing processes integrating new technology in knowledge management as well as new information can be hard.

But these common challenges can be overcome by;

- Developing clear, precise strategies to capture records and share business knowledge;
- By properly defining the intentions and objectives of any new knowledge management system before being initiated;
- By creating a better environment between the employee and management for easy sharing of knowledge;
- The goals should be clear and all the strategies should be well planned to enable proper utilization of the knowledge collected;
- Allows put in the budget, strategy, and training needs of any new knowledge management that should be installed; and
- The management strategies should be changed constantly to enable the new introduction of the knowledge management process.

4.7. BENEFITS OF COMPUTER KNOWLEDGE MANAGEMENT

4.7.1. In Business

Through fast access to KMS, it is easier for organizations to find their information and also its stalk holders. Hence creating an environment that is so easy for them to work in because all the information is there and they don't need to repeat it.

It greatly improves the decision-making process within the organization because the information is readily available and very easy to access enabling the management to decide quickly on what to do and how to do it best.

It greatly promotes cultural change and innovation whereby people are open to sharing new ideas, access the latest information and enhance collaboration within the staff of a particular.

The business organization needs to be more efficient in its business process and within its operating units, there is no excuse for small performance within them because they already have knowledge that is open and flows freely.

Using KMS by increasing customer satisfaction can greatly increase the productivity of an institution.

4.7.2. In Healthcare

It has greatly helped to turn information overload into educative and easy decision making with the new flow of technology the healthcare team gets an overload in the data managing and storage but with the new knowledge management they can be able to store their data and information safely and be able to retrieve it easily and when they need it.In the medical field there is no room for mistakes. With the help of knowledge management in the health care institution important and life-saving information is easily available to any expert or doctors hence helping greatly but also keeping confident the patients' details.

4.7.3. In Farming

Knowledge management is being used by agricultural organizations to help farmers improve their yield by making better decisions. It has become an important tool in capturing, storing, and processing data and information. The introduction of an online plant clinic has greatly helped farmers to adopt new technologies and even learn more about how to improve significantly. In creating a good knowledge management system for agriculture expert analysis and observations are needed for its development. The knowledge management has also provided an extensive information base where farmers can learn from and a portal for them to sell their products.

4.7.4. In Organizational Behavior

Organizational behavior is concerned with all aspects of how an organization influences the behavior of individuals and how they in turn also influence the organization in return. This field draws freely from several behavioral sciences such as anthropology, sociology, and the likes. However, its most important concept is to apply behavioral science to the most pressing issues in management.

There are 13 types of knowledge as listed below;

- Posteriori knowledge: This is derived from a Latin word which means 'what comes after' so it means its experience which comes after practice.
- Prior knowledge it means from before: This is the assumption that comes before an argument, analysis or assessment. This system is normally used in logic thinking, mathematics, physics, and thought experiments especially scientific theories that are developed and proved using this prior knowledge.

- Dispersed knowledge: This is knowledge with no reliable truth to back it up because it is derived from many sources and a good example is a financial market due to its fast-moving nature many people tend to develop a different opinion about it. Creating mixed ideas among investors.
- Domain knowledge: This is concerned about a specific area like an expert in that particular field.
- Empirical knowledge: This is derived from qualitative and quantitative observations, experiments or even measures. Its normally used to prove the truth about a point or proving the falsity of an argument.
- Encoded knowledge: This is also known as collective explicit knowledge. Which mostly is entitles symbols, signs, such as books, documents, manuals, notes, and codes of practice. Thus, helping to predict the patterns or behaviors in an organization.
- Explicit knowledge: It is also referred to as expressive knowledge, it can easily be expressed, organized, and verbalized. The best examples are the encyclopedias and documents.
- Known unknown knowledge: This is the type of knowledge that one knows but you don't know yet. This knowledge is very beneficial because it allows one to research and enhance oneself.
- Metaknowledge: This type of knowledge about knowledge is normally used to describe tags, models, and taxonomies which are used to say more about knowledge. Metaknowledge is a fundamental instrument in fields like knowledge engineering and knowledge management.
- Procedural Knowledge: This is the knowledge to do something. This type is very difficult to convey because it depends on the job nature. It's also considered as the intellectual property of an organization and it can only be acquired if accompany is procured. Involves more sense such as practical experience in solving problems. This procedural knowledge is very different from descriptive knowledge because here everyone has a different approach to do a similar task and hence descriptive knowledge is obtained by doing that.
- Propositional knowledge: This is also known as descriptive, declarative, and constantly and it can be represented in a natural or formal language such as mathematics or propositional logic.

- Situated knowledge: Normally comes from a viewpoint; it reflects content that can be used to explain a difficult analyzed history of a particular culture to an outside.
- Tactic knowledge: This is very difficult to attain or explain. It is associated with a unique experience that allows selective people to achieve mastering abilities in that particular artist, such as playing musical instruments or even solving puzzles. The other good example of tactic knowledge is emotional knowledge because it comes naturally and achieves excellent results. Other kinds include strategy, problem-solving, intuition, and also decision making.

In psychology, philosophers have divided knowledge into 3 classes and these are personal, procedural, and propositional. In this field knowledge consists of 3 basic elements;

- The human belief or mental representation about the actual state of affairs;
- The accurately corresponds to the actual state of affairs, e.g., is it true or false; and
- Legitimized by logic and empirical factors such as a scientist can be able to back or support his work fully as opposed to some is not a scientist and just repeats words without even having fully understood the concept. Justifying what one knows should have solid evidence to back it up.
- Philosophers also have two angles in their scope of the field and this is;
- Ontology: refers to the study of reality which is used to determine what exists in reality; and
- Epistemology: refers to how humans see things from their point of view.

In marine biology, computer knowledge management plays a very big role in services like handling the marine life, filtering, and visualization of large-scale marine life. This particular scope of field emphasizes the exchange of scientific and technological information for the success of government projects such as food security, biosecurity initiatives such as restriction of fish diseases that migrate from one area to another. Most institutions have used knowledge management to improve documentation, operational efficiency, and information sharing. Others have taken it as a way to fully transform their companies, e.g., from a multi-platform to single-platform. In the coast region strategies have been laid down to develop and implement desired activities that will include all the stalk holders in different levels like locally, national, and international levels. The lessons learned from different case studies can greatly help in changing the coastal tourism area. With the use of knowledge management themes in the coast which will provide useful products which will disclose information to tourist which are the best place to attend to and these themes include: the coastal local voices, coastal bets practices and technologies, coastal environmental economic dynamics and the coastal policy change processes (Fernandez and Sabherwal, 2014).

Computer knowledge management technologies are information technologies that contribute to knowledge management. The key technologies are communication and collaboration that are web-based for internet and intranet usage as well as mobile technologies such as telephones and video conferencing. For an effective knowledge management process to be initiated it needs a few things in place;

- The knowledge portal: This is a gateway of information that enables the user to use one or many ways for assessing the information. It contains software technologies that support the process of team communication and collaboration.
- Knowledge profiles: This is a portal whereby the user can create their profile which is personal but is specifically on their needs, area of interest and their frequency of distribution.
- Collaborative Workspaces: These are workspaces created within organization workspaces that can be set up for new team members or projects, this will act as knowledge portals where new knowledge will be stored in an orderly manner and when needed it easily found and can be shared across other teams within the organization.
- Urgent requests: The portal should have a facility that enables urgent requests to be sent and be received within the company without worrying who will know.
- The document libraries: The document libraries are the locations where all the documents are stored. Most organizations today have employed the use of Electronic Documents and Record Management systems (EDRMS) and it should flow smoothly with other information and knowledge sources.
- To improve knowledge across the whole organization and to support knowledge processes a centralized knowledge server

is needed to facilitate easy communication between people, for the easy access, creation, and sharing of knowledge among the organization teams.

Knowledge management system refers to any kind of IT that normally stores and retrieves knowledge that is intended to improve collaboration, locating knowledge sources, find all the hidden knowledge, uses the knowledge to improve the knowledge management process. The structure of knowledge management consists of 8 elements: knowledge management strategy, human, and social knowledge management issues, knowledge management organizational, knowledge management processes, knowledge management technologies, knowledge management performance measurements, leadership in knowledge management, business cases and implementation in knowledge management. Adoption, acceptance, and assimilation are the 3 stages that make knowledge management implementation successful.

Knowledge management is considered a very important tool especially in the growth of the economy. It also depends on the organizational structure thus organizational structure determines how roles, powers, and responsibilities are divided and to what extent to ensure proper flow of information in an organization. A good example is in the traditional hierarchical structure where the senior management makes all the decisions. Hence this kind of knowledge management system greatly affects sharing and creation of knowledge within the organization and interactions between the individuals' decreases. While in decentralized structures decision making power is distributed among various departments creating diverse information availability. Communities of practice can be well facilitated in the organizational structure. These communities of practice are groups of people who have already organized themselves but they are dispersed in different places but they communicate regularly to discuss important issues. Communities of practice have a large group of individuals as opposed to traditional departmental boundaries, in turn, they are also well informed about the new technology that is available like blogs and social networking technologies (Fernandez and Sabherwal, 2014).

Knowledge management in education is becoming one of the most important academic tool, improving the academic systems and resource patterns within and outside the organization. Teachers or education providers should be knowledgeable about changing and introduction of knowledge management to pass positive information knowledge to their students. Knowledge is the most important intellectual capital in an organization and is normally stored deep inside their brains. The advantages of knowledge are that it enhances competence, improve decision making, strengthening the commitment of an organization. To help teachers' grow and enhance their knowledge is very beneficial to an institution but most information that these teachers have originated from their many years of experience and this in turn when passed down to these students them are enlightened with knowledge. In developing countries education has developed very fast than other knowledge-based institutions the likes of software, pharmaceutical, architecture, and management consulting which will require a big push up so as improve. Knowledge management has greatly supported the growth of knowledge management in schools and turns improving the culture of learning organizations, hence enhancing E-learning and manages the legal and intellectual property of a school. More, however, knowledge management cannot be bought or used within a given time frame because it is a dynamic and continuous process implemented over some time depending on the human relations and their culture (Wallace, 2007). It is very possible to study knowledge management in school in 3 phases and this is as follows;

- Information technology (IT);
- Human resource; and
- Integrated perceptive.

Given the rapid change in curriculum, teachers have to manage knowledge from different sources and spend a lot of time collecting data and information and turning them to use teaching materials. The teachers can greatly reduce their workload by sharing knowledge within them.

Computer knowledge management in the nursing field has greatly improved its performance; nurses are the largest group of the first care health providers and play a large part in improving healthcare services. The success of nursing has greatly improved due to the ability to apply current and the most relevant knowledge needed. Technology has helped nurses to organize and update their information from different sources to help them improve in giving standard healthcare services. IT has significantly improved the quality of the healthcare IT improves collaboration between nurses as well as the sharing and creating knowledge that improves the timeliness of quality of and access to a variety of healthcare services. Healthcare services were based on six elements which are safety, timeliness, effectiveness, efficiency, equity, and patient-centered. While equity is concerned with closing the gap between the healthcare system and justice in which healthcare is and should not be influenced by the characteristics of the patient such as gender, geographical location or even the social-economical statues whereas efficiency is entitled with care that is useful to avoid misuse or underuse of services, effectiveness deals with matching science to care; timelines deals with avoidance of delays within the healthcare system (Wallace, 2007).

The organization not only needs comprehensive strategies but the information should be relevant to many different employees to be able to understand and properly implementing it. The basic structure of a school includes its daily activities, procedures, and IT infrastructure. A learning organization can use the human resources provided to improve knowledge sharing and decrease the wasting of time sourcing for knowledge. Knowledge management in schools is normally involved in acquisitions, accumulation, sharing, transformation, application, innovation, integration, and diffusion which is emphasized by the school leadership management. Even if this knowledge management has greatly helped teachers some still use the traditional methods to teach or even solve their problems.

Knowledge management strategies and applications are about how organizations can create knowledge, share the old or new knowledge effectively and distribute it amongst its shareholders or employees, managers, customers, and suppliers. Knowledge management has become a very important tool in strategy hence accelerating globalization, digitalization, and services of new products and services.

Knowledge management strategy is a plan that is detailed on how the organization will manage company data, information to increase production and efficiency. There are several ways to improve the knowledge management strategy and this include by dividing everything into small spaces, setting monthly setbacks, finding new ways beyond customer service, by doing extensive research, by using simple and understood training procedures, creating a good plan for content creation and encouraging community actions To achieve all this implantation should be a success by identify all the problems within the business, preparing for change, having a dedicated team, by acknowledging the major attributes of the system and rolling out all the building blocks (Wallace, 2007).

In sharing information either internally or externally in an organization is aided by the right knowledge management tools used. Examples of these tools include customer relationship systems, learning management systems and knowledge bases.

The 4 main pillars of knowledge management are leadership, organization, technology, and also learning. There are 3 components of a knowledge management system which include the input of knowledge, people or even tools; the interaction of knowledge, people, and tools and lastly is the output of the information acquired. Knowledge management is divided as follows explicit knowledge; document management intelligent gathering, data mining, text mining IT is very useful in this field; tacit knowledge involves the tools, practices such as knowledge surveys, questionnaires, individual, and group interviews.

Knowledge management cycle is the orderly process of transforming information into knowledge within an institution explaining how knowledge is captured, processed, and even distributed within the institution. Key drivers of successful knowledge management strategy include:

- Increasing awareness and proper understanding of the organization;
- Breaking down the business case and to identify important benefits;
- Communicating proper practices; and
- Giving a solid base against the measure of progress.

A knowledge management plan is a document used for a specific project, department or organization that is based on the knowledge needed by the project or what knowledge will be created by the knowledge. Organizational behavior is a science that incorporates knowledge of social and behavioral science. Knowledge management is very useful because it enables an organization to better protect or even exploit what it knows and to improve its knowledge of what it needs most. It is a way of helping an organization to detect their mistakes and how best to tackle them to achieve success. Knowledge helps the human race not to repeat the same mistakes they did in the past and even providing new survival tacks for them. What becomes a big problem is when this information cannot be accessed. Knowledge management is very important to the success of the business because it helps in first decision making, by building learning institutions by making learning routines and by creating cultural change and innovation.

Below are five reasons why knowledge management is necessary;

- Customer satisfaction is greatly increased because these customers can get their answers quickly and in a short period. Customers can contribute their ideas or views, which makes them feel like they are part of the organization. In turn, they invest heavily in these organizations, which increases profit margins significantly.
- It improves the efficiency of an organization's operational unit

and business processes due to knowledge available.

- By proper sharing of ideas, collaboration, and access to the latest information it will greatly promote cultural change and innovation.
- By accessing knowledge with ease decision making tends to become easier and quicker due to wider access to opinions of different people and also of experts.
- Knowledge management has helped in speeding up access to several information' and knowledge hence increasing productivity.

Service now knowledge management is a process that helps clients to browse pieces and later on leave feedback. Reasons as to why modern companies should use this service now field service management simple by just replacing spreadsheets', by boosting productivity within the company, promotes a bigger knowledge-sharing base and by having ready user information which increases customer satisfaction.

4.8. IMPACTS OF COMPUTER KNOWLEDGE MANAGEMENT

- People – Knowledge management impacts employee learning, adaptability, and job satisfaction;
- Processes – Knowledge management increases effectiveness, efficiency, and innovativeness;
- Products – Knowledge management increases the range of value-added and knowledge-based products; and
- Organizational performance – Knowledge management helps increase return on investment and achieve sustainable competitive advantage.

Computer knowledge management is essential for the storage and sharing of information to the organization. Knowledge management provides the tools for the team members to acquire information easily and it becomes helpful when an IT provider is getting information from someone who is not on site. The knowledge management team has significantly improved by the use of documented procedures that were created earlier on and stored, they can be able to access them and use them to solve any problem that had occurred and hence enabling a smooth flow of work without wastage of time.

The most important reason for the introduction of KMS within an organization is to reduce the risks or to eliminate them. By having the correct procedures and checklists documented they eliminate the chances that something may be missed. Besides, it can help detect an organization's management changing and also it can detect the management finances that are behind or even the productivity levels. Update knowledge management processes give protection against the loss of a key staff member or even a staff. In turn, safeguarding the key informationand documentation the organization needs to retain and if a key staff or supplier leaves the organization the information is not lost to rest (Nonaka, 2005).

Knowledge management is essential for storing and sharing information that is crucially important to an organization or company. The effectiveness of this system helps to assist in both small and big projects that are being run to become successful. Allowing easy transition of knowledge within the organizations' team members hence it helps to eliminate any gaps that may be developed within the organization if a key team play is lost or if moving to an external IT provider, knowledge management system can make this transition much easier.

Data mining is about the discovering of new patterns from a wealth of data in the database by focusing on the algorithms to acquire useful knowledge. While knowledge discovery database (KDD) is the process of discovering useful knowledge from the data. Data mining has aided different in various fields and below are some of its examples;

- In health care institutions the use of disease KMS in-hospital case studies was normally used. Data mining tools are widely used to explore diseases, operations, and tumors relations. They are used to build KMS in clinical medicines to improve the quality of treatment.
- Retiling is used normally in knowledge by customers in the household for the product line and brand issues. Data mining has greatly helped by giving suggestions and solutions to improve a firm's production and brand, in turn, fulfilling the customers' demands.
- In the financial or banking institutions data mining can help banking institutions to make decisions support and knowledge sharing processes which will greatly help within the institutions.
- In the small and middle businesses like the food company and the food supply industries with the integration of data mining and

knowledge management together they can help in proper decision making.

- In entrepreneurial science data mining, knowledge has been used to facilitate the extraction and has helped to guide managers in determining strategies on knowledge-oriented organization competition.
- Data mining can find hidden patterns between knowledge management and its performance for better knowledge management implantations from the data collected from questionnaires to improve the business field.
- Data mining techniques can help in the smooth flow of teamwork and collaboration.
- In construction industries, text mining techniques to handle the text information sources for industrial knowledge discovery and management solutions.

Below is a look at eight knowledge types in organizational domains for data mining collaboration in knowledge creation;

- In the health care sector, the dataset is composed of three types; the basic health care providers' dataset; the outpatient health care statistics dataset and the medical statues database and also the source is from the hospital inpatient medical records.
- In the construction industry, this was a simple sample data set in the form of post-project reviews that define good or bad information. Multiple key phrasal knowledge sequences formation was created through the application of text timing and was used as an essential part of text analysis in-text documentation.
- In the retailing domain is customer data and the products purchased have been collected and stored in the databases to mine whether the clients buying habits and behavior can affect the product line and brand extensions
- Knowledge sets are contained in strings of data, models, parameters, and reports for each analytical study to help predict changes of bonds, cluster data of bond features in the financial domain.
- In the small and middle business domains to solve the food supply chain network problems which are made up of several components like the knowledge base, task classifier and template

approaches, user interface and others. By the use of this system, it has helped for decision support models and also helped managers to make appropriate decisions.

- The research assets domain is mostly focused on the management of knowledge assets by applied knowledge and information network approaches. It provides three types of research, like human resources or intellectual capital and research programmers.
- In the business domain, it has four main domains for knowledge management which include the explicit-oriented, the tacit-oriented and the success factor. The decision attribute is one dependent attribute of the knowledge management process.

The application of data mining has been widely implemented in various institutions like healthcare institutions, construction industry, food companies, from the retailing companies to financing companies. Each field has been supported by different data mining techniques which include classification, clustering, and dependency modeling.

Management of knowledge of resources has lately become a big demand for development. By getting the most useful knowledge has a very big impact on management and decision making. Below are the aims of giving a research summary on the application of data mining in the knowledge management technologies domain. This includes;

- The publication rates and research on the application of data mining in knowledge management will increase in the future and cover the interest in different areas.
- The classification of data mining tasks is usually the employed model in an organization for description and prediction. Nevertheless, hybridization techniques, e.g., association rule and clustering; classification and clustering, etc. are used to solve different knowledge management problems. This trend will give rise in the future.
- In the healthcare department, a particular article used the visualization technique as a supplement to other data mining tasks. The visualization system could enhance and lead to better performance in decision making.
- Knowledge management is an interdisciplinary research area. Nevertheless, the future of knowledge management development may need integration with different technologies and demand more methodologies to solve many knowledge management

problems. Knowledge management applications development tends to support expert decision making and will be the application of a problem-oriented domain.

In the knowledge capturing, this is the process in which knowledge is converted from tactic to explicit forms and vice versa through sub-processes of externalization and internalization. The knowledge capture can be acquired even outside the organization or institution boundaries either from consultants, suppliers, customers, and competitors. Externalization is the process through which an organization captures the tactic knowledge its staffs possess which is later documented, verbalized, and sharing. While internalization is the process through which workers acquire tactic knowledge. It represents the traditional method of learning and can also be acquired outside the institution or organization. Knowledge can come in many styles but when it comes to bring change and development. With good knowledge management and correct application can lead to better life and achievements. In the organization set up, knowledge can enhance the expansion of activities and the creation of new domains and by improving the organizational culture and practices. However, on the levels of society knowledge brings technology and economic progress. Expansion of companies or organizations can greatly create economic growth which contributes largely to job employments among people. It will greatly enhance knowledge sharing, contributions among company staff, managers or suppliers hence leading to knowledge growth among the population and creating a sharp diverse and open-minded society.

In conclusion, knowledge can be acquired from different sources, e.g.,

- Superstition and intuition a based where knowledge is acquired through subjective feelings, interpreting random events or even believing in magical events this is superstition while intuition means knowing something without even knowing its source.
- Knowledge can also be attained from an authority, when they say a positive thing we learn from it. The authority figure may not be an expert in the field but what they say can greatly impact knowledge.
- Knowledge from tenacity – this involves hearing a piece of information so frequently tending to believe it so true despite evidence that it can be a lie.
- Knowledge from rationalism is the logical reasoning, ideas are precisely clearly stated and logical rules are applied to arrive at a logical sound conclusion.

- Knowledge by empiricism is knowledge gained from observation, objectives, and trusting our senses such as people who don't believe until they see it. This kind of knowledge is used in psychological research normally because psychologists use data and believe in probabilistic conclusions. Most people behave mostly in the same way in most institutions due to what they see and share.

Knowledge by science involves the combination of rationalism and empiricism. This is whereby scientist collects data and a hypothesis is a study regarding the outcome of the study. This is the best way for scientists and researchers to gain the information they require.

Then there is the use of descriptive knowledge which is very useful in discriminating, measuring or even defining various behaviors or even characteristics. Predictive knowledge is used in determining a relationship between two behaviors and if they are connected. Proper knowledge in understanding changes in behavior or characteristics is very important while descriptive knowledge is used in hypotheses and is accepted as a source of knowledge in defining behavior and characteristics. Understanding is used in causal hypotheses and is useful in determining if there is probabilistic evidence that one behavior or characteristic affects another behavior or characteristic (Maier, 2007).

At times in the school set up, students don't know the difference between hypotheses and theory. Hypotheses this is the prediction regarding the outcome of a single study while a theory is an organized system of assumptions and principles that try to explain a particular concept and how they are related and how each one of them can be solved.

However, knowledge management can be abused and in turn, lead to incorrect sources of knowledge either from the teachers or the tutors or even the students can misinterpret the information to something that is not right. In order not to get wrong impressions of the knowledge a better understanding and examining cultural beliefs, attitudes, and attributes should be well understood and well researched before introduction of a new knowledge management being implemented (Maier, 2007).

CHAPTER

ICT and the Society

5

CONTENTS

5.1. INTRODUCTION

Information and Communication Technology refers to the installation of computing devices and communication facilities for the purpose of sharing information. It encompasses all uses of the modern technology that exist to help people with their personal activities. It covers the sending, receiving, use, and storage of any information that is transmitted electronically in machine language which is in 0's and 1's and commonly known as binary computer language.

The famous platforms of Information and Communication Technology have been existence for as so long as we human beings have been around. This is because, there has always been a way of communicating with each by use of technology available at that point in time despite the ages. It is only that the latest age of electronics has affected us the most.

The first age which was the "pre-mechanical" age. During this age, alphabets were invented and used to keep records of information by writing on scrolls such as the famous Egyptian scrolls.

Numeric numbers were also invented during this age and the first calculator, the famous abacus system used for counting purposes was invented by the Chinese. It was the first machine to be used to process data into meaningful facts.

The "mechanical" age lead to the invention of more complex machines which were more of a combination of our current technology with the first age technology. Machines like the Napier Bones used for multiplication and division purposes was developed by John Napier, who was a Scottish Mathematician.

The Analytic Engine having been developed by Charles Babbage (an English Mathematician) was the first computer-like device to be developed for the purposes of data processing.

Currently, the "electromechanical" age is the age closer to our current age. It did lead to developed of the first telephone handset, the most popular means of communication up-to-date only that it is more advanced. The first radio set was also invented and developed in this age for the purposes of sharing information amongst the audience.

The current age, referred to as the electronic age, has been growing at a rapid speed, with invention of new technologies day in day out. These technologies are more of the advancements of the prior ones, making the human lifestyle easier.

5.2. CATEGORIES OF INFORMATION AND COMMUNICATION TECHNOLOGY

There has been invention of two categories of Information and Communication Technology based on their area of use and what specific task they are supposed to perform.

The first category refers to traditional computer-based technologies which are acitivities you can do on your computer without the help of anyone (Haftor, 2010). Most of the tasks performed by use of traditional computer-based technologies are in the category of special-purpose computers which aim at accomplishing only one task without the help of anyone. Most applications found in our personal digital assistant computers are under this category. They are further categorized into two sub-groups.

The standard office applications which include: Word processor, such as Microsoft Word, which is used to write letters, essays, reports among others; Spreadsheets, which is an electronic version of a manual ledger book; Database software, which is the electronic version of the old filing system used to manage data in many forms from basic lists; Presentation Software, which has replaced the use of projectors during presentations; Desktop publishing, such as the Adobe InDesign used to produce publications such as magazines, newsletters, magazines, and other complex documents; Graphics software, which has replaced the use of drawing tools used to create and edit images such as logos, drawings, and pictures for use in different areas (Haftor, 2010).

The second category of traditional computer-based technologies is the Specialists applications which include: Accounting packages, such as Sage, are used to manage an organization's accounts; Computer-Aided Design is used to assist the design process such as architectural, engineering, electronics, and roadways designs among others; Customer Relations Management is used by businesses to understand their customers better by collecting data to monitor the buying trends of customers. Customer Relations Management technologies are mostly connected to applications that run centers which are in direct contact with the customers during transactions for better monitoring of customer purchase trends.

The second category of Information and Communication Technologies are Digital Communication Technologies which refer to the exchange of data through electronic means over some distance. Under this classification, there are aspects which are critical to the communication of information, such as network types and ways of accessing the internet.

The most crucial types of networks include are categorized into two: The Internal networks and External networks (Haftor, 2010).

The Internal network mostly referred to as Local Area Network (LAN) consists of a few hardware devices (used for both input and output purposes plus for data processing) in an organization. The main reason for use of a LAN is to enable sharing of hardware facilities such as printers, scanners, software applications and data within an organization with ease hence reducing time invested in performance of activities.

The second category is the external networks which allow a user to communicate with someone outside your internal network. In such scenarios one requires connection to the Wide Area Network which allows sharing of information within a bigger geographical area for it is basically an interconnection of different network.

5.3. DIFFERENCE BETWEEN DATA AND INFORMATION

Since Information and Communication Technology deals mainly with information, there is need to differentiate between data and information, many people confuse the two terms to mean one and the same thing.

Data are raw materials or collections of different details, which need to be worked on thoroughly before it can be converted into something meaningful and helpful to the end user. Data does come in different forms such as numbers, words, symbols among others. A perfect example of data are the numbers we use during calculations before we get the required output after the calculation process is done. Once data processing is done, the output received is information (Bradley, 2017).

Collected data undergoes four stages for it to be converted into meaningful facts. First and foremost, data is recorded in a certain place. The recorded raw facts are the analyzed by distinguishing the most relevant parts with the least relevant ones. The most relevant parts are then recombined to produce meaningful facts which are output through different ways such; compilation of a report, writing an essay or article among other ways.

Information is basically data that has been processed in such a way that it is meaningful to the person who receives it. Information cannot be referred to be information simply because it is data which has been processed, rather it needs to be information that is of some importance to the end user (Bradley, 2017).

In Information and Communication Technology, the information relayed must be of good quality and meeting the clients' expectations. Some of the characteristics of good information are discussed in the section below.

- One of the qualities is that, information relayed across such a platform must be relevant for most of it is used for decision-making in different setups. By being relevant it means that, your information should clearly meet the objectives of any information reports and it should focus on areas considered to be exceptional in information gathering such as pros and cons in a certain areas and areas where limits have been exceeded.
- The information shared via Information and Communication Technology platforms should be up-to-date if it is to be actioned. This quality improves on the rate at information is produced.
- You should ensure that your information is accurate as possible and free from errors whosever. In cases of uses of any assumptions or estimates, users should be informed. This quality can only be achieved by use of more and more time as possible for data collection for it to be checked regularly for any errors.
- Users are different hence they have different needs. The information provided on the Information and Communication Technology platforms should address the main points, be well detailed rather than being a short summary of how things are done. The format should be more of that of reporting about something rather than explanations.
- Your target audience requires to be availed with information that is easy to read, understand, and also be able to use in other areas. This is so because, not all among your audience are of the same academic level hence your information should be presented for all to use by being clear and communicated through the right medium to reach as many people as possible.
- Information does cost money. Money is required for data collection, data analyses and compiling of reports from collected data. Users need to know if the information they have invested in, is worth their time and cost incurred in acquiring the information.
- Users need to access information that will always be accessible at any time of the day, hence it is advisable that your information comes from an authoritative source. It is also ethical to state the source used and in case of any citations made in your information, proper referencing should be done.

5.3.1. Different Purposes of Information

Information is used to serve different purposes in different areas of businesses, organizations, and other platforms.

Information is required for use in planning sessions in an organization. For effective planning to take place, an organization needs to be aware of all of its resources, what it needs, if any advancement is required in its current system, the cost to be incurred, the profit or the main objective of its activities and all this can only be achieved through data collection which leads to combination of a full report, information of the entire organization.

Information is used for record each and every transaction event in an organization for proper management of the business for future use in case any references required.

Information does help in monitoring the progress of an organization by checking against the plan you came up with. This ensures proper use and management of resources. This practice does help in confirming if things are going better or worse than expected and to find ways in which corrective measures can be put in place (Sreekumar, 2011).

Performance must be evaluated for an organization to deliver to the society more so in the world markets. Proper detailed information is required for evaluating performance which can only be obtained by gathering and analyzing information on different areas of the organization.

Most information is mainly gathered to help in decision making. This information is categorized into three categories.

Strategic information is used to help draw the goals and targets within a certain duration of time. It can also be used to evaluate how well those goals are being accomplished with time. Strategic information deals mainly with the profitability of a business, its current size, growth rate and competitive layout of the markets the business operates in and the achievements made by the business and returns from those achievements (Sreekumar, 2011).

Tactical information is mainly used to rule out how the resources can be used efficiently to maximize the profit.

Operational information is used to make sure that specific tasks are carried out as it was planned without any delays or errors whosever.

There are a variety of information requirements relayed via the Information and Communication Technology platforms. For example, for different businesses, depending on the various ranks in, each ranked office does have its own information standards. Senior managers need information to help their businesses in planning, middle management need more detailed information to help them monitor and control business activities and employees with operational roles need information to help them carry out their duties.

Information gathering can be a costly and tiresome activity, but some strategies must be followed. Before deciding to venture into data capturing process, one must have a clear idea of what information they are really going to collect, the tools they will use to gather the information, specify in what format the data will be collected in; have a clear outline of the data collection process and ensure they meet the privacy specifications of data collection. Information verification is a very crucial practice in any organization. It ensures that the information collected is authentic by checking and confirming its real sources, date of compilation of the different data items, and in what format and ways it was made available to the right audience.

Gathered information can be stored in different ways for future use. There is the private information which is a collection of related data items which have not undergone the final compilation for it to be presented to the public. Public information is produced once all data items have undergone the final stages of compilation and its worth to be presentable to the society.

Once information has been collected, it does need to be guarded from access by unauthorized users who may temper with it or cause its deletion from the storage areas.

With the increasing development of the Information and Communication Technology platform, information is under lots of threats hence the development of different information security programs which are designed based on different goals.Confidentiality being one of the goals does deal with protecting any form of information from being availed to unauthorized user by any means.

Information should be integral, meaning that it should not be altered or changed from its original form no matter the circumstances.

The third goal of information security systems is that, information should be made available to the target audience at all times in the easiest and efficient way no matter the situation at hand.Ways in which information is accessed should be accountable in the sense that they should be able to keep a record of who accessed the information, at what time, and from which location. This allows easy tracking in case of any illegal access to any form of information.

5.3.2. Invention of Different Information Systems for the Purposes of Communication

With invention of Information and Communication Technology, there has been invention of different information systems for the purposes of communication.One of them is the Executive Support System (ESS) which is specifically used to help senior management staff make strategic decisions based on the summary of the most important information in an organization. This summary is obtained through use of data analysis and modeling tools such as the "what if" analyses available in the ESS to help in strategic decision-making.

The Management Information System (MIS) is primarily deals with the internal sources of information. It usually takes data from the transaction processing systems (TPS) and summarizes it into a series of management reports which tend to be used mostly by the middle managers and supervisors who deal with operation tasks.

Decision Support Systems (DSS) are specifically designed to help the management in decision making process more so in situations where there the outcomes of those decisions are not predictable. This system uses tools and techniques which help in gathering relevant information and analysis of options and alternatives available. It mostly involves the use of complex spreadsheet soft wares and database soft wares for the creation of a "what-if" models.

Knowledge Management Systems (KMS) mainly exists to help businesses create and share information in different platforms. Most of the information shared by use of this system is mainly fresh content which has been researched on thoroughly and approved to be worth sharing for commercial purposes. These systems are developed around systems which allow efficient categorization and distribution of knowledge (Haftor, 2010).

The TPS has been designed to deal with daily transactions and activities within an organization efficiently and accurately. This does avoid the errors which occur once such tasks are performed by humans and as we all know, we as humans tend to get tired easily and monotonous work is kind of boring to us.

Office automation systems tries to improve the productivity of employees who need to process data and information in offices. This does reduce the work load for employees allowing them to perform many tasks within the shortest time possible with little energy being invested in the task.

5.4. THE RELATIONSHIP BETWEEN THE SOCIETY AND INFORMATION AND COMMUNICATION TECHNOLOGY

The relationship between the society and Information and Communication Technology (ICT) has led to the development and growth of the already existing social business. Social businesses are businesses which deal with helping the community grow and better the lives of the community members. They are more concentrated on giving back to the society rather than making profits.

ICT has made the social businesses more affordable to set up. This is because it is difficult for social businesses to find investors if they are not-for-profit organizations. The ICT help advertize the businesses on different social media platforms so that well-wishers can contribute a fraction of their earnings (Proenza, 2015).

Many social businesses use the ICT platform to reach millions of people instead of having to offer their services to only one community. This makes the businesses more scalable. They also do use ICT related solutions to perfect their deliverance of services. For example, the social businesses which have majored in agricultural practices may decide to use drones to eliminate pest and diseases by spraying the farms in an easier and fast way making their produce be of high quality.

The stories of social businesses may be distributed among the different social media platforms encouraging more and more people to take part in their growth or motivate them to setup their own social businesses which will have more positive impact to the society at large.

It is said that everything does have two sides in its life time. There is the good side and the bad side. This principle does apply to Information and Communication technology for it does have both positive and negative effects to the society.

We cannot really say that the positive effects do out way the negatives ones, or that the negative effects do out way the positive ones, but it is better we look at both the positive and the negative effects in details.

Access to information is one among the greatest positive effects of ICT. Information is being made available to users in different platforms at a cheaper cost and in an easy format which does not have any problems during its access. This has increased people's knowledge for whatever information they are doubtful is confirmed to them in a touch of a button. This information is made available via the internet which is an interconnection of different computers some of which act as the server computers (Proenza, 2015).

(computers which contain information requested on the internet) and others act as client computers (computers which ask for information from the server computers on the internet).

There has been improved access to education services and materials. E-learning has been introduced in many institutions availing distance learners a platform to participate in classwork through online tutorial videos and online exams. Laboratory experiments which are dangerous to carry out in school laboratories are being presented to students through videos which are elaborated to a greater extend hence easy for students to understand. These impossible laboratory experiments may also be carried out by use of simulations. Study materials such as e-books and past examination papers are being availed to students on via the internet. This does enable students to have their own personal learning equipment instead of having to share in class. With this platform, the more abled students academically maybe electronically isolated from the less abled students by assigning to them more challenging assignments, and for the less abled students they be offered remedial online classes which are more elaborate to them. Academic scholarships are also being availed via the internet and people who meet the qualifications listed are offered a chance to pursue or better their dreams in well-known facilities in the world which offer the best quality of education.

Figure 5.1. With the advancement of ICT, more and more tools have been invented to help with daily activities.

Source: https://teamctf.com/internet-marketing-strategies-have-to-be-aligned-to-the-newest-market-trends/234/.

Processes which had been out of reach are now revived. The world of photography being one of them. With the invention of digital cameras, features, such as photo editing can be done using a photography software.

For people with eye-sight problems, screen magnification enables them to see clearly and read effectively ordinary text without the use of the Braille system.Organizations are communicating at a lower cost than before with the introduction of VoIP programs which use the internet to allow voice communication instead of the use of telephone which require airtime for one to communicate. Email messages has reduced the cost which was incurred in mailing letters for it allows sending of both official and friendly letters with the touch of a button at a much lower cost. Video-conferencing which is also a means of communication has increased the connection and togetherness of business stakeholders for it allows them to conduct their meetings at the comfort of their homes without having to incur transport cost traveling to a common meeting point. It only required a camera and voice software to enable the members present in the meeting to participate in the agendas of the day. Website is also one of the most effective ways of communicating an organization's services on the internet. It is accessible throughout the day, allows flexible responses to be communicated to the organizations either through the contact information availed on the websites or the fill up forms presented on the website. This allows customer services to be improved based on the responses the organization receives from its clients via the websites. It does promote customer relations, ensures good supply of goods and services and development of newer and better products opening new growth opportunities to businesses (Proenza, 2015).

Figure 5.2. Organizations can sell their products worldwide through e-commerce platforms, which connects people around the world. This leads business growth worldwide.

Source: https://www.cbinsights.com/research/direct-to-consumer-retail-strategies/.

Business information is being managed effectively with the invention of Information and Communication Technology. Customer information is monitored keenly to help in production of advertisement programs. Business stock is being controlled well in terms of its rate of usage, and the cash flow it is generating for the business and does help to reduce wastage of resources and increase of profit generated.

Data encryption does protect access of data by unauthorized people. This is enabled by use of either physical security system such as use of fingerprint to access a certain device's records, use of facial or iris recognition to enter a data room which might be the main backup area for data.

Information and Communication Technology does connect individuals from all parts of the world through the internet which is a global network. This platform does open a worldwide opportunity to people in different parts of the world in spite of how remote your location might be. The interconnection is growing day in day out due to the use of social media platforms which allows sharing of ideas, interacting, and knowing each other even to an extend of some people meeting their soul mates on the internet (Proenza, 2015).

With ICT, people are able to communicate in real time at high speeds without having any time lags between the distance separating both the receiving and sending end. Information communicated is also precise for with lack of time lags, the chances of alterations to information are low.

ICT is versatile in the sense that it can perform multiple task at once by use of multi-media platforms which might be integrated in many different areas of the business world increasing the rate of production.

5.5. NEGATIVE EFFECTS OF INFORMATION AND COMMUNICATION TECHNOLOGY

One of them is that it has led to job loss more so to the computer illiterate people in different workplaces. People who do not have basic knowledge on how to handle computers are being forced into early retirement with the integration of ICT in different workplaces. This occurs due to replacement of manual operations with automation processes by use of robots.

People who conduct their office task from the comfort of their homes are at a high risk of suffering from depression effects. This is because most of them do not have much will to get out there and interact with their fellow human beings, because what is the use of having to spend transportation money in traveling to meet people yet you can still earn more and more money from the comfort of your home.

Before the electronic age of technology was fully integrated into the society, people did find ways of getting to their place of work. Some did use to cycle to their place of work, others had to walk a few miles, all of which this means of getting to work were in one way or the other a form of physical exercise. With the use of ICT in workplaces, and with many people having to work at the comfort of their homes, cases of: obesity, heart attacks, all of which are caused by lack of physical exercise and eye-sight problems caused by excessive use of laptops and mobile phones have increased.

Integration of Information and Communication Technology is costly for their expenses incurred during the purchase of both hardware and software devices for an ICT system to work effectively without any errors. An ICT expert is also required for the setting up of an ICT system in an organization. Further costs are incurred during the maintenance of the system and during the attempts to keep up with the ever-advancing technology. The sum of all these costs if not well managed could cause a disaster to the financial system of an organization (Proenza, 2015).

Many people think that the integration of Information and Communication Technology into the business world will be a great step ahead of the competition world, but for some organization, it is a great disadvantage to them. This is because with the integration of ICT there will be increase in price of offering services to restore the money used during integration which might discourage many customers and make them opt for businesses offering cheaper services to them. And loss of customers, leads to the downfall of a business.

Organizations which have bought in the idea of using ICT in their place of work do have a greater task of having to protect their information from security breaches. Customer information needs to be handled and protected with the uttermost respect. Such security breaches may occur through attack of information systems by malicious programs which target the vulnerabilities of an organization's information system or the weak points of the internet connections in an organization (Proenza, 2015).

With the integration of ICT in the education sector, it does lead to the disadvantaging of students who do not have access to internet due to their economic status. This at large does lead to low education delivery to the world increasing the rate of illiteracy which the current generation is greatly trying to eliminate. More teachers are buying the myth that the tutorials offered on the internet are far much better than the kind of knowledge they do offer to their students. This myth might be 20% true, but what of the remaining 80% which it has not qualified imply? It implies that, some areas of the education curriculum will benefit from the use of ICT, but large areas of the curriculum are not really benefiting, instead they are being destroyed slowly, day in day out because the manner in which a subject is being taught has a larger effect on the student than how it is being presented by ICT. Some of the educational information availed on the internet is incorrect leading to low levels of education and low understanding of different facts.

The availing of information by Information and Communication Technology platforms has led to digital divide. This is a situation whereby those who can access information via the internet are separated from those who are unable to access information. Availability of information on the internet does also lower the standard of quality education for some of the information provided is misleading and contrary to what the original sources of educational information said (Proenza, 2015).

ICT has availed all forms of information via the internet, and as we all know, some forms of information are to be restricted based on age of access. This kind of information is misleading and does lead to immoral and unethical practices by people who access it, more so the underage. All of this does lead to the degradation of the society core believes and principles for human behavior is made to be more and more pathetic.

This area of Information and Communication Technology does have a bright future. This is because many projects on ways to advance ICT are still underway and they are based on superb inventions which will be of great impact to the society.

Drones have already been developed and many more advancements of them are still underway. They are or they will be used for aerial surveillance, filming, used by the military to setup attacks among other activities.

Autonomous cars, commonly known as self-driven cars, are still being developed at high rate. In future, people will not have to worry about refueling or performing service check-up.

Machine learning (ML) will also be introduced to humans whereby they will be able to understand exactly what a robot does, and why it has to do so. ML nowadays is only done by robots, but with humans being introduced to it, many activities carried by robots will be effective and with minimal errors under the supervision of humans.

Blockchain which is a series of different information blocks interlinked together will be used for data security purposes. This is because this series of blocks is highly resistant to modification of data hence preventing alteration of data by unauthorized personnel.

The famous 3D printing still an underway project, will be of great use to engineers and architectures, this is because it will help them design actual house designs and print them on a piece of paper with the help of 3D technology. 3D technology works by building a three-dimensional object from a computer-aided design model, mostly by adding more and more layers to a certain shape.

Quantum Computing will be a great technological advancement once it will be introduced to the world of computing. The normal processing of data which is processes data in the form of 1's and 0's will be replaced by a form of processing which first examines the probability of data state before its processing, known as quantum technology, meaning that it will have the potential to process more data at a fast speed.

Robotics has already been introduced to the system, but more advancements of robots are still underway. With robotics, tasks which might be dangerous to humans such as chemical manufacturing will be handed over to robots, hence saving more human lives loss through interaction with poisonous chemical elements.

Biometrics will be used as means of access identification to a certain device or rooms. The iris or fingerprint pattern will be used to prevent access to private rooms or personal devices from access by unauthorized users. Biometrics might also be used to determine the different internal body structure of humans without having to visit a health facility, hence detection of different diseases in advance and early treatments reducing the mortality rate (Proenza, 2015).

Artificial Intelligence (AI) which is a computer program used to create robots that are able to reason out and act based on their judgment without human intervention is one of the main reasons for existence of robots. AI gives a robot the ability to learn humans through ML. Depending on the tasks assigned to a robot during its manufacture, different type AI are being used to develop them.

The weak AI enables a robot to process thoughts as a human and react based on their judgment. It allows a robot to respond to commands assigned to it despite the fact that the robot itself does not seem to understand the commands. This is possible because the robots have been programmed with already predefined commands and the possible responses. A suitable example of a robot produced through Weak AI is famous Siri and Alexa found mostly in Apple products.Strong AI creates robots which perform their task on their own without any supervision. The robots are programmed to do their task correctly. This AI is widely used nowadays as many things are being automated to perform tasks on their own such as the self-driven cars among others.Specialized AI creates robots which perform only a specific specialized task. Industrial robots are mainly in this category for specialization is required to improve the quality of products produced without having to face the threat of inaccuracy in measurements or any other form of inaccuracy performed by humans for specialized task are tedious because they are repetitive.Virtual reality which is the use of computer technology to create a new unique environment which is not real but one is able to use virtual reality tools to interact with objects in that new environment (Sreekumar, 2011).Augment reality can be used during advancement projects of objects in the real world. It modifies the features in a real-world object by use of computer-generated perceptual information giving the real-world objects a new look on the computer. The design capture on the computer will then be used to make proper adjustments to the real object and convert it to be similar to the design.

With the invention of Information and Communication Technology, many legal considerations have been made. Issues to do with online payments systems, data privacy concerns, business torts, ownership of property (intellectual properties), and contracts made via online platforms, and criminal liability such as hacking are a big threat to the society. The legal firms in the world are doing their best to try and curb this cyber war and make the integration of ICT to the society a good experience to its users.

Knowledge on use of different devices found in the field of Information and Communication Technology is being offered in different schools, starting from primary level where students learn how to use a computer, going to high school level where students learn about the different areas in the world of computing and then to campus studies where students specialize in different computing fields and learn them in depth.

To sum it all, ICT has great impact on the society and we have to be . Both positive and negative effects, for every existing thing in this world does have two sides.

CHAPTER

Ethics and Professional Responsibility in Computing

6

CONTENTS

6.1. INTRODUCTION

Roles and jobs performed by professionals in computer science (CS) vary a lot. Some of the tasks that computer professionals perform include:

- Writing specifications of new computer systems;
- Designing instruction pipelines for superscalar processors;
- Diagnosing timing anomalies in embedded systems, software system validation and testing;
- Restructuring the back-end databases of inventory systems; and
- Analyzing package traffic in local area networks (LANs) and recommending policies for medical information systems regarding security.

It is the duty and obligation of the computer professionals to undertake these roles diligently and meticulously. This is due to the fact that the performance and functionality of this computer systems are heavily impacted by their decision making and therefore everything they do needs to be precise and accurate. Overall, this normally has an impact on the system users directly and other people indirectly. For instance, in motor vehicles the software is installed in order to control the automatic transmission of an automobile and should ensure the safety of the driver. In different fields, professionals receive special training to perform their job.. This is similar to a computer professional. When these obligations from different fields are combined, they are known as professional ethics. Obligations related to ethics have vastly been studied over the years by philosophers and they have been well elaborated and analyzed by religious leaders. In the field of philosophy, ethic has been given a definition. It is a branch of philosophy that is involved in codifying, safeguarding, and recommendation of ideas of good or bad behavior. It heavily deals with issues of value as it seeks to resolve questions of human morality. It studies the behaviors that a principles person should have, the practicability that a principled person should practice and the personality that a person who has virtue should contain (O'Regan, 2018).

Normally, there are personal and cultural values that an individual is expected to possess, such as honesty, fairness, loyalty, respectfulness, concern for others, self-respect, self-fulfillment, and courtesy. Apart from this, one needs to be aware that professionals normally have stakeholders in their businesses and this implies that professionals have added obligations that they need to perform for their clients, employees or other professionals and the public in general. In the field of CS, the ethical obligations required to be performed by professionals surpasses the laws and regulations of the country. Normally rules that have been put in by the country slows down the advancement in mechanization. Taking into consideration, before 1986 the electronic communications privacy act in the United States of America did not provide laws that would require a search warrant in order to enable authorities to collect information which is personal that was being transmitted over the computer communication networks. Even though there were no laws that used to govern the privacy issues of personal information being transmitted over the computer communication networks, it was the obligation of the Professionals to be aware that there is private information of users and it requires protection (O'Regan, 2018).

6.2. DEFINITION OF PROFESSION

Profession is defined as a job that was derived upon specialization of a concept through academic training and experience and the main objective is to instill services to others and thereafter an agreed upon compensation is given to the profession. In CS there are a couple of computing professionals and they include: software engineers, database administrators, computer system analysts, computer scientists and hardware designers. Is there a resemblance between the occupation of computer professionals and other recognized professionals such as lawyers, doctors, engineers, and accountants? We also need to ask ourselves the question which is in what other ways do professions in the computer sector resemble other occupations that are traditionally not thought to be a profession for example electricians, fashion models, plumbers, and secretaries?

There are professions that portray specific characteristics and such professions are known as strongly differentiated professions. Search professions have the permission to perform certain roles that are not available to other types of professions for example prescriptions of drugs by doctors, performing Court orders and this involves judges and lawyers and other parties. They have special rights and responsibilities. The main criteria that will be used to differentiate strongly differentiated professions to others are the specialized knowledge and skills, arranged investigation, professional autonomy, a strong and firm professional association and a comprehensible social good associated with the profession. Parties who are members of the strongly differentiated position normally have a body of knowledge. This means that they have specialized knowledge or skills to a related field of study and as earlier mentioned such skills are gained through formal academics and practical experience. Although in some professions there might be the passage of education which is formal and practical experience, they are still considered as apprenticeship training rather than formal training. An example of such a profession is plumbing and electrical repairs (electricians). In apprenticeship the students are not taught the theoretical basis of the profession which is usually taught in formal education thus the reason why it is not considered as a strongly differentiated profession. Also, a professional school introduces students to the values and practices that are required for one to be a professional and this is not gained through apprenticeship. For example, students in the engineering department are normally taught the value of being efficient and to always reject half-baked work, in medical school the students are taught how to become reliable physicians and finally in law school, the students are taught how to be future attorneys who will be able to understand the law and practice it professionally. When it comes to professional work there is normally a huge attachment to intellectual properties and components and because of this an individual ought to have studied a degree and after the degree the person is required to have a post-baccalaureate of the degree such as Masters of economics or doctor of philosophy in project management. Professionals normally heighten their level of knowledge through systematic research and this means that they do not necessarily depend on the transfer of craft traditions from one era to another (O'Regan, 2018).

Professional research is normally done by academic members belonging to a specific profession and by the practitioner members to physicians of the academic profession. Normally there is usually advancement of professional knowledge and one cannot be satisfied by the knowledge they already possess and because of this, professionals normally engage in the continuity of academics by reading publications and attending conferences. Professionals are advised to share their knowledge regarding their fields instead of hiding secrets of a guild. Although sharing is recommended, professionals are also advised to keep particular information about their clients in the event that they are confidential. Usually, other professions for example plumbing requires that the customers' desires should be satisfied but in the case of a strongly differentiated profession the professional should always try to meet the needs of the client optimally. For instance, if the doctor has diagnosed a patient with a certain condition, let's say a flu. The doctor is required to give the particular medicine of the diagnosed illness rather than what the client wants. Due to the specialization of knowledge, clients normally don't have the full knowledge of the services that are being provided by the professional and therefore they cannot evaluate their choices though other professionals in the same sector can analyze and evaluate the quality of services being provided. This is how analyzing is done where by professional peers review your accreditation and Licensing activities. They evaluate the quality of the academic program for accreditation and they create a criterion that will determine the requirements for the licensing of individuals. For instance, in the field of law, the lawyer is required to pass bar examination in order for them to be given a license so as to practice their profession in a particular state. In the United States of America, once the license has been given, the professional license granted by one state is recognized by other States. This license comes with professional legal authority and privileges that are not available to individuals who don't have a license. For example, a doctor in surgery can perform surgery to a patient in different areas of the world and such activities should not be performed by individuals who are not medical professionals and don't have the license to do so. With the responsibility and obligation that comes with the process of accreditation and licensing, the public completely gives control over a profession to members of the profession but in return the profession must do their part and promise to serve the public with utmost professionalism. The engineering department works towards creating a safe and a more economical way of constructing objects, the Department of law works towards creating a reliable and an efficient justice system, and professionals in the field of medicine also work towards creating an environment where patients will heal and they will get all the services they require so as to survive. Professions come with different purposes and values and some of these include its commitment to a public good. These values are clearly expressed in the code of ethics. One indicator that will perfectly describe how occupation into a professional has transformed is the creation of the code of ethics (O'Regan, 2018).

The National Professional Association has the privilege of being able to develop and update the professions' code of ethics and they do this through the publishing of journals and periodicals and hosting of conferences in order to enable the professionals to have a learning program and create a network with different professions. The international Professional Association also has the ability to create organize accreditation of Educational program and individual licensing of professionals. The question that comes in mind is, does the computing profession level up to this criterion for a strongly differentiated profession? The answer is yes but in order for one to become a computer professional he or she must go to school and acquire a baccalaureate degree in CS, computer engineering, information systems or any other related field and master the specialized skills needed. Some of the skills are discrete and algorithms, database theory related to CS, specialized skills such as digital system design and techniques of software development. The foundation of knowledge related to CS develops through intense research in computing which is normally carried out by universities, colleges, Industries, and government Laboratories. To elaborate this, take an example of a mechanical engineer. A huge number of mechanical engineers work for an employer rather than a professional client. This can be done through the creation and development of a program that uses application software to control car parts. The computer professional that is the software engineer also has a role of ensuring that the end-user of the appliance is safe while using it. This creates an indirect relationship of the computer professionals with the end-user that is the clients and the general public. Several codes of ethics normally express the obligations and responsibilities of a professional in the sector of CS to its employers, clients, and the general public. The topic of code of ethics will be reviewed in the later sections of the book and this will involve two codes because they apply to computing professionals. Even though other professions and the computing profession have a similar criterion, they are defective in a significant way. You will find that other academic programs for example engineering, law, and medicine are greatly accredited unlike the computing programs which have few accreditations. Take for instance in the United States of America computing professionals cannot be license unless the professionals have taken software engineering and this is only done in Texas. The Association of Computing machinery has enabled computing professionals to earn proprietary certificates which can be offered by corporations for example microscope, novel, sun, and Cisco and have reaffirmed its opposition to sponsor the licensing of individuals. In the United States of America, other professions have bodies that control the professional departments take for example the American Medical Association dominates the Medical Profession and the American Bar Association has created dominance in the legal profession but when it comes to computing profession, there is no organization that has come forth and established dominance (O'Regan, 2018).

The case on the ground is different because multiple distinct organizations exist and some of these organizations include the Institute of electrical and electronics engineers, Association of information technology (IT) professionals and ACM. These organizations remain largely distinct although they operate on the same projects with different publication and codes of ethics. Despite the fact that there's a debate whether computing professions are strongly differentiated or if they are not strongly differentiated, the computing profession has an objective which is more important and this is to ensure they have observed and practiced their ethical obligations and this will be explained in the next article.

6.3. DEFINITION OF MORAL RESPONSIBILITY IN COMPUTING

Moral responsibility is defined as the caliber of deserving moral commendation, rewards or consequences due to an action or not including activities that were in accordance with one's moral obligation. Philosophers often describe people who have a moral responsibility for an action as moral agents. As a moral agent one should have the capability of being able to reflect upon their life situation and to create intentions of how to act upon the situation and then to carry out the action eventually. It is also important to note that moral responsibility does not really equate to legal responsibility. With this definition let us look at the question below. The atomic energy of Canada Ltd manufactured and sold a cancer radiation treatment machine in the early 1980s. This machine was known as the therac-25 and it heavily relied on computer software to control and manage its operations. During its usage at around 1985 to 1987 the therac-25 LED to the deaths of three patients and it contributed to serious injuries to other three patients. The question being posed is who was responsible for the accident? Is it the operators who might have probably given out large doses of massive radiation which produced intense burns or the software developer who designed, tested, and evaluated the software which contained several errors that proved to be serious? Or the system engineers who ignored and neglected installing backup hardware during manufacturing which provided safety mechanisms that had been used in previous versions of the machine? The government? The manufacturer that is an AECL? With these questions being asked we can distinguish amongst different types of responsibilities (Duquenoy, Jones, and Blundell, 2008).

6.3.1. Causal Responsibility

In this type of responsibility, obligation is attributed to the causes for example "the earthquake was responsible for the damaging of the swimming pool." In the case of therac-25, the proximate cause of each accident was caused by the operator that is the person who initiated and performed the radiation treatment. Just because the operator deems to be blamed, the therac-25 operators cannot be completely blamed because they followed the standard processes that are provided and the information displayed in the computer monitors was complex and confusing. It's just like in the case of the earthquake situation. The weather cannot be blamed for a moral failing.

6.3.2. Role Responsibility

To make sense out of role responsibility, take an example. If a garbage collector is given the duty of disposing chemical materials even if the operator who's using the forklift is the one who is actually transferring the toxic waste from the plant to the truck, it is the garbage collector who is responsible for the job. This means that a worker or an individual who has been given a job to perform is considered the responsible person for the task. In the case of the therac-25, the system engineers and software developers were the people who were given the responsibility of creating a program that will help in the effective usage of the radiation treatment and this means that the deficiencies and the in capabilities of the machine is to be blamed on the engineers. Role responsibility does not necessarily encompass the full extent of a professionals' responsibility.

6.3.3. Legal Responsibility

The parties involved that is either the individual or the organization can be legally responsible or liable for the difficulties that were incurred. This happens in the event where the parties are charged with a crime or the organization could be liable for damages in a civil lawsuit. Legal responsibility applies in all professions for example in the case of a doctor. In the event that he or she performs surgery and during the process of operation a malpractice is done, the involved parties can file a lawsuit against the doctor where he or she will be sued if it is true. Taking the case of therac-25, the atomic energy of Canada Ltd could have been sued. A category found in the legal responsibility is strict liability. Street reliability implies that in the event that a product that was made by a certain company leads to harm of the end-user, it can be either injuries or any other kind of damage, the manufacturer of the product can be found liable and responsible of the injuries incurred by the end-user and a lawsuit can be charged against him even though the product was in good condition and met all the standards that are required which is safety and application standards. The objective behind strict liability is to encourage manufacturers to be extremely careful during the manufacturing of products so as to provide safety during its application and also it provides a way in which victims can be compensated in the event an accident happens (Kizza, 2007).

6.3.4. Moral Responsibility

Moral responsibility is different from the other types of responsibility that is causal responsibility, legal responsibility and casual responsibility. This is because the other responsibilities are mutually exclusive that is if one individual has been responsible in their duties, then that means the other individual has not been responsible in their duties. But in the case of moral responsibility it tends to be shared amongst all the parties. In engineering, numerous engineers that were involved in the manufacture of a certain product are responsible for the safety of the products that they have designed and not only is the safety engineer responsible for its safety. Moral responsibility tends to focus on what parties need to do in the future in order to ensure that there is safety in product design rather than blaming what has happened in the past. In other words, this shows that responsibility is a deed. A responsible person possesses qualities such as being consistent, they don't complain, they control their emotions, they are well organized, they rarely make excuses and they canceled plans ahead of time. Irresponsible people are usually rude, they are not considerate and they cannot be trusted in whatever they do. Sharing of responsibility normally occurs in the event that there are a number of parties that need to collaborate as a group in order to create something such as a software engineering team. Sharing of responsibilities is designed in a way that everyone being involved in the group has a portion of responsibility that he or she is required to take care of. This enables the parties in the group to be accountable to the other members of the group and to those whom the group work might influence. The influence can be either the individuals on actions or the impact of their collective efforts (Kizza, 2007).

Suppose that a company that is involved in computer network monitoring has to analyze network traffic data. If the monitoring team made errors in a complex statistical analysis, these errors have the potential of changing the results and interpretation of the data. If the team members responsible for the error are not able to rectify the mistake, they have a legal and moral obligation to consult other professions who are more experienced, for example statisticians. A statistician can be hired to analyze the data and rectify mistakes where necessary. Team members can work with the statistician in optimizing the performance of the product but at the end of the day every member of the group is held accountable for the individual roles in correcting the mistakes. During processing of the first report there were errors made and the stakeholders were already given the reports and they had read it and they had analyzed it. It is the responsibility of the team members to inform the stakeholders that there was an error in the report and that corrections have been made. When an individual has owned up to the moral responsibility for being reckless and negligent, this does not mean that it is a mitigation process by the presence of good intentions or by the absence of body consequences. For instance, if a program tester feels too analyze and evaluate a new module sufficiently and the module fails. Even though the negative consequences due to the neglect of the program tester has been experienced and it was not his or her intention, the software tester is still held responsible morally for the harm and damage caused by the defects of the module (Kizza, 2007).

Another example is supposing a hacker installed a software that is meant and designed to steal passwords and vital details from a public computer. In the event that the software fails to perform its job the hacker is still considered to be morally responsible for the situation. Moral responsibility applies in both failing to act and acting. For example, if a computer has been designed and an engineer is required to set up memory chips inside the device. In the event that the engineer notices that there's a fault in the manufacture of the device let us say the fault and defect can lead to electrocution of the end-user and still goes ahead to install the microchips without rectifying with the problem, the engineer will be held responsible and accountable for failing to act in accordance to ethical practices even though this was not the task assigned to him in the first place. The engineer is required to call attention to the design flaw before performing his specified duty. Due to the technical and complicated nature of computer systems, it is difficult for accountability to be clearly expressed and easily understood. A perfect example is the embedded system of the therac-25. The computer in the therac-25 that is used to control the device is hidden internally and due to this, software developers and computer engineers tend to refuse to take responsibility of the defects and errors that might cause intermittent crashes and loss of data. Bugs in a computer system whether small or big can lead to fatalities that are very dangerous. Errors and defects during coding are known as bugs. In addition, due to the autonomous nature of computer systems people normally try to put blame on the computer system instead of the software developers and engineers who failed in the design, programming, and the deployment of the computer systems (Kizza, 2007).

6.4. RESPONSIBILITIES OF PROFESSIONALS IN COMPUTER SCIENCE

6.4.1. Responsibility to Clients and the End Users

When a computer professional is working on a certain project, it can be either as a consultant or as an employee in a company. The professional is required and obligated to undertake tasks in a competent manner and according to the standards provided in his or her professional threshold. Some of these standards are paying attention to the excellence in terms of technicalities of the job and also taking into consideration the concern for the social effects and impact of computers on the public operators and the end-user in general. During assessment of how capable the computer system performs and how risky they are, the professional is required to be honest. The professional is required to give findings that are accurate and honest and relevant in the manufacturing process. During the manufacturing of products, the main objective is usually customer satisfaction and it is due to this, the professional must consider not only the specifications of the client but also how the system may impact the quality of the standard of life of the end-users. Take for example a computer professional who is designing an information system for a bank should allow for speedy access by customers and clients and at the same time safeguard the client's personal records from unauthorized access. Although there might be challenges that might be faced along the way, that is the technical requirement to provide a quick access may be at loggerheads with the social obligation to ensure there is privacy of client's information. Professionals in the computing sector normally enjoy a noticeable amount of freedom when it comes to deciding how to make a user specification of a computer system. Most of the computer professionals choose to invest resources in order to decrease the response time rather to enhance a graphical user interface or vice versa (Kizza, 2007).

Computer professionals should figure out the biases that are available in the market and utilize that gap in their design choices. For instance, in an online store, for example, Ali Express the software designer can create a search engine which displays the most expensive items first to the least expensive items. This might come in handy in profit maximization for the retailer over the interest of a customer to minimize expenses. Due to the complex nature of software's, not only small software's but also moderately large software's like computer programs it is safe to assume the notion that software's contain errors. Even so, a program does not have errors that can be detected it is still hard to prove its correctness. With such reality is coming in to play, software engineers ask themselves how can they design a product that does not contain errors in the future. You will find that most engineering artifact sooner or later fail in performance. Most engineering artifacts fail due to wear and tear that is physical failure but, in the event, that software artifacts fail it is due to the fact that there were faults during its initial design. Some software errors can be easily detectable for example in light bulbs and I -beans. This is because it can be statistically predicted.

Software developers and engineers are encouraged to acknowledge responsibilities and obligations for the failures of software artifacts. And this can be done when software developers practice due diligence during the designing of programs and should be as honest as possible about both the unknown defects and the known defects in the program especially the program that deals with safety-critical systems which might threaten the lives of people in the event that there is failure. When software developers practice the quality of being open and honest, it will trickle down in enabling software users to make reasonable decisions when purchasing a certain software. Just like in the department of medicine, Miller advocates for the establishment of "software informed content" as a means of formalizing an ethical principle that will require software developers to be open and candid. The requirements of software informed consent is that software developers should convey using elaborate explanation which the customer can be able to comprehend, the risks that are involved in using the software including the chances of known defects and the probability that faults might which have not been discovered still exist. The idea behind software informed consent plays an important role in that it motivates software developers to be candid and frank in their operations and it gives the opportunity of continued research into procedures of finding software faults and measuring risk.

6.4.2. Responsibilities to Employees

You will find that most computer professionals normally work for employers. The nature of employment can be contractual or non-contractual. There is normally a consensus where the professional promises to perform duties for the employer and in return the professional is paid a certain amount of money and any other related benefits. During working, professionals often get access to the employers' personal information such as sales records and other sensitive data. With this comes great responsibility and the professional must be able to keep this data confidential. Other information must also be honored by the professional such as intellectual property that is owned by the employer. The professional is under no obligation or right to benefit from the information he or she knows regarding the employer, for example, the professional has no right to profit from Independent sales by use of his intellectual property and the resources of the employer. The professional should be able to identify conflicts of interest in order to create loyalty with the employer. Every employee is obligated to work loyally on behalf of the employer. Conflict of interest arises when the professional is required to give sound judgment and evaluation regarding a certain job but the professional has some self interest in the job. The interest can be either financial or personal interests. For example, a professional might be given a job of purchasing computers for the organization from a specified third party but the Professional's wife also has a company that sells computers. Instead of the professional buying the computer from the required third-party, he or she goes ahead and purchases the computers from the wife's company. In such a situation the professional should remove himself from the decision-making process and let another person handle the situation. You will find that most professionals have administrative posts. This is expected because managerial roles supplement the responsibilities of computing professionals (Kizza, 2007).

6.4.3. Responsibility to Other Professionals

In ethics everyone is taught to respect others but when it comes to respect of professionals, one is required to practice collegiality. This means that if one profession borrows the ideas and concepts of another profession, it is only right that the one who has borrowed the idea gives credit to the other profession whose ideas were borrowed from. For example, when a professional is writing a research article he or she normally gives credit to the initiator of the idea by citing the sources of the content in the article from previous publications. Although the professional has borrowed the concepts and ideas of another professional, it is also important for them to edit their work in order to not plagiarize the content. In the field of academic plagiarism is considered to be unethical because this implies that you took someone's ideas and represented it as yours. Due to the fact that clients do not have the capabilities of evaluating the standards and how good their assignment is, other professional colleagues have the responsibility to evaluate the work of their fellow professionals. Such a form of evaluation normally takes place in both investigation plus practice and it is known as peer review. In the profession of Computing, after research has been done it is then presented at a conference in front of people and then published in a scholarly journal. Once the research has been done and the manuscript has been made, their peers who are expert in the subject of the manuscript usually review the manuscript and after the manuscript has been reviewed and deemed worthy it is then reported and it is then presented in a conference or publicized in an article. Professional Standards must highly be observed by the computing professionals since they are working together (Duquenoy, Jones, and Blundell, 2008).

Hypothetically standards are deemed to be very appropriate but in computer science, the term standard raises a lot of controversies this is because it is informal and non-existent. This can be Illustrated when there were difficulties during the licensing of software engineers when IEEE and ACM tried to standardize software engineering. In professionalism, senior professionals are expected to tutor and guide junior professionals. Although professionals have vast knowledge, junior professionals usually lack experience when it comes to professional judgment. Tutelage of a senior professional is the best learning procedure that can develop and enhance the professional judgment of junior professionals. In the field of Engineering, for an engineer, e.g. a civil engineer attains professional engineer license, this senior professional is required to supervise a junior professional for at least four years. In order for a professional to maintain their license, it is important for the professionals to tutor one another in order to bring about continuation of academics and growth in profession. Committee of volunteers comprises of professionals who want to volunteer in the peer review of research publications and other activities like editing and this contributes to fulfillment of professional obligations.

6.4.4. Responsibilities to the Public

Normally, the public as the most important stakeholders because they are the end-users of a product. The code of ethics emphasizes that there should be safety in terms of welfare and health to all users. It is known that it is everyone's responsibility to ensure that other people are safe but for engineers, they have a more special duty to ensure that there is complete harmlessness of commodities that is being produced. This applies to Professionals in their computing department. Computer professionals are mandated to provide safety to the public and to improve the quality and standards of life to those who use computer and information systems. Due to this Duty, that computing professionals have been given the role of enhancing the public's comprehension of Computing. Educating the public is a responsibility that is collective and all the computing professionals have a role in participating.

The computer professionals can educate the public in many ways. An example of such a responsibility and ways in which professionals can educate the mass is by advising a group of people for example congregants on buying computers and also noting down publications to the relevant institutions regarding a prospective law on internet regulation. When it comes to matters regarding public computing policies, it is specifically vital for computing professionals to have a say and contribute their expertise to such discussions. There have been numerous controversial policies in our communities. This is where computing professionals can come in and contribute in decision making by providing technical fact. Controversies that have been brought by technology on the social impacts of computers is a topic that needs to be discussed. In the event that a professionals' due diligence of loyalty to the general public is at loggerheads with a professionals' duty of integrity to the user, it is the professionals' responsibility to consider whistle blowing the situation and alerting people and parties who are not involved regarding the issue.

6.5. CODES OF ETHICS

In every profession, there is a rule that governs professionals' behavior and obligations to employees, clients, and general public. Association of Computing Machinery (ACM) was collectively accepted by the societies in computing fields.. In 1992 ACM adopted its rules accompanied by guidelines that interpret them. For example, the guidelines show that law compliance might be put into play. In computer professions the ethics codes of the ACM state the ethical obligations of the leaders of the organization who are mostly technical managers. The principal regarding program design was produced from the collaboration of the ACM and other societies. The software engineering principle has similarities to the principle of ACM code in that the obligations of the technical managers have been included. These codes are distinct because they were the first codes to exclusively focus on software engineers and not on other computer professionals. From the long version of coding, this code has been broken into a shorter version. The short version consists of eight principles and a preamble. The long version clearly expounds and heightens the eight principles with multiple clauses that apply to particular issues and scenarios. You will notably find out that codes of ethics and usually not complete this is because no document can be able to address every possible outcome. Despite this, a code of ethics must be written in a language that is general and each statement in the code of ethics will require interpretation in order for it to be applicable in particular circumstances. According ethics serves many functions. A code of ethics has the ability to act as an inspirational element as it inspires members of the profession to work hard and strive for the professions ideals. It educates new members of the profession of their responsibilities and obligations and informs non-members on what they should require and expect the members of the profession to do. A code of ethics also sets up standards that every professional or member is required to adhere to and it provides a foundation for which members can be expelled when they violate these standards. When a professional want to decide he or she can use the code of ethics as a support tool. During the decision-making process, take for example in the event that an engineer is designing a product and notices that the product is not safe to be used by the end user the engineer can object the creation of the product and will be fully backed up by the code of ethics consensus (Duquenoy, Jones, and Blundell, 2008).

6.6. PRINCIPLES MAKING OF DECISIONS FOR COMPUTING PROFESSIONALS

Over the years there has been the emergence of unsolicited bulk commercial messages commonly known as spam when using emails. This has stirred up a lot of controversy in the computing world. This is because there's no legal and ethical definition of the word spam which has been accepted universally. One broadcast sperm can send millions of messages to different emails at the same time. There have been minimal laws that restrict senders from sending spams because they argue of practicing their liberty of speaking. Before the introduction of some legislations the United States of America had no rule that prohibited spamming. Even with the introduction of the legislation, the law still does not apply to spam messages that have been sent from other countries. In as much as there has been prosecution involving the CAN-SPAM act, most people have made complaints that they still receive many email messages that they consider to be a spam message. You will notice that spamming is normally made to be misleading and it mostly includes data that is not accurate but others normally have accurate information. In many countries, spam messages are considered not to be illegal but in terms of ethics, they're mostly considered to be unethical by many people and such people have given reasons as to why. Spam is considered to be time-consuming this is because once the recipient has gotten the spam messages he or she must delete the junk email messages as these messages waste unnecessary space on computers. In addition, spamming greatly reduces the trustworthiness of emails. Spamming is not reversible that is, the sender is able to send the spam to other users but the sender cannot receive spam from other email users. Finally, the usage of spam cannot be incorporated into the general practice of emailing and this is because if everyone is allowed to send Spam messages from one e-mail to another, there will be intense traffic flow which will lead to the clogging of the system and eventually no one will be able to send email messages (O'Regan, 2018).

Using the three reasons that describes the disadvantages of spamming, an action of morality can be evaluated from this. The morality questions being asked is first, whether the results of sending spams has more good consequences than bad consequences second, is the person sending the sperm willing to trade places and put him or herself on the shoes of the people receiving the sperm or the people affected by the action and finally, whether the people being affected by the action of spamming and the people sending the spam can choose the process of spamming as a general rule. There is a huge correspondence between the three kind of moral reasons illustrated above and the three of the many traditions in philosophical ethics that is the golden rule, duty-based, and consequentialism ethics. Analogies to more relatable situations and scenarios can be used in the evaluation of ethical issues in the use of computers. For instance, a hacker might argue that hacking of unprotected data is legal because the data was not protected in the first place but put the same situation if a house is closed but left unlocked. In the event that a person enters the house without permission, the person is deemed to have committed the Crime of trespassing and trespassing violates the privacy of the occupants of a house. During decision-making when it comes to matters regarding ethics, computing professionals can not only rely on general moral reasoning but also in particular guidelines that have been provided in the code of ethics such as the ACM code of ethics. Using this, let us have a hypothetical example: company Z is planning to secretly monitor the pages in a website that has been visited by its employees using a software that mines data to analyze their access records. An engineer working in company A comes up with the recommendation that the company should purchase the data mining program from David who is an independent contractor but the engineer fails to mention that David is her husband. At the same time, David designed and developed this software while previously employed at company B and company B is not aware that company A wants to purchase that program. When we analyze such a scenario, we first see that accessing the web details of the employees means that they are invading their privacy. This is synonymous to a situation where one is eavesdropping another person telephone call. In the code of ethics, professionals are advised to respect the privacy of individuals. Secondly, there is a conflict of interest between the company and the engineer. This is because the sale and purchase of the software will benefit David who's a domestic partner to the engineer. The engineer was disingenuous by failing to mention this relationship. Finally, because David developed the program will still be working in company B, chances are that the rights of the program is still owned by company B and it is contractual. Professionals are obligated to honor property rights and contacts. A clear solution to an ethical problem cannot be fully achieved by applying code of ethics because different principles in a code might conflict. For instance, when it comes to principal of honesty and confidentiality, there will be a conflict when a professional is asked to explain and give information about the technical details and information regarding the prospective product that the employer wants to design and the engineer must choose between answering the question completely and keeping the information secrets. This is caused by loyalty issues.

Due to the emergence of ethical problems during decision making a more advanced method has been developed for solving such problems. Manner has studied, investigated, and collected what he describes "procedural ethics, step-by-step ethical reasoning procedure that may prove useful to computing professionals engaged in ethical decision-making. The procedures and processes that have been mentioned above appeals to problem-solving of ethics in engineering and aids professionals in the avoidance of particular traps that might otherwise alter judgment of a professional. The Professionals involved in issuing decision-making have been advised not to interpret the procedures as allowing complete objectivity or providing a mechanical algorithm for reaching a conclusion about an ethical problem so because all these ethic issues of any complication, they need subtle and objective judgment.

6.7. THE ETHICAL CHALLENGES OF ARTIFICIAL INTELLIGENCE AND AUTONOMOUS AGENTS

You will find that most of the time different professions have similar ethical issues such as conflict of interests and others. There has been an emergence of unique ethical issues in the engineering and computing departments. This is due to the designing of machinery whose outward behavior resembles human behavior that is, it is considered to be intelligent. With the advancements of machinery as they are become more flexible and sophisticated and they are increasingly taking on jobs that were once assigned only two humans, professionals in the engineering and computing department have the obligation of rethinking the relationship to the artifacts they synthesize, develop, and then deploy. For many years, artificial intelligence (AI) has stirred up many ethical challenges which have been greatly discussed. There are two classic examples that have been used to elaborate the discussions that have been brought about by AI. These references are by Norbert Wiener in 1965 (18) and by Joseph Weizenbaum in 1976 (19). In the 1990s, there has been the introduction of complex autonomous agents which are online robots and physical robots and the emergence of such agents have increasingly heightened the ethical debate. There has been two basic issues that are of immediate concern: the first one is the responsibility that the Professionals involved in the designing of such advanced machines have and the second one is the assumption that the machines that have been designed by the engineers will have the level of sophistication and advancement that will enable them to be considered moral agents by themselves without blaming engineers and scientists who developed them. This concern of ethics is very controversial and it is actively investigated. This article will not even be able to cover the discussion regarding the advancement of AI and the ethical issues that goes hand-in-hand with its advancement. Influential ideas in the area have been published in recent essays by Floridi and Sanders (20) and Jimmy (21).

6.8. ACM CODE OF ETHICS AND PROFESSIONAL CONDUCT

6.8.1. General Moral Imperatives

Bring a contribution to the community: It discusses on the enhancement of standards of the community. The duty of professionals is ensuring there is protection of basic human rights and respect the vastness of different communities. The objectives outlined in this principle involves the minimization of negative consequences of computing systems and this includes threats that might impact the user health wise and in terms of safety. Keeping this in mind, engineers are required during the designing and implementing of systems to ensure that products of their efforts will be utilized in a responsible way socially and will meet the needs of the end users and at the same time avoid harmful effects to health and welfare. The products being designed should also be environment-friendly. Thus, computing professionals who designed and developed systems must inform the users of any potential damage to the environment.

Avoiding damage to others: The term harm is defined as a deliberate infliction of damage and this can be the loss of data and undesirable environmental impact. The code outlines computer professionals should not in any way design technology that might cause danger to the community in general. Some of the actions that might be deemed harmful include modifying files, intentional destruction of files and modification of programs that may lead to extreme wastage of Manpower and Resources for example time and attempt needed in patching the system with "computer viruses." There are times where actions that might be well intended and mean no harm to anybody might eventually lead to unexpected harm. In such a situation the professional who was given the obligation perform this specific task is required to mitigate the negative consequences and as much as possible to the best of his or her ability.

Unintentional and unexpected harm can be avoided by carefully considering potential effects on all those affected by the decisions made during design. During the developing and designing of software, professionals are advised to follow all the known standards of system design in order to reduce the chances of harming others indirectly. Computer professionals should also investigate and analyze the social impact of systems being developed in order to foresee the chances of any serious harm occurring to others. In the event that the features of a system are misrepresented to the end-users, the computing professional is held liable for any injuries or harm that might happen.

During designing of the products, the computing professional is required to give reports and findings on any personal and social risks. In the event that the supervisor do not act to mitigate the dangers that have been reported, the computing professional is advised to blow the whistle in order for the problem to be fixed or reduced.

Before the computing professional reports any dangers, he or she must have properly assessed and analyzed all the relevant aspects of the incident. This is because misguided reporting can be by itself harmful. The credibility of the assessment of risk and responsibility must be maintained. Assistance canhave asked for from other experts during the assessment of the reports (Kizza, 2007).

Enhancing trust and honesty: Being honest builds up trust full stop Trust is required in an organization to ensure that it is effectively functioning. An honest computing professional is required to provide full disclosure of all parts of the systems limitation and problems and should avoid making deliberate false claims about the system or system design. A computer professional is also required to be honest about his or her own capabilities and qualifications and about any other situations that might make him seem dishonest like conflict of interests.

Being just and avoiding discrimination: Computing professionals must practice merit regarding fairness to others and tolerance. Discrimination shows itself in many forms. It can be racial, gender, religion, disability, origin or others and such factors is considered to be breaking the rules and regulations set by the ACM and this will not be entertained. Lack of equity amongst different Communities of people may lead to the use or misuse of data and mechanization. Regardless of age, disability, sex, religion, national origin and race, a fair society would give equal opportunity for every person to benefit in the use of computer resources. Despite these ideals there is no justification for unauthorized utilization of computer systems and such ideals do not give a reason to violate the ethical values.

Respecting the rights of property which includes copyright: Violating rights that have been put in place to safeguard copyrights has been restricted by law. This is applicable even when the program is not so protected. Software can be copied but under the right authorization.

Giving credit to intellectual property where due: Honesty of people's intellectual property needs to be safeguarded. This means that no computing professional should take credit of another person's idea even in the situation that there is no copyright protection for the work.

Honoring the confidentiality of others: With the increase in technology there has been the Enabling of gathering and transfer of private information on massive scales and therefore computing professionals have a responsibility of safeguarding the privacy and the integrity of information that describes individuals.

This can be done by providing accurate data and protecting it from access by an authorized individual in addition procedures must be put in place to allow individuals to review the records and rectify errors. This principle implies that a legal amount of personalized data should be collected from a system and the disposal period after the retention of the information should be clearly elaborated and enforced and there should be a reason for the collection of personal data. Consent from the owner of the data should also be gotten.Honor confidentiality: A computing professional should be honest to clients when he or she is accessing private information that belongs to the clients. The principle behind this is honoring the responsibilities regarding privacy to the customers, workers or user besides the law States otherwise.

Other specified expert duties.

- Work hard towards achieving high standards of being effective in the duties assigned. Professionals should strive to be excellence in performance.
- Gain the ability of being an expert. Once the expert has obtained excellence, he or she must go a step further and maintain the ability he or she already has. This can be done by setting up standards and the Professionals working hard towards achieving them.
- Be aware and honor roles that involve executive duties. Parties are compelled to become law-abiding citizens and respect the authorities. The rules and regulations of the ACM should be adhered to.
- Reviews from an expert should be accepted and provided. Peer review is important as it helps in creating a qualified duty mostly in the computer sector as it heavily relies on expert review.
- Provide rigorous understanding on the evaluation of Computing technology together with its effects. Computing experts should practice being impartial during the evaluation process of the framework and provide options as the professional must be able to figure out any conflicts of Interest that are available.
- Honor contract agreement together with the duties allocated. Computer professionals should be integral and honest in the job they have been assigned to and this involves making sure that the components of the system undertake its duties as deliberated. Furthermore, professionals are also obligated to give performance updates on a product when they're working with other people.
- Enhance community comprehension on computer technology together with its repercussions. It is the mandate for computer experts to divide their expertise with other professionals and the community in general in order to help them comprehend computer-related knowledge and their limitations.

- Have access to computer systems under authorization. Computer system experts are prohibited from trespassing and operating a computer unless given authorization and destruction of electronic assets is also prohibited. Trespassing involves accessing information that is deemed to be private and confidential without any authorization.

CHAPTER

7

Gender Differences in Computer Science and Technology Profession

CONTENTS

7.1. INTRODUCTION

Gender differences in any profession normally come from social factors that end up influencing how men and women behave. There are many organizations that involve and welcome diversities in gender, and also encourage for both sexes to be included when decisions are being made in the company and also in offering promotional opportunities. However, there are also other organizations that do not encourage the inclusion of gender and end up promoting bias in the workplace. There are many companies that have acknowledged the fact that the differences in gender help in adding value and different perspectives to an organization.

Both physical and emotional factors are involved in gender differences. These factors are what normally influence how males and females behave in the workplace. Most of these influences maybe due to previous factors that are psychological such as physical factors, for example, how capable an employee is to perform a job, or even how the employees were brought up.

Figure 7.1. It is important to understand the gender differences that occur in the workplace so as to advocate for gender equity and equality.

Source: https://www.ft.com/paidpost/CBS/gender_differences/index.html.

Stereotypes in relation to women and men may also be a reason why gender differences occur. One of the stereotypical assessments that a couple of people believe in, is that women are supposed to stay in the home while men are working and providing support. These stereotypes normally end up in gender discrimination.

There are many legal problems that come from the unfair or different treatment that men and women get in the workplace. There are a couple of labor and employment laws that help in governing discrimination on the basis of sex and also ensure that practices in the workplace that treat a certain sex in an unfavorable manner due to gender, are prohibited (Jaschik, 2018). Employers are also expected to ensure that they provide accommodations that are special for issues that are related to gender, such as breast-feeding and pregnancy.

There is also the Equal Pay Act which make sure that women and men are paid equally for any similar job that is performed in the company.

There are many concerns globally on gender disparities in the computing profession, and these have become much more important with the emergence of the information age.

Due to these concerns, there have been many public policy debates that are talking about gender equality, considering the fact that computer applications have led to an increase in influence on the society.

These debates have helped in expanding innovations in information technology (IT) as well as reducing the consequences of sexism.

In the earlier times of computers and computing, there was a good representation of women in the field.

They often were able to work as "human computers," allowing them to make calculations that were complicated, as well as work in big groups, such as Harvard computers.

Women were also able to work on cryptography and ballistics calculations. However, female human computers were paid less than male human computers (Jaschik, 2018).

Most of the human computers were female by the year 1943. At the same time, most of the fast programmers on machines such as the Electronic Numerical Integrator and Computer, were mostly female.

One of the major reasons why women were given jobs in programming and human computing was due to the fact that programming was considered a clerical function that required low skills, while creating the hardware, which was done by male engineers, was considered they harder job.

The six women who programmed the Electronic Numerical Integrator and Computer, designed the demonstrations to the public, and ensured that the machine was well prepared for introduction to the public, were hardly recognized for the work they did.

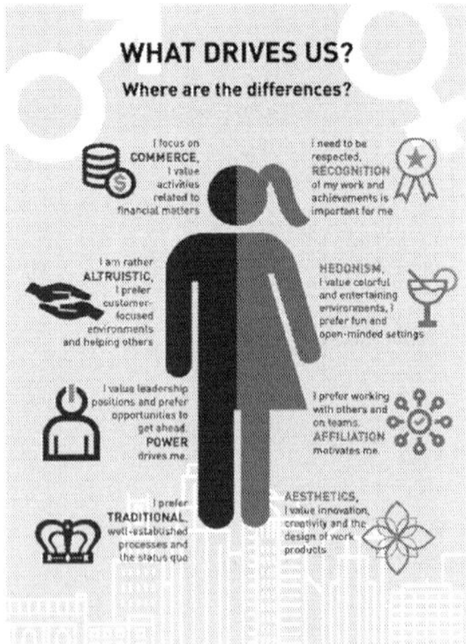

Figure 7.2. Gender differences can influence how people act in the workplace.

Source: https://asystems.as/what-drives-us-are-there-gender-differences-motivation-and-values/.

There were certain major shifts that were taking place, and these were helping in pushing women out of the computer programming field, in around the 1960s, despite the fact that it was a profession that was considered good for women to venture into. The field was made much more prestigious by men who were programming by the creation of professional associations, requirements to do with a level of education for work, and by actively not hiring women in the field. There were certain tools for hiring that were started, where the answers would be shared in groups and clubs that only had male members (Jaschik, 2018).

In addition, they were able to develop a personality test to push women out of the field. These tests discriminated against people who were keen on collaborating with others, which favored mostly male applicants. The entrenchment of these trends in the industry has led to these practices being perpetuated into the modern day. In the mid-1960s, there were several CS program, such as the one at Princeton University, which did not accept females.

7.2. THE GENDER GAP

A survey conducted by Supporting Women in IT involved asking the participants about their choices in career. This survey found that fewer women had interest in pursuing a career in CS. Several other studies also provided a strong base for a correlation between perceived ability and level of interest when it comes to making career choices (Ehrlinger et al., 2017).

The "Strategies of Inclusion" project that dealt with "Gender and the Information Society" was able to release some findings on from a survey conducted in Europe in 47 case studies. The main finding was that techniques used to recruit and retain women in the computing field. seem gender neutral. Some of these techniques include advertisement campaigns, introducing role models, and allocating quotas. There are also calls for educating reforms which will aid in increasing the quality of technological facilities.

Many individuals place high value on job security. The previous generation strongly believed that IT sector would flourish and offer many job opportunities, which led to parents encouraging their children to consider computing as a career without any concern regarding the gender of the child (Jaschik, 2018).

Despite the fact that there has been a major rise in computing in the last 50 years, introduction to the Internet, and the continuous need for technology in the world today, it is evident that women still have a lower level of engagement with CS comparison to men. A report showed that only 9% of girls in comparison to 44% of boys choose computing at the A-level.

Statistics done by the digestive education showed that the number of females who studied CS in undergraduate career had risen to 37% from 14% between the years 1971 and 1984. However these numbers have declined gradually to 18% in 2011.

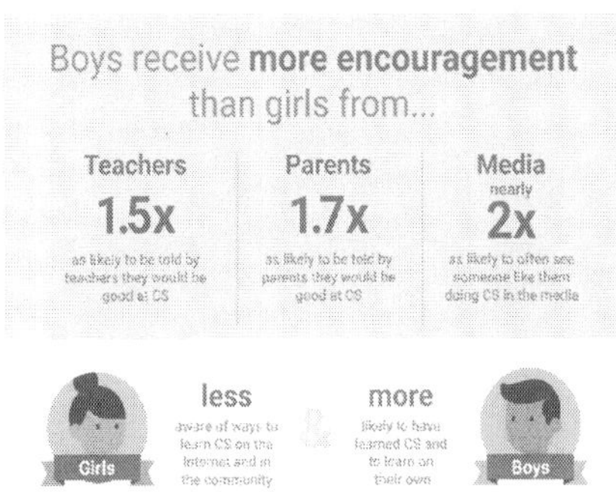

Figure 7.3. This shows an example of the gender gap that is there in CS, and this affects girls the most.

Source: https://blog.google/outreach-initiatives/education/racial-and-gender-gaps-computer-science-learning-new-google-gallup-research/amp/.

Considering the fact that it is becoming much more important to be a computer scientist instead of a computer illiterate, the statistics are becoming much more depressing. It is important for all genders to have an appreciation and engagement with deep learning, big data, artificial intelligence (AI), and machine learning (ML) (Jaschik, 2018).

There is a geek culture that surrounds CS and this is one of the main factors that is putting off women. Many people see computer scientists as nerds who have little to no social skills. Even the smartest people in CS, including Bill Gates, who formed Microsoft, were able to personify the meaning of the word geek.

Therefore, despite the fact that many people would like to achieve Bill Gates' financial status, they don't necessarily aspire to be like him, no matter how much he has changed the world. This also applies to Steve Jobs who founded Apple.

Another field where men are dominating is video-gaming. Despite the fact that gaming computers were invented 25 years ago, men still make up a majority of game users and designers.

However, men wish that more female computer scientists were working on designing video games. However, female video gaming professionals are not seen as smart and clever as their male counterparts. Instead, female professionals are perceived in a sexist way. However, even though these stereotypes still persist, things have started to change with 49% of gamers in the UK being female.

No matter how much things are improving for women in technology, we still have a lot of work to do before girls in schools think of CS as their career choice. Many initiatives have been started to empower girls, such as Girls Who Code and Code First. Yet, there is still a need for the society to change its perception and push more women into pursuing these careers in the future.

Back in the days when programming involves dials, switches, and cables to rewire a machine physically, two of the first computer programmers were female.

These were Ada Lovelace and Jean Bartik. Some of the female role models we see today in CS include Dame Wendy Hall and Sue Black OBE. Both of them have received honors for the body of work they did in the CS field (Jaschik, 2018).

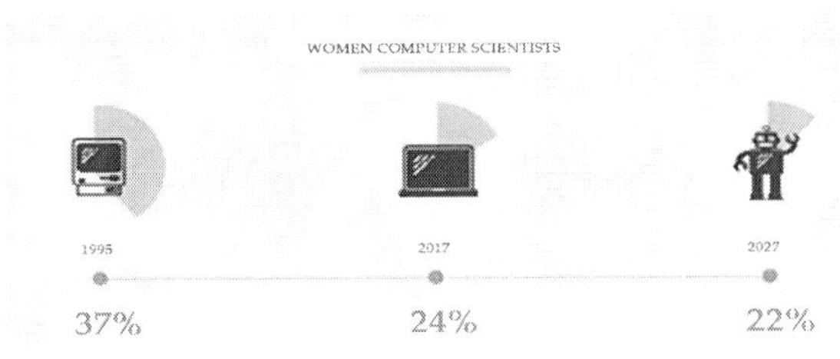

Figure 7.4. The picture above shows the percentage of women who were and will be in computer science between the year 1995 and 2027.

Source: https://www.goodreads.com/author/show/3105592.Jackie_C_Horne/blog?page=7.

The women, who have been recognized as pioneers in the computing field helped to create, develop, and imagine the ways in which electronics and computers can help in the modern world. They have acted as role models for many young girls today and have spread the word that computing in this modern world is not just for males (Jaschik, 2018).

7.3. GENDER DIVERSITY CAN BE BENEFICIAL

Technology organizations and departments that are gender balanced and gender diverse tend to perform better when it comes to financials, especially when women have a significant number of positions in the top management. They are also able to improve team dynamics, productivity, work efficiency, and ultimate corporate revenue.

A diverse workplace will aid in expanding the pool of qualified employees. United States Department of Labor showed that there will be over 3.4 million jobs opportunities related to computing by 2026. This might be a major problem considering the fact that those jobs can only be filled by 17% of the people who are doing a bachelor degree in computing by 2026. There are not many women who are choosing CS as a career choice and this means that we are not taking advantage of our diverse workforce. We need to better attract talent in the computing industry (Trauth and Eileen, 2006).

Gender diversity helps promote equity. Technology can break down any economic inequalities caused by gender and race. Jobs that are not specifically involved with IT are requiring the employees to be knowledgeable about computing. Acquiring in-depth skills computing through studies can be a valuable investment, which is important in today's economy of information.

In addition, the customer base is a reflection of gender diversity. Most of thecompanies have a variety of people as their customers, and therefore it also makes sense to have a variety of people who are skilled and intelligent working on the products and services (Trauth and Eileen, 2006).

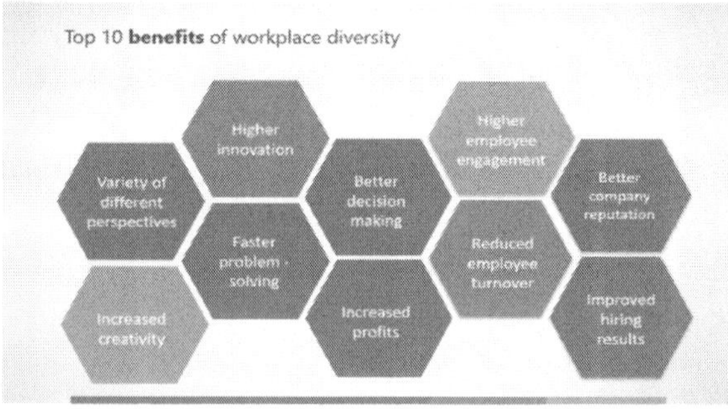

Figure 7.5. The picture above shows advantages of gender diversity in the workplace. This underscores the importance of having a workplace that is gender diverse.

Source: https://www.talentlyft.com/en/blog/article/244/top-10-benefits-of-diversity-in-the-workplace-infographic-included.

A team that is gender diverse has more chances to create products that will meet the requirements their diverse customer base. When there is an underrepresentation of women, most of the technical decisions are based on experiences, judgments, and opinions that the men have had. This results in a bias that is skewed towards male judgements. Research shown that diverse teams tend to be much more creative, productive, and able to keep up with changing schedules.

7.4. FACTORS THAT CONTRIBUTE TO WOMEN NOT PARTICIPATING IN THE COMPUTING FIELD

7.4.1. Education

Since 1984 there has been a decline in female participation in computer-related fields. This was after personal computers were mass-marketed as toys for predominantly boys. Giving the boys the chance to fiddle with computers ended up in a higher level of interest and readiness when it came to studying computer science.

A study in Canada on 7,000 high school students showed that the level of interest that young women had in the computing field was much lower than that of the young men. There is a similar effect that is seen even in higher education were only 4% of female students in college showed an interest in CSs in the United States (Trauthand Eileen, 2006).

Studies have proven to us that there are some aspects in computing that make women lose interest in the field. One of the greatest discouraging factors is the geek factor. There is this misconception that choosing a career in computing means being stuck in front of a computer writing codes all day. Both male and female high school students are affected by the geek factor, however, it has shown to have a big effect negatively on the female students. In addition to this, the popular media depicts computer programmers as males and that has led to a lack of role models for those female computer programmers that exist. In Stanford University, there has been a great change showing that female students are now choosing CS, making it the most popular major since 2015.There are many countries that now focus on making sure that students are well learned in mathematics and reading in addition to computing matters. This is because it is hard to get a job in today's world without knowledge in computing. One of the major issues in schools today is that it is hard to teach computational thinking as a subject on its own, such as mathematics or biology. There are some organizations such as the National Center for Women and IT, that have helped in distributing free resources that will increase awareness on the need to teach CS in schools (Trauthand Eileen, 2006).

Figure 7.6. Education has a major influence on the number of women that are in the computing field as of today. There are many women who did not get the opportunity to major in computer sciences due to the misconception that women should stay at home and not study.

Source: https://elearningfeeds. com/the-history-and-future-of-women-in-computing-simplilearn/.

There was a study that was conducted in 2014 in Romania that examined the gender disparity in computing. It showed the statistics of female enrollment in programs to do with computing. Some of the main aspects that were discussed included equity versus equality and the image of computing, which is normally masculine, and how it has led to a negative effect on computing opportunities for women.

7.4.2. Male and Female Perspectives

There are many studies that have shown that men and women view computers in different ways.

One of the studies was able to show that female interviewees are much more likely to say that they viewed a computer as a tool that should be used within a larger interdisciplinary and/or societal context in comparison to men who are also interviewed. In comparison to this viewpoint, men are more likely to show an interest in computers as machines.

Most of the women who were interviewed in this study stated that most of their friends or colleagues who had jobs in CS were geeks and had very few social skills. Women tend to dislike the concept that a career in CS makes computers their life (Jaschik, 2018).

Another study that was done in 2000 by The American Association of University Women showed that the female gender tended to approach the computer as a tool that is utilized mainly for what it can do, however, the male gender was able to view the computer as an extension of itself.

Men normally find the computer to be interesting while women are only interested in the possibilities of the computer as an instrument including how it can be used as a medium that is artistic.

The study showed that girls tended to dislike boys who confused real power with Power on a screen.

They thought that video games were stupid and showed how little the boys knew of the real world. The study also showed that both boys and girls utilized computers at around the same rate, however, they use them for different jobs (Jaschik, 2018).

Figure 7.7. Women have a negative attitude towards computer-related subjects. This is one of the main reasons why there are not many women in the computing field right now. They believe computing is nerdy and not feminine.

Source: https://www.hospitalitynet.org/opinion/4095431.html.

The University of Akron interviewed around 1000 students and found out that the women had a negative attitude towards computers in comparison to men. A similar study was done with 300 students in the University of Winnipeg and the results were similar. This has been seen to play a huge role in the gender disparity phenomenon when it comes to the computing field, especially with the females who lack an interest in the field at a very young age.

7.4.3. The Obstacles to Advancement

There are certain factors that have been highlighted in a research on the obstacles that women face in an undergraduate computing degree. These include:

- The methods of teaching that are used in the undergraduate classroom have practices and policies that privilege competition instead of cooperation, and this tends to be much more advantageous to men.
- The climate in the computer laboratory in undergraduate education sees women as foreign and not belonging, and this makes the women experience a high level of hostility as well as sexism.
- People who mean well but unknowingly create a stereotypical threat by constantly reminding female students that women are able to compute just as much and as well as men can.
- Certain practices that are subtle are continuously reproduced

due to the strong resistance to making changes in the system that undermines and under-represents women.

Just like in situations before college, there is implementation of solutions outside the main stream such as provision of role models, providing mentorship, and women's groups, which can lead to the creation of a perception among women, the professors, as well as their male colleagues, that for women to be successful, they required to get additional help so as was to graduate.

Most of these people do not come to the realization that additional help does not have anything to do with academics, but it helps the women to gain access to the various networking opportunities that male students access with much more ease. There are many female students who refuse to participate in these support groups that are extracurricular due to the fact that they do not want to seem deficient. Women and other underrepresented minority students study computing under conditions that are not similar to those that men experience (Ehrlinger et al., 2017).

7.4.4. Lack of Promotion and Acknowledgement of Skills

Figure 7.8. Not being acknowledged in the workplace is one of the main reasons why women quit their jobs in the computing field. Most male bosses have a backward mentality that only advantages the male workers.

Source: https://www.forbes.com/sites/womensmedia/2016/04/20/gender-bias-and-how-to-recognize-and-navigate-warning-signs/amp/.

Women in the computing field tend to feel that their skills and feedback are not as valued as those of men in the same workplace. A study that was done showed that 64% of women in computing roles felt that the people they were reporting to where responsive and receptive to their ideas, in comparison to 76% of women who are not in computing roles. The statistics are also similar when it comes to retaining women in the industry as women will tend to quit their jobs when they are not well valued for the work that they are offering to the company (Trauth and Eileen, 2006).

Women in the workplace tend to feel like they would prefer to be a part of more projects than they currently are in, making them feel like they are not well utilized. They would prefer their supervisors to present them with opportunities that will help in expanding their skill sets and also their level of responsibility at work.

It is however not enough to just acknowledge the skills that they bring to the table. They also do not have enough support and advocacy that they require for the promotion of their skills. Women also tend to feel like they are alone due to the fact that they do not have enough role models, mentors, and networking opportunities. These systems are meant to support the women and also help them in developing talents and opportunities for advancing their careers in addition to ensuring that the women can be promoted to roles that are much more senior. The advancement of females into senior technology roles can only be achieved using advocacy as its major player (Trauth and Eileen, 2006).

7.4.5. Stereotypes

There are many stereotypes in the computing field and this can mostly be changed using media to help in influencing the interest of women in CS. The image that is seen of people who are pursuing a major in CS in the popular opinion today, is a person who is very smart, mainly is obsessed with computers and has very few social skills. The opposite of this image is considered to be people who have more social skills and are traditionally feminine.

This stereotype continues to be propagated and generated by students when they are asked to give descriptions of people who study CSs. In the study, women who were given two articles to read, one with a stereotypical story in CS and one with a non-stereotypical story, tended to enjoy the one that was not stereotypical. This study helped to prove that women being underrepresented in CS is not because they do not have the interest. All in all, the conclusion showed that women tend not to choose CS as a major due to the prevalent stereotypes that are generated and propagated in campuses (Trauthand Eileen, 2006).

Stereotypes have shown to bring a negative consequence seeing as they prevent women from choosing technical fields due to a lack of interest. The stereotypes have shown to be unattractive to women and this would change if they had real representations of computer scientist and also female role models from the field of CS.

Another form of stereotyping is racial stereotyping which is a major problem and it can be seen with the high number of white or Asian males in the computing field. This makes it harder for people outside these ethnicities, women especially, to find jobs. Women who are not white or Asian women have a hard time getting jobs because they do not meet either half of the stereotype. The race of a woman has a low probability of affecting her choice in pursuing a computer-related career.

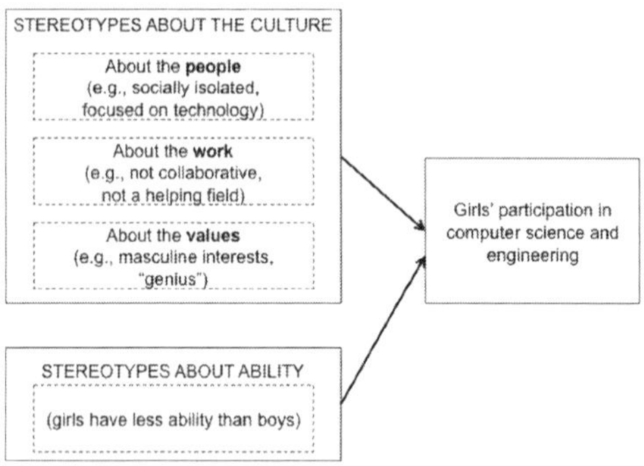

Figure 7.9. These are some of the common stereotypes that are found in the computing field. These can be very discouraging and can lead to girls not choosing computer science.

Source: https://www.washington.edu/news/2015/02/11/how-to-interest-girls-in-computer-science-and-engineering-shift-the-stereotypes/.

Women who come from a higher socioeconomic status have a higher chance of choosing a computing or computing-related field. This is the same case as a woman who comes from a family that already has members who are in the CS field. At the same time, most companies that deal with computer-related aspects normally look for employees who come from schools that are prestigious, which leaves the other people with less opportunities (Trauth and Eileen, 2006).

7.4.6. Psychological Differences Between the Genders

Women normally prefer careers that are people-oriented, while males normally show an interest to careers that other thing-oriented. Gender-egalitarian countries have a larger gap between the female and male interests in comparison to countries that are non-gender-egalitarian. This means that it not possible to conclude that gender differences are due to societal roles. This conclusion would be considered a naive interpretation of results.

7.5. HOW TO BRING THE WOMEN BACK INTO COMPUTER SCIENCE AND TECHNOLOGY

Most of the information that has been collected about women in IT and computer-related careers has been through case studies and interviews. Many programs help address the level at which women in IT have been under represented.

Some of the suggestions that have been incorporated into encouraging more women into the information and technology career include employee referral bonuses, formal mentoring, providing them with training opportunities, multicultural training all female employees in IT, as well as educational programs that target women.

There has been a decrease in the number of female students in colleges that are interested in studying CS as a major since the 2000s.

The nature of this problem was investigated by Alan Fisher and Jane Margolis. Some of the major issues that came up in regards to retaining and keeping women interested in CS were pedagogy and interest in curriculums, the experience gap, peer culture, and confidence doubts.

There are many universities in the United States that are making sure to change the programs in CS so as to ensure they are retaining the interest of women.

Figure 7.10. Bringing women back into computing can be very beneficial for many reasons. One of them being an increase in the level of innovation and ideas.

Source: https://www.cc.gatech.edu/news/596712/state-women-computer-science-investigative-report.

Providing exposures that are positive and proactive to earlier experiences in CS has shown to be very effective when it comes to retaining and creating enthusiasm for women, allowing them to later put CS into consideration as a career field. This is seen in The Alice Project which is a programming activity that is based on blocks and it makes it easier for students to make animations, create narratives that are interactive and even programming simple games that are in 3D. Universities and colleges are also starting to change processes and accessibility to mentorship for women that are majoring in computer-related fields.

Another way in which schools are trying to address this problem is through reaching out to elementary and high school girls at an early time. This includes incorporating after-school computer clubs, computer camps that are for girls, and even creating girl support groups so as to motivate girls to gain an interest in CS at a younger age. There is a program that was started in Canadian schools called the Canadian Information Processing Society outreach program. This program normally works by sending representatives to primary schools to talk to the girls on the importance of careers in IT. The main goal of this program is to educate the girls on the advantages as well as the opportunities that are available in the computing and IT field (Trauth and Eileen, 2006).

There are also some companies such as IBM that have helped in encouraging young women to gain an interest in technology, science, and engineering. They have started camps for younger women between the age of 11 to 13 so as to show them some of the opportunities they would have if they chose CS as a career.

In addition, there are many efforts that are being put into ensuring that the work that other female computer scientists are doing is visibly recognized, so as to provide more role models for younger women. An example of this is the Grace Hopper Celebration of Women conference series. This conference gives the opportunity to female computer scientists to meet, promote collaboration, and be able to show the work that they have done to the public.

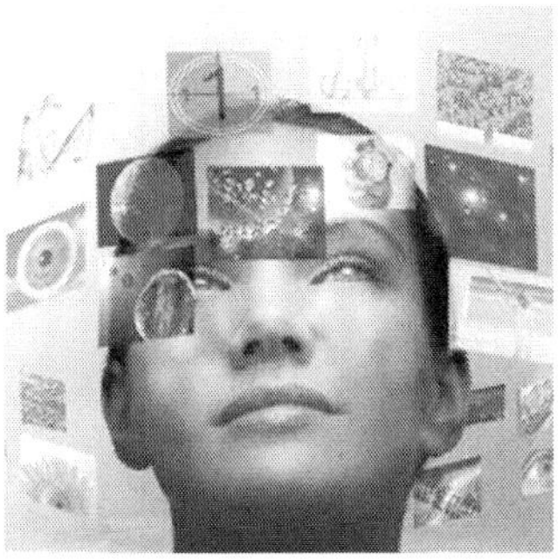

Figure 7.11. One of the main ways to increase the number of women in technology is through motivation. Many organizations have been created specifically to motivate women to choose computer science as a major, and this has proven to be a very efficient strategy.

Source: https://m-cacm.acm.org/magazines/2014/7/176222-european-women-in-computing/fulltext.

The Association for Women in Computing has also helped in providing many opportunities for women in computing to grow professionally through programs that are based on career-oriented and technical topics as well as the ability to network. There are also some organizations in the United Kingdom that have helped in promoting the cause of women in the computing field such as the British Computer Society Women's Forum.

7.6. THE NATIONAL CENTER FOR WOMEN AND INFORMATION TECHNOLOGY

This organization is as of now the leading supporter of entry and retention of women in computing. They aim at helping to create work and academic environments that are fair and able to welcome women into the computing field. They have also done research that has been able to show us that encouraging women is one of the main ways in helping them join the computing field, which is primarily dominated by men.

The research was also able to show us that women who join computer-related fields do so out of the influence of a friend, teacher, or family member, in comparison to the male counterparts who do not need much encouragement to do so. The conclusion showed that supporting women can be very advantageous in increasing a woman's self-esteem allowing her to believe that she is able enough to join the computing field (Jaschik, 2018).

This research by this organization is what led to the development of the Aspirations in Computing program that has helped in providing girls with the encouragement they need, networking opportunities, and female role models. Girls normally feel uncomfortable when they are the only ones in a certain class or group and this program has helped in enabling them to have a lower feeling of isolation in such situations. Being able to create a sense of belonging is important for women retention and interest in the CS field.

national center for
women&
INFORMATION
TECHNOLOGY

Figure 7.12. This organization has provided numerous opportunities for women in computing by promoting changes in the system, which predominantly favors men. Making women comfortable in a classroom or workplace is important in retaining them in the technology professions.

Source: https://www.wikiwand.com/en/NCWIT.

The organization also created an award that has helped in involving women in national competitions that involve computing and IT. The women who are awarded are selected for their academics, leadership skills, the aptitude in computing and IT as well as their plans after graduating school. The program has been able to achieve a 55% increase in the girls applying for computer-related majors since they started.

7.7. ORGANIZATIONS AND ACADEMIES

Ada Developers Academy is a school in software development that provided free tuition for women in the one year it takes to study the course. This school was started in September 2013 by the Technology Alliance. It also allowed the students to apply for a stipend of $1000 every month.

There is also a network of city chapters called the Girl Develop It and this has helped in teaching women from different parts of the United States on the ways in which they can develop software using JavaScript, CSS, and HTML, and other frameworks and languages. There has been development of the structural and content resources that are utilized for the teaching of these programs and they are also offered at no costs on their website.

In San Francisco, there is an intensive programming course for women only called the Hackbright Academy. This course takes 10 weeks. This academy also provides scholarships for mothers who previously worked in the information and technology field and require retraining to go back to work.

In 2006, an organization called Geek Girl was started. Its main purpose was acting as a resource of technology for women. This organization aims at empowering women of different ages and making it easy for them to use and understand technology. In addition to this, all the services provided are done so by women. Despite the fact that the main audience was meant to be female and this organization was created specifically for the empowerment of women, they also encourage men to take part in services as well as events that are being offered by the organization. They also host conferences, events, and meet ups that I look at most. They have a video channel that helps in providing workshops on tools that women can use to promote their technological skills as well as providing coverage for conferences and events that some people may not be able to attend. In addition, they have a website where they post blogs that are able to give news that is related to technology and information that a reader can access with the lowest level of experience in technology (Charles andThébaud, 2018).

Another programming school in the United States, that is immersive and only takes in women is the Grace Hopper Academy. Their curriculum pays attention to MEAN stack and aims to make sure that women are helped when they are beginning their careers in software engineering through mentorship and education.

Figure 7.13. These provide entrepreneurs with an opportunity to sit a course that allows them to successfully open businesses. It has really helped many women with their startups in the technology field.

Source: https://grasshopper.com/academy/.

There is another nonprofit organization that pays attention to educating young girls in underserved communities on CS. It is called CodeEd. They form partnerships with programs and schools with the aim of helping to provide teachers who would be volunteering, computers, and CS courses. They help by providing courses in CSS and HTML as well as providing cost material and a curriculum at no cost. The classes that are offered by the organization are normally run by two teachers who are volunteering, where they provide lessons in a manner that the school they are teaching in can accommodate, in addition to providing projects that are fun and experimental for their students to enjoy.

Sheplusplus (she++) is an organization that has helped with the facilitation of a community that is working to make sure that women are inspired enough to take up roles in CSs. It was established in 2012 when they held an inaugural conference which stared female computer scientist who had high positions in technology companies such as Facebook and Google as speakers. This conference helped in inspiring those who organized it to add on to the organization which now has helped in facilitating participation initiatives by being able to host more events. In these events they normally display a video that has stories meant to inspire women from female professionals in the technology field, in addition to providing a program for mentorship.There is a group of female engineering students that represents an organization called Nerd Girls each year, which helps in encouraging women to take up roles in the technology and engineering profession. This organization helps in celebrating women in the technology and engineering field. Members who participate in this organization help in solving problems in the real world, as a group, by being able to address and fix issues that are related to technology in the community. This organization has gained the attention of very many people nationally since it was established and there is even a reality show that was created to show the public the activities that the organization does to solve technological problems. The Institute of Electrical and Electronics Engineers sponsors this organization (Ernst and Horwath, 2014).

In 2007, Femgineer was initially developed as a blog whose main aim was on female engineers, but it however developed into an organization that helps in supporting women in careers that are in the technology field. This organization is now focused on education and helps in offering free teaching resources on technology, workshops, supporting meetups and forums, and they have also been able to develop a team to help in continuing the expansion of the original blog. Femgineer was founded by Poornima Vijayashanker who speaks avidly and regularly on issues that are related to technology and even about the organization. She also founded an organization that supports startups, and helps in teaching technology using workshops all around the United States.

Figure 7.14. This organization brings women into the computing field by empowering them through providing mentors and role models they can look up to. They also provide courses that can equip women in the industry to develop in their careers.

Source: https://femgineer.com/press/amp/.

A group in Europe called the Organization for Security and Co-operation has helped in supporting gender equality by proposing policies that favor women in the technology field.

7.8. ORGANIZATION OF POST-SECONDARY SCHOOL EDUCATION

There are many organizations that are run by students in a couple of post-secondary education institutions that mainly deal with advancing women in CS. Women in Computing is an example of this.

This organization is supported by the Rochester Institute of Technology. Students, staff, and faculty at the Institute are part of this chapter and work at supporting and furthering the development of the computing culture to women. They do not only do these in the campus but even in the community at large. They normally organize events in both the campuses and in others that are around their institution. This institution is among the top of the list of schools that have a chapter that supports women in CS.

Figure 7.15. Giving female students an opportunity to see the benefits and opportunities of a career in computer science early in their schooling times increases the chances of them choosing this field. This includes providing school activities that they can attend with female role models they can learn from thus beating the narrative.

Source: https://study.com/articles/10_Things_High_School_Students_Should_Never_Post_on_Facebook.html.

Harvard Undergraduate Women in CS is an organization that is hosted by Harvard University and it focuses on promoting women in the field of computing in many different industries and schools, educating women in computer-related sciences, and even providing more opportunities to women in computing fields. They also provide support for the WeCode conference which helps in promoting the involvement of women in computer-related fields.

7.9. PACESETTERS

This is a program that was created by The Women in IT so as to help in improving the gender composition in computing. Since this program was created in 2012, there has been an increase of women in more than 20 corporate and academic organizations.

Most of these women are women who were in the science field but not keen on majoring in CS. This program allows organizations from different parts of the world to come together to find ways to effectively increase the level of participation of women in computer-related sciences.

As of now, there are so many government agencies, nonprofit organizations, corporations, and academic institutions that are working together with pacesetters to solve the problem of including women into the computing field.

They have been able to work together to create teams that will help in developing and funding the required programs and later on in sharing the results.

There are many prestigious companies that are working together with pacesetter organization including Microsoft, Google, and Intel among others.

These are some of the results they have achieved while working with this organization:

- Google has helped in building newer programs for women in their undergraduate level and they have also created a panel of engineers, for career development which has helped in giving women an opportunity to participate in mock interviews before their real job interviews. This has helped in increasing the number of women applicants and also increasing the number of women who participate in an internship program that is run by Google for software engineering.
- Intel has helped in piloting a program that has helped in allowing women to participate in training that is specialized. This program is called Command Presence Workshop.

Figure 7.16. The command presence workshop provides female students with computer training so as to professionally develop their careers. This training is specialized and set to meet their specific needs.

Source: https://allevents.in/surrey/executive-presence-workshop/1000079262045913.

- Virginia tech has helped in creating a team of CS faculty, student mentors, and advisers who promote interaction with female undergraduate and high school students who will potentially choose CS as a major. Since they started this program, they have seen a 57% increase in female participation.

CHAPTER

Computer Science and IT Professional Associations

8

CONTENTS

8.1. INTRODUCTION

Organizations that are considered the main contact point for those professionals who work in the corresponding fields are called professional associations. Professional associations aid in defining professions and also in assisting members of the association to grow in their profession through research, quality control and ongoing learning. They also work to make sure that standards are maintained within the profession, providing professional development that is ongoing to the members, and even representing the interest to the community and the government.

Professional associations have websites that provide information to the public about occupation and the industry in question. There are various different services that are offered to members in the professional associations, but in general, they provide a safe space for those who are working in the same field so as to promote interaction with each other and also learning from each other. In the computer industry, professionals are asked to join relevant associations especially as students as it is always the first step in the development of one's profession.

Figure 8.1. Professional Associations have helped in the development of many people's careers. They all aim at providing their member with the means they need to achieve their career goals.

Source: https://pointroadgroup.com/join-professional-association/.

Professionals in the computing industry who are able to list the professional memberships and even development courses have the highest chance of showing their potential employers the commitment that they have to their careers. Even when one does not have much work experience, these can help them in gaining a step forward when it comes to getting a job, by setting them apart from their competition.

There are a couple of benefits that come with joining these associations. Some of these include:

- When one joins as a student, they get highly discounted membership fee.
- Members of these associations are able to attend conferences, events, and even get many opportunities to network and for development professionally.
- They get opportunities to perform research on the specific areas that they practice in and therefore learn to improve on their level of innovation and provide quality work.
- They also have an opportunity to receive journals on the regular as well as other different publications that they can subscribe to.
- They are able to gain access to information on the salary based on the conduction of surveys by the association, and also get advice on agreements in the workplace.
- The associations provide schemes for mentorship, advice on the careers, and information about the industry.
- They get to see the different job vacancies that are available in the industry in real time.
- The association can provide scholarships for those who want to continue with further learning and they also provide awards and prizes to the employees who do well over the year.
- They provide the members of the association with information on the requirements that one needs for professional registration.
- The members are able to get assessments of the qualifications that they would need overseas.

Below we will discuss some of the Professional Associations in the Computer Science (CS) and Information technology (IT) industry.

8.2. ASSOCIATION FOR COMPUTING MACHINERY

The Association for Computing Machinery helps in bringing together educators in the computing field, researchers, and computing professionals with the purpose of providing inspiration for dialogue, sharing of resources, and addressing the challenges that are in the computing field. The Association for Computing Machinery is the largest computing association globally and it helps in strengthening the collective voice of all computing professionals through promoting high standards, a strong level of leadership, and being able to recognize technical excellence. The association helps in supporting the growth of its members in a professional manner by being able to provide opportunities for the development of their careers, continuous learning, and being able to network with other professionals.

Figure 8.2. Association for Computing Machinery (ACM) promotes networking amongst people in the computing field, allowing them to share information and discuss the matters affecting the field.

Source: https://www.acm.org/.

The Association for Computing Machinery was founded just as computers were gaining their popularity, and this association has been able to open doors all over the world and it now has more than 100,000 members who live outside the United States. This growth in membership has caused the development of councils in many different countries including China, Europe, and India which has helped to foster opportunities for networking that are strengthening the bonds within and across technical communities and countries. The association has help in raising awareness on the important educational, technical, and social issues around the world to do with computing.

Special Interest Groups: The Association for Computing Machinery has special interest groups that have helped in representing the main areas of computing, and therefore being able to address technical community interests that help in driving innovation. These groups help in offering away range of conferences, activities, and publications that focus on various specific sub-disciplines of computing. They allow the members to share what they discover, their common advantageous practices and even expertise.

The Association for Computing Machinery has 37 special interest groups that have major network opportunities that are always undergoing expansion, reflection on the growth of the discrete disciplines of computing and technical communities. The Association for Computing Machinery is able to use the special interest groups to sponsor conferences that are held annually, symposia, and workshops, so as to serve practitioners and constituencies that are based on research. Most of these events have become Premier global events due to the fact that they have been providing objective spaces for innovative competing ideas.

Local neighborhoods: The Association for Computing Machinery has infrastructure that is best broadly and helps and supporting over 900 student and professional chapters globally. These are what are referred to as local neighborhoods and they provide an opportunity for members to have the accessibility to research that is critical as well as the opportunity to establish networking systems that are personal.

Volunteers; Members and non-members of The Association for Computing Machinery get to have many different opportunities for volunteering, that help in the creation of networking possibilities as well as enhancement of the development of the career. The volunteers in The Association for Computing Machinery help in serving as a international community of researchers, practitioners, and students, that is growing almost daily. These people are able to lend assistance that is valuable at conferences, webinars, publications, and other events.

The Association for Computing Machinery's governance is directly and critically impacted by the volunteers in the association. This is through the council which is the highest governing authority. The volunteers also help in the executive committee and many other different task forces and boards of The Association for Computing Machinery.

Figure 8.3. Most of the members in this associations are volunteers in peer reviews. This gives opportunities to develop their careers and also promote networking.

Source: https://enafrica.org/career-application-2/.

The volunteers, both those who are members and those who are not members, have roles of leadership in the journal publication of The Association for Computing Machinery, as reviewers, associate editors, and event editors in chief. They are also many who are part of the education board which helps in providing recommendations for the curriculums, especially for the universities that provide computing courses for four years, as well as community colleges. They have even been able to provide a curriculum that has undergone translation Chinese.

The Big tent: There is a lot of diversity in the community, quite similar to the variety of subfields that are comprised in the computing field. These include: students, educators, practitioners in project management and software development, researchers in academia, engineers, and application designers.

Apart from the diversity of different occupations, it also extends to the religion, ethnicities, and even gender. The Association for Computing Machinery has a women's committee that helps in the advocating of full engagement of women internationally in all computing aspects.

There is also a committee that is sponsored specifically to celebrate diversity in computing, and this has helped in the bringing together of researchers, students, faculty, and even professionals from all over the world with different backgrounds. It has helped in providing a networking environment that is supportive for groups that are underrepresented across a wide range of fields in IT and computing.

Supporting students: The Association for Computing Machinery has student chapters that have helped in enabling students to be a part of professional activities. There are many students from many different colleges and universities (over 500) from all over the world who have had enhancement of the learning through exchanging of ideas with fellow students and professionals who are established.

The Association for Computing Machinery has helped very many students by offering over $1.6 million in one student membership that is affordable as well as scholarships. Both students who are looking to do their masters and even those who are looking doing their undergraduates are able to participate in the competition for student research. These competitions are recognized internationally and are normally sponsored by Microsoft. The students gain an advantage by being able to share the work with the other fellow students as well as professionals, allowing them to gain recognition and experience as well as earn prizes.

Recognition of excellence: The Association for Computing Machinery is very good at recognizing excellence through the many different awards that they give for both professional and technical achievements as well as contributions in IT and CS. Apart from members who have been able to gain professional accomplishments, they also award those members who have brought in a contribution that is significant to the mission of the association.

They have an award which is normally accompanied by a $1 million prize, and this award is normally given by Google, due to the contributions that are long lasting and are also very important technically to the field of computing. There are other major awards that help in recognizing achievements by young professionals in the computing field, innovators of software systems, educators, pioneers who have helped in making contributions that are humanitarian and Cross-discipline and theoretical computer scientists.

Provision of advocacy for public policy issues: The Association for Computing Machinery is known for leveraging the respect it has internationally as well as its leadership, for the shaping of public policies, all over the world. The association has policy entities that are distributed geographically in North America and Europe and this helps in the development of statements to do with policies, briefs on issues, white papers, and reports that help in providing policymakers with analyses that are based on knowledge, and thus helping the acceleration of innovations that are useful in the computing field, which in turn benefits the society. It also helps in the delivery of expertise on policies to do with education, women in the computing field, and ensuring diversity in computing.

Figure 8.4. Advocacy has always proven to be a means to achieve resolutions for issues. Thus association is using its well-known name to advocate for issues in the computing field that are affecting the public all over the world.

Source: https://www.iaml.info/advocacy-committee.

Publications that have helped to advance technology, innovation, and research: The Association for Computing Machinery is a well-known and acknowledged major source for scientific information globally and it has helped in the promotion of research and also innovations to do with CS, due to its magazines, journals, and all the conferences and symposia that are held annually (over 170 of them).

The authors in The Association for Computing Machinery are some of the leading innovators and thinkers in IT and CS field globally and they have provided research that is original and also in their own well knowledgeable perspective. The Association for Computing Machinery has also helped in providing access to their digital library which is a database of literature that is comprehensive and expanding and it also has bibliographic resources that are well detail for professionals in the computing field from many different publishers. The digital library as of now has over 1.1 million articles that have been written by leading researchers in the computing field globally.

In addition to this they have a magazine that helps in providing news on the industry, observations, commentary, and practical research. This magazine is called the flagship magazine.

Ethics and Conduct: The association has a code of ethics that helps in making identification of the elements of the commitment that each member has to the professional ethics conduct. It helps in outlining the major aspects that promote the contribution to the well-being of the society and humans and also those that focus on the relation that these considerations have to the responsibilities of the professional, complying with the code, and imperatives of the organization.

The Institute of Electrical and Electronics Engineers: This is a professional association that has members in electrical and electronic engineering. The main offices are located in New York City and New Jersey. This professional association was created in 1963 after the American Institute of Electrical Engineers and the Institute of Radio Engineers was amalgamated. It now referred to as IEEE.

Since 2018 it has become the biggest technical professional association in the world with more than 450,000 members in more than 150 countries. It mainly deals with the technical and educational advancement of electronic and electrical engineering, computer engineering, telecommunications, and disciplines that are related to any of these. This association was founded in 1884, first as the American Institute of Electrical Engineers. The rival institute was founded in 1912. They later on amalgamated.

The amalgamation occurred in 1963. By the time they were merging, they had around 140,000 members, most of whom came from the United States (around 93%). They have grown to around 240,000 members by 1984 with a minimum of 21% from outside the United States. As of today, this professional association has more than 430,000 members in over 150 countries, with 45% of them from outside the United States. They still continue to grow.

Figure 8.5. IEEE produces more than 30% of global research papers in computer science, electrical and electronics engineering. In total, it published more than 110 journals and magazines reviewed by peers. It sponsored more than 1700 events and conferences.

Source: https://www.pngfly.com/png-bm7r97/.

8.2.1. Their Core Values

One of their most important values is trust. Many professionals believe that if they can be trusted, it adds to their value as individuals. This virtue includes being able to invest in continuous education and creating a long-lasting pipeline of students that will be able to ensure preservation of the profession.

IEEE also aims to ensure the cultivation of vibrant, active, and honest exchanges between interdisciplinary global communities and cross-disciplinary communities of technical professionals. Partnerships are important in any field and one of the things they are aiming at, is being able to promote a culture where employees and volunteers respect each other, value contributions at the various levels of the association, invest in training and development for the enhancement of skills, ensuring empowerment of members to promote a positive change, and also being able to build a membership organization that has a strong partnership between staff and volunteers in serving the profession.

The aim to perform all this while still being of service to the human race by being able to leverage science, engineering, and technology to advantage the welfare of human beings. This includes their ability to promote public awareness and also making sure that the public understand the engineering profession. Lastly, they also believe in integrity. This means that they are able to foster a climate that is professional where the scientists and engineers gain continuous respect for the volunteerism and their great ethical behavior.

8.2.2. Educational Activities

The association is able to provide opportunities for members to learn a variety of sciences to do with engineering, technology, and research. They have many different educational opportunities that they are able to offer to the members, including:

- The Education Partners Program;
- IEEE e-Learning Library;
- Standards in Education; and
- Continuing Education Units.

Figure 8.6. This library has more than 400 courses and education video packages in the field of engineering.

Source: https://lib.metu.edu.tr/announcements/ieee-e-learning-library-database.

The e-learning library has online educational courses that have been collected and designed in a manner that allows one to read at their own pace. The Education Partners is only for members of the association any provide degree programs, certifications, and specific classes with a discount of 10%, all which one can do online.

The Standards in Education site helps in explaining the meaning of setting standards and how they are important as well as ways to develop and use them. This site also has modules with tutorials and illustrations of cases that help in making introductions of where the standards came from, the terminology that is generally used, how they are used, and the impact they have on products. In addition to this, the site also provides any information that is new in relation to the standards, reviews of books, and links to other sites that have information on standards.

So as to ensure the maintenance of a professional engineering license, there are around 28 states in the United States that require one to have Professional Development Hours.

This encourages engineers to look for Continuing Education Units so that they have the ability to participate in Continuing Education Programs. Continuing education units can be translated into Professional Development Hours, where 1 Continuing Education Unit is the same as 10 Professional Development Hours. There are now other countries outside the United States, such as South Africa, that require continued professional development credits, and this association is planning on featuring some courses that can be listed in South Africa for these members.

The association also works to sponsor a site that has been created in a manner that helps younger people understand engineering in an easier and better manner, as well as understand how a career in engineering can integrated into their future wants.

The association also allows for students between the age of 8 years and 18 years, teachers, and even the parents to go to the site so as to have the ability to prepare for a career in engineering, be able to question experts on questions that are related to engineering, play games that are interactive, go through links that have information on the curriculums, and review the lesson plans.

The students are also able to use this website to search for degree programs in engineering that are accredited in the United States and in Canada. Those visiting the site have many different search options they can choose from, including country, state, location, etc.

The professional association also helps in the facilitation of partnerships between activities between students and all of its entities, through Student Activities Committee.

8.3. THE IEEE FOUNDATION

IEEE Foundation

Figure 8.7. This Foundation is providing services based on philanthropy in supporting the main purpose of the professional association in fostering technological innovation and excellence for the benefit of humanity.

Source: https://give.everydayhero.com/us/ieee-foundation.

This foundation is a charity foundation founded in 1973. It was established with the main purpose of supporting and promoting education in technology, excellence, and innovation. It has a separate incorporation from the IEEE although they have a very close relationship. It is compulsory for the members in the board of directors of the foundation to be actively involves with the IEEE. They have to be members of the association as well. One of them is actually required to either have been or be in the board of directors for the IEEE.

In the beginning, the foundation was established to ensure the acceptance and administration of donations for the award program of the association, however, these donations became much more than what was necessary for this job, and therefore, there was a broadening of the scope. Not only is the foundation able to solicit and administer unrestricted funds, but also administer funds that are designated by donors so as to support the programs that are dealing with education, humanitarianism, preservation of the history, and recognition of peers.

8.4. AMERICAN SOCIETY FOR INFORMATION SCIENCE AND TECHNOLOGY

This is the only professional association that bridges the gap between practicing and researching information science. For almost 80 years, this professional association has at the forefront of developing new theories, techniques, and technologies.

Their members include thousands of researchers, students, developers, practitioners, and professors in the information science and technology field, from over 40 countries globally. These members have helped in the development of this professional association and they are an important part of their professional development as well. All the members in this association have one main aim and purpose, which is improving the manner in which the society is able to store, retrieve, analyze, manage, archive, and disseminate information.

asis&t
EUROPEAN STUDENT CHAPTER

Figure 8.8. This association built an infrastructure exchange programs and student internships that created networking opportunities with students all over the world.

Source: https://www.asist.org/chapters/student/esc/.

The vision entails the establishment of information professionalism that is newer and better, in a place where information is very important to social, personal, economic, and political progress. They plan on achieving this by:

- Being able to advance knowledge on information, including how it is used and created.
- Providing an analysis of practices, technologies, and ideas.
- Ensuringing that theory, research, service, and application of information is valued.
- Being able to nurture new ideas, interests, and perspectives.
- Creating awareness by informing the public on the importance of information sciences and technology, as well as the benefits they bring to society.

The main mission is to advance information sciences by ensuring that there is a provision of focus, opportunity, and support to professionals and organizations that deal with information.

Some of the functions of these professional association include:

- Providing the development of careers and opportunities to do with leadership through the regional chapter as well as their students' chapters.
- Connecting students, researchers, practitioners, and organizations from different aspects of the field through events and special interest groups.

- Editing, publishing, and disseminating publications that are dealing with research and development.
- Using webinars to share professional education that is important.
- Promoting development and research and also for information professionals to be educated.
- Creating opportunities for networking through the community of the professional association.

The American Society for Information Science and Technology is able to provide all these services to professionals in these fields: information science, CS, management, law, linguistics, medicine, engineering, education, and chemistry.

8.4.1. Their History

The American Society for Information Science was established on March 13, in the year 1937. It was initially referred to as the American Documentation Institute.

At this time, the members had to have undergone nomination by and should represent affiliated societies that were scientific and professional, Government agencies, and foundations. It was initially created to deal with developing microfilm so as to promote the dissemination of information.

The number of people who were interested in the development of new techniques and principles in the specific aspects of information services and documentation, increased.

This led to the amendment of the bylaws in 1952 so as to allow the admission of individuals and also members that were institutional.

This means that the American documentation institute became the national professional society for those who had concerns with all the aspects and issues of information science.

These years (1950's) also had an increase in the level of awareness when it came to the work that automatic devices could do, when it came to searching for literature as well as storing and retrieving information.

There was a lot of growth in the variety of professional interests due to the growth in magnitude and potential of these concepts.

Figure 8.9. Information science has allowed us to analyze, collect, classify, manipulate, store, retrieve, move, disseminate, and protect information.

Source: https://www.istockphoto.com/vector/word-cloud-information-science-gm576725790-99103117.

There was a major increase in membership during the 1960s as the issues that were caused by the "information explosion" became a major concern nationally. There was later a vote to change the name to American Society for information science from American Documentation Institute due to the fact that information science became and identifiable discipline. This happened in 1968. The team members in the association at this time, were dealing with the process of information transfer, utilizing IT and systems, and creation of a national professional organization for those who had a concern with matters to do with how to design, manage, and use IT and systems.

In the 1970s, there was an acceleration of the shift from processing of batches to modes that are online and also from mainframe to minicomputers in microcomputers. At this point, the traditional boundaries that had been set among the various different disciplines started fading away, and the term "information" was added in the titles of many library schools. The association then made the meeting that used to occur on each Mid-Year, an annual event that focused on one main topic that was of current interest.

Later in the 1980s people were able to use the personal computers to access large databases such as user-oriented services such as Dialog. The association then had to add to and revise the special interest groups so as to deal with the shifts, and therefore had to establish groups on information systems in the office as well as personal computers in addition to information issues internationally and information services rurally. By the time the dickhead was ending, special interest groups were accessible involving media not printed, social services, community information systems, and energy into the environment. At this point, the association had its first chapter that is not North American.

As the proliferation of information and communication technology continues, members of the association are now able to examine the social consequences; technical bases; understanding of online databases in a theoretical manner; the use of databases in education, industry, and government; and also Internet and World Wide Web development. The litter changed their name to the American Society for information science and technology in 2000, so as to account for the many different members in the association. Thereafter the name was changed to Association for Information Science and Technology so as to account for the growing international membership.

8.5. ASSOCIATION FOR WOMEN IN COMPUTING

Figure 8.10. This association has helped empower women by giving them the opportunity to fulfill their careers in computer-related fields. This has proven to be very effective considering women are always left behind in these fields.

Source: https://www.awc-hq.org/.

This is a professional organization whose members are mostly women in computing. It was established in 1978 and it is part of the Institute for Certification of Computing Professionals. It was originally called The National Association for Women in Computing.

The professional association deals with professionals who play a role in technology and information, with the dedication to ensuring promotion of women in this field of technology. They have chapters as well as a continually growing network of members who are independent, thus being able to offer camaraderie with professionals who have similar thought capacities.

The chapters provide outreach to members and opportunity to network across various job functions, personal interests, and business segments to do with computing and technology. The association provides programs and opportunities, which are very valuable tools in promoting opportunities in continuous education, that help in developing the careers of the members, and also promoting the enhancement of relationships and mentorship with the other members in the association.

The association has chapters that provide a long history of using social investments to give back to the community. The members of the association are leaders who have a passion in the youth who are interested in careers to do with computing and technology, and therefore always find time to volunteer and teach at workshops that are dealing with technology and computing, as well as providing opportunities for the youth to shadow their jobs. There are also some chapters that help in offering women who seek to do careers in computing and technology with scholarships. There are also other chapters that provide clothing drives, so as to give a chance to women who are seeking a chance at a new computing career, to find ensembles that are suitable for interviews. The association also has some chapters that help in collecting technology for organizations that are either national or local, so as to be able to publish and ensure distribution of the technology to communities that do not have enough resources.

8.5.1. Purpose

The association for women in computing has a purpose in providing opportunities for women in technology and computing to grow professionally through mentoring, networking, and continuing education. They are able to make this an accomplishment using their ability to promote awareness on the different problems that affect women in the technology and computing industry, so as to improve the level of women development professionally and advancing women in technology and computing. In addition, they make it their purpose to make sure that they encouraging women to go after careers that are involved with CS.

This professional association is nonprofit, and it takes in both men and women who are interested in IT. They have an award called the Ada Lovelace award, which is normally given to members who have performed greatly in either: remarkable service to the community of technology and computing through participation in and accomplishments in computing and technology for the benefit of women and/or a scientific technical achievement that was outstanding.

Figure 8.11. The main aim of this organization is to ensure that there are many more people, males and females included, taking part in supporting women in computer science.

Source: https://www.cs.montana.edu/~awc/.

8.6. COMPUTING RESEARCH ASSOCIATION

This professional association is a North American non-profit association that deals with certain academic departments such as computer engineering, CS, and other related fields that are related. This professional association was established in 1972 and is based in Washington DC, United States.The mission is to ensure the enhancement of innovation by working together with the government, industries, and academia. Their goal is to strenghten research is and education in computer-related fields. They are able to achieve this by being at the top of the computer research community. They have the power to inform the public and policymakers and push for the development of talents in the computing field.

8.6.1. Policy

This association helps in assisting policymakers to come to an understanding on the matters that are affecting the federal networking and IT research and development program, which is a program that has put in a lot of effort to make sure that computing research is well supported. The Computing Research Association has also worked to make sure that the Members of Congress are well educated, and also ensure provision of testimonies from experts in the areas that deal with CS research, to policymakers. The Computing Research Association together with their Computing Community Consortium have helped by sponsoring the Leadership in Science Policy Institute, through a workshop that run for one and a half days in Washington DC. They also have maintenance of a website for government affairs as well as policy blog for computing research.

8.6.2. Professional Development

This professional association has worked to ensure that computing researchers are supported all through their careers, so as to make sure that the need for a supply of researchers in the computing field as well as advanced practitioners who are talented and well educated, is continuously met. They have also assisted with the development of leaders within the community of research in the competing field, in addition to promoting the changes that are required so as to advance education. On top of that, they have encouraged members to participate in groups that are was not well represented.

Figure 8.12. CRA runs under the commitment of ensuring that industries, academia, and governments are united in promoting the advancements of research in computer science so as to positively impact the world.

Source: https://www.hmc.edu/about-hmc/2016/12/16/computing-research-association-recognizes-two-harvey-mudd-students/.

Some of the other work they do include:

- Offering academic and career workshops;
- Supporting the CRA's Committee on the Status of Women in Computing Research; and
- Running the Distributed Research Experiences for undergraduate projects.

8.6.3. Leadership

They have also been able to support the development of leadership in the communities dealing with research. They are also working to ensure that it is promoting cooperation amongst the different elements in the community that deals with computing research.

The Computing Research Association has also been able to support the conference at Snowbird, which is a conference that is held biennially, where the leaders in the departments for computing research come together for the purpose of networking and addressing the common problems in the field. The Computing Leadership Summit is also supported by The Computing Research Association.

8.6.4. Collection and Dissemination of Information

The Computing Research Association is able to collect and disseminate information on the reasons why computing research and the policies that relate to it are important, to the communities that deal with research and policymaking. They also look at developing information that is relevant and also make sure that the information can be accessed by the public, computing research community, and policymakers.

The Taulbee Survey is normally published by The Computing Research Association, and it is a major source of information on the enrolling, producing, and employing of PhD s in computer engineering and CS. It also provides data on the salary and demographics of faculty in computer engineering and CS jobs in North America. Some of the statistics that are provided include the breakdowns of the ethnicity and gender of the professionals. The Computing Research Association also helps in providing the computing research news which undergoes publishing around 10 times every year for researchers in the competing field, and The Computing Research Association Bulletin which is used for the sharing of news, information on the initiatives of The Computing Research Association, and matters that the general community would be interested in.

Figure 8.13. This survey solicited valuable data from members to publish the statistics of the survey.

Source: https://cra.org/2017-cra-taulbee-survey-another-year-of-record-undergrad-enrollment-doctoral-degree-production-steady-while-masters-production-rises-again/.

8.6.5. Committee on Widening Participation in Computing Research

This committee aims to ensure that success and participation of groups that are not well represented in research in the computing field and education are increasing at all levels. In general, the committee makes sure that groups that are not well represented have positive benefits from CS and engineering activities. It also deals with making sure the rate of success of all engineers and computer scientists in the working environment is improved. It was initially referred to as the Committee on the Status of Women in Computing Research. This was changed in 2019.

One of the awards they have been able to receive include: The National Science Board's Public Service Award for their programs that are well oriented on actions, that were aiming to increase the number and success of the participation of women in research and education in the CS and engineering fields. This was in 2005.

8.7. EUROPEAN ALLIANCE FOR INNOVATION

This is an international professional community which is non-profits. Their goal is to promote the empowerment of the information and communication technology research globally as well as the innovation community. They also help in promoting the corporation between international and European information and communication technology communities. The headquarters are located in Belgium and other offices are in China, Boston, Shanghai, United States, Bratislava, and Slovak republic. The office in Bratislava was created together with the Slovak University of technology through being able to sign the memorandum of understanding. This association was founded in 2010 by Imrich and it has over 150,000 members from all over the world.

The organization helps in organizing conferences and events as well as providing support for their members, so as to try and raise their rates in which innovation is reaching the market. The European alliance for innovation is an organization that is helping to empower innovation and global research.

The main mission is the creation of environments that will help to improve research and to ensure transformation of the greatest ideas into propositions in the commercial level through corporations in the community. They have certain guiding community principles that have helped them get to where they are including openness, objectivity, equality, and transparency. They have been able to create an environment that is rewarding excellence in a transparent manner through unique corporation methodologies. These have also helped to build recognition in an objective manner regardless of age, origin, economic status, etc. without the negative influence of no membership fees and also closed-door committees. This means that they do not let anyone or anything come in between their members' research careers.

The European alliance for innovation has been able to lead the way towards the advancement of research and innovation through these shared values. In addition to research and innovation advancements, they have also been able to empower individuals as well as institutions, so as to benefit the society in the advantageous digital revolution.

EAI
RESEARCH MEETS INNOVATION

Figure 8.14. They have been able to collaborate and form a partnership with the International Federation of Inventors' Associations.

Source: https://en.wikipedia.org/wiki/European_Alliance_for_Innovation.

The European Alliance for Innovation publishes scientific magazines and journals through their own publication platform that is driven by the community, which is called the European Union Digital Library. They also use their E-script system to post publications online in addition to having a database where the European Union Digital Library has their scientific publications that have been reviewed by peers

8.8. ASSOCIATION OF INFORMATION TECHNOLOGY PROFESSIONALS

This is a professional association that aims to quantify IT education for professionals in the business field. It is a nonprofit organization based in the United States, however, its activities are run by around 60 chapters locally. It also has 280 students' chapters at different universities and colleges.

It is the largest organization that represents executives in information management all around the world. It was the first organization in the field of data processing to initiate a certification program that is for professionals.

They have very many established student chapters on different campuses. These chapters operate as bodies that are autonomous with complete corporation from the headquarters of the Association of IT Professionals.

The organization provides very many benefits, considering the fact that IT has any effect on every aspect of business. Some of the benefits include:

- Being able to interact with other majors and faculty in the information systems field, outside the setting of the formal classroom.
- The members are presented with the opportunity for learning about the profession of IT outside the scope of the coursework that is required of the student in school.
- It helps the students develop and enhance their personal and professional skills that they require so as to compete in the job market, giving them a step of head if they are part of the association.
- It is an extracurricular activity which may also provide an upper hand in the job market especially included in the resume.
- The members get very many opportunities to network and develop friendships in contacts at the various levels of Association of IT Professionals, as well as the industry in IT.
- The members gain the opportunity to go to conferences that are both national and regional.
- The professional association runs a consumer electronics show in Las Vegas which members have a chance to attend. This is considered a great opportunity.

Figure 8.15. This association has a great dedication to professionalism and ethics in the data processing field.

Source: https://Twitter. com/aitphq/status/567677383965437953.

Some of the activities that members should be ready to attend include:

- Meetings or socials.
- Speaker meetings which include professionals in IT presenting their opinions on IT and computer and information science issues.
- Activities that are related to computer and information science that are held by the Association of IT professionals.
- Conferences held by the chapters in regional and national groups of the Association of IT Professionals.

The association of IT professionals is open to all majors, especially those who are majoring in computer and information science. They require the members to have an interest in technology as well as its applications professionally. All the members are also expected to comply with the requirements that are set by the code of conduct, that is adhered to buy that association members.

8.8.1. History

The association was initially established in the United States in 1949. It was previously referred to as the National Machine Accountant Association. Disassociation was then granted a charter in 1951 where it had over 20 chapters.

The Association of IT professionals had its first certification program, which was debuted with a certificate in data processing; a professional examination that was initially held in New York City in the year 1962. They were later able to add an examination in registered business programming in 1970.

This association was part of the establishment of the Institute for the certification of computer professionals, and it played a major role in administering the examination program and stimulating the acceptance to the examination by the industry. As of now, this certification is referred to as Certified Computing Professional.

The Association of IT professionals was able to create an award that was given to the man of the year in 1969. This award was given to the person who was able to provide the most accomplishments by the end of the year in the information and technology field.

The professional association was later bought by CompTIA in 2017. They later rebranded it as CompTIA IT Pro and Student Membership.

The Association of IT professionals always expects the members to follow the code of ethics that has been put in place and has been existing for many decades. There is also standard of conduct that the members are expected to operate by, which is specific for all IT professionals.

8.9. COMPUTER PROFESSIONALS FOR SOCIAL RESPONSIBILITY

This is a global organization that promotes the use of computer technology in a responsible manner. It was started in the year 1981 and was mainly formed to educate policymakers as well as the public on the many issues that are associated with computer technology. It was initially founded by computer scientists in the United States and as of now has around 25 countries from six continents as members.

CPSR Computer Professionals For Social Responsibility

Technology is driving the future...
It is up to us to do the steering

Figure 8.16. Their main aim is to ensure that computers are used in a responsible manner. They achieve this by providing the public with expert judgment couples with scientific information that can help influencing public choices.

Source: http://www.publicsphereproject.org/content/computer-professionals-social-responsibility-cpsr.

There are many projects that the computer professionals for social responsibility has been able to incubate, including:

- The Public Sphere Project which helped and us still helping in the creation and supporting of equitable and effective public sphere globally.
- The Electronic Privacy Information Center which focuses attention of the public on the privacy and civil liberties issues that are emerging and also helps in protecting privacy, democratic values in the age of information, as well as freedom of expression.
- Computers, Freedom, and Privacy Conference which is an annual academic conference that is held on how computer technology, privacy issues, and freedom intersect.

- Privaterra which aims at providing technological education as well as supporting civil society organizations when it comes to privacy of data, communications that are secure and security of information.
- The civil society projects.
- The 21st Century Project which dealt with campus housing.

Their Computer Professionals for Social Responsibility is an alliance with people from the public who are interested and concerned about the effects that information and communication technology has on the society. They work to look through decisions that are made with concern to the development and use of computers, due to the fact that those decisions have consequences that are far-reaching and also reflect on the priorities together with the basic values.

The members of The Computer Professionals for Social Responsibility are experts on issues to do with information and communication technology and are therefore able to provide assessments that are realistic of the promises, limitations, and power of computer technology. As citizens who are concerned, they help in directing the attention of the public to making choices that are critical when it comes to the applications of computing, and the manner in which those choices have an effect on the society.

The Computer Professionals for Social Responsibility have been able to serve as a catalyst for discussions that are in-depth, as well as actions that are effective in major areas. This has been achieved through sponsoring local, international, and national projects.

They have five major principles that they follow in every project they undertake:

- Fostering and supporting discussions by the public of, as well as responsibility of the public for choices to do with the utilization of technology in systems that are critical to the society.
- Working to get rid of myths that are popular about the manner in which technologies are infallible.
- Challenging the assumptions that only technology is able to deal with the problems that we have socially and politically.
- Critically examining issues that are both social and technical within the profession of IT both internationally and nationally.
- Encouraging the utilization of IT for the improvement of life quality.

The Computer Professionals for Social Responsibility has members whose interests are mainly those of the computing profession, governance of the Internet, Internet access, civil society and the Internet, privacy, and intellectual property. Some of the main topics that they deal with include:

- Intellectual property – they believe that there is a substantial effect on trademark laws and copyrights, due to Digital Communications and global online systems. The main issue being whether the laws that were initially created to ensure the protection of copying physical objects can still be enforced in a world where it is cheaper, easier, instantaneous, and perfect to copy these materials. The Computer Professionals for Social Responsibility support laws on copyright that help in protecting the ability of the public to ensure pursuing of ideas through asserting utilization of rights in a fair manner.

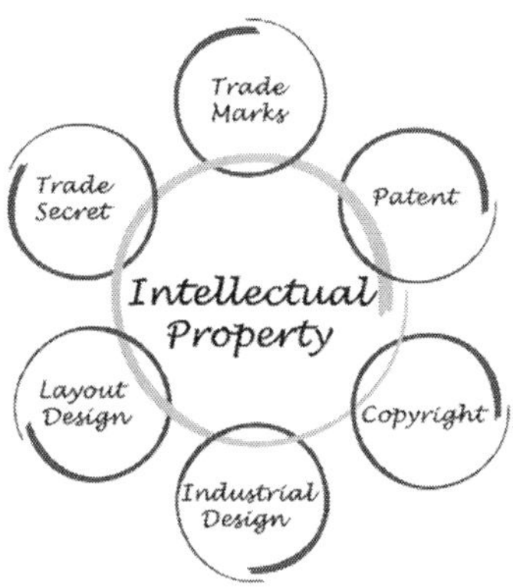

Figure 8.17. This refers to the creations of the human intellect that are intangible. Above are some of the well-known examples.

Source: https://kit-llp.co.ke/intellectual-property/.

- Computers and the environment – There are many changes that have started to happen due to the development of technology, social changes, and the large amount of production and consumption of computer equipment. It is evident that the environment is closely tied to the use, production, and disposal of a computer. There are many trace metals and other substances that are involved in the production of computers which may pose health hazards to the environment and the public. Computers can be both very beneficial to the environment and also very hazardous at the same time due to its difficulties in recycling. The Computer Professionals for Social Responsibilities are exploring these issues and trying to look for ways to make a computer as part of the solution for a world that is much more sustainable.

- Internet Governance – there are many different issues that are encompassing Internet governance. Even organizations that relate to the financing, governing, and control of the Internet together with its protocols have many different issues that they need to solve. The Computer Professionals for Social Responsibility have been involved in many issues to do with governance of the Internet. Some of these include the World Summit on the Information Society process and also the Internet Corporation for Assigned Names and Numbers.
- Community Networks – they believe that public communication as well as information systems are very important to how democratic societies are maintained now and especially in the future. They also believe that the core values of other communities such as economic development, health, cultural identity, and education can be served in a proper manner through public systems that have been designed appropriately. They also believe that these can achieve their inherent potential with the help of wealth citizens acting through public interest groups.
- Weapons and Peace – The Computer Professionals for Social Responsibilities have been working at the creation of a world that is much more peaceful with the use of their technical insight.
- Privacy and Civil Liberties – The Computer Professionals for Social Responsibility were able to broaden their national program to include privacy and civil liberties in 1986. Since that time, they have been able to play a major role in the promotion of privacy and civil liberties, in addition to creating resources that are important on this issue.
- Voting technology – The Computer Professionals for Social Responsibility have been studying the machines that are used for voting as well as the human machine interface that is used to vote since the 80s. They have been able to research the system of elections, observe elections, comments on the standards of

voting systems, and participates in election administration. They were even a part of South Africa's historic election in 1994. They have been able to write many different papers and she puts on the systems of election and have also spoken at conferences meant for election administration. Their work has been featured on different magazines, newspapers, and broadcast media.

8.10. SOFTWARE DEVELOPMENT FORUM

This is an international community that has several sub forums which involves different topics on software development. It normally looks for, and attracts people who are interested in developing software. This forum initially started as a conference before attracting very many different members both internationally and locally from all over the world.

Figure 8.18. There are so many people who have been able to benefit from this forum. It has helped in providing its members with a great opportunity to achieve their goals by providing them with ideas and advice on their startups.

Source: https://www.af.mil/News/Article-Display/Article/111811/software-development-forum-to-shape-future-of-network-capabilities/.

It is a forum that deals with many different aspects including development of software for the most trusted and secure websites or even development of software for payment security.

The initiators of this forum had always had an interest in the history of software development and also software engineering. Software engineering has grown and it has become a profession that deals with the correct manner in which, and also the best possible way to ensure maximum quality of software and also the creation of software in a proper manner, so as to suit and fit the needs of both the international and local market. In this situation, software quality is mainly referring to the level at which your software is maintainable in terms of its stability, usability, security, size, readability, and also the number of flaws and bugs it has.

Software development forum started just like any other event. That is, they started as a small community gathering with a few people who had an interest in the development of software and the matters that revolve around it. They had many ideas when it came to the development of software, and their main goal was to launch an event that would attract many people from Silicon Valley, who would be able to listen and act on their ideas.

They were able to meet their goals in a short period of time due to their devotion and hard work, and that is how they have reached where they are today. As of today they help members gain opportunities in a scene that is highly competitive. They are able to provide guides and tips for members who have start up projects. They also provide many different tutorials that have information that helps in expanding the members' point of view, allowing them to know the industry from different points of view. Embracing this new perspective allows them to improve their level of innovation as well as develop professionally in software development and software engineering.

They have a team of members that are fully invested in developing their perspective so as to promote innovation, allowing them to come up with the best ideas to solve our current issues in the world right now through software developing. Their goal is to bring together people from all over the world who are interested in the expansion of their own business opportunities. They also want to fulfill their goal of the creation of a networking place that is going to be at the top of the list attracting clients from all over the world. They are able to achieve this by having networking events that help in bringing people together and also promoting sharing of ideas.

CHAPTER

9

Personnel Issues in Computer Science and IT Professionals

CONTENTS

9.1. INTRODUCTION

In business community, many problems that arise were initially small problems. These problems may create even bigger problems that lead to the fall of an organization. Since it is not the dream of any business owner to watch the company fall, they mainly work to ensure that their organization is safe and secure to ensure that the business organizations have a friendly and palatable environment for the workers. Personnel is an individual who is employed in a business organization as an employee and the issues they may face that may hinder them from carrying out their duties appropriately may bring rise to the so-called personnel issues. Individuals who are in the computer science (CS) and IT oppressional are not guaranteed that they can avoid this issue hence they also encounter personnel issues in the course of their work. When personnel issues are dealt with it will prevent a lot of complaints from the employees and also the employers will be able to prevent themselves from falling into the wrong hands of the law or even getting arrested by the police. Personnel issues in CS and IT professions include the following as discussed:

9.2. HARASSMENT

Harassment is the process where an employee is neglected his rights in a way that he is seen less worthy than the rest. It violates the Civil Rights Act 1964. Harassment can be in many different forms such as it can be sexual harassment where an employee is harassed sexually. In every organization both genders exist and every individual has a right not to be harassed sexually at any one time. Some employers may get malicious and they may harass their employers sexually in a bid that they will not promote them if they do not have sex with them. It may even go to some certain extent of saying that they will suck the employee and this may create a fear in the employees that they may end up getting sexually harassed for the fear of losing their source of income. Sexual harassment may also arise when the business workers harass one another, for example, a rape case may be planned in an organization. Any employee who has been harassed sexually in any organization has a right to fight in a court of law and seek justice and that is why most employers tend to avoid such a scene by ensuring that the organization is free from any sexual harassment. The feminine gender is usually more prawn to sexual harassment but it may also face the male gender at certain circumstances since the female gender is more fragile and delicate. If sexual harassment is eliminated in an organization, it may hinder a lot of misfortunes that may arise later on. Any individual in any career even in CS-related and IT oppressional may fall victims at any one time and therefore causing a lot of damage (Shinder, 2005).

Harassment may also exist where a person is harassed due to the color of their skin. Color discrimination is mainly found in the white countries where they discriminate individuals with a black color and origin. The black in such countries where discrimination takes place are not given their rights such that a dark person may fail to get employment in a company on account of his color though they are highly qualified and an unqualified individual can get the same work and therefore it may pose as an unfair deal to the black individual. The laws of the world states that color discrimination is a crime and any organization or individual who is named with such an offense may be dealt with ruthlessly and therefore every organization has to campaign against color discrimination or else they may face the consequences ruthlessly which should be avoided at all costs. Individuals are educated that color of someone's skin is not a definition of someone's character. Other individuals who may be harassed due to the color of their skin is the individuals who are suffering from albinism condition as they may face opposition from individuals who are not well informed about this illness.

Another Harassment may exist in the sector of race where people from a certain race are not given their rights. According to any countries rights it states that any individual must be given all full rights that other individuals have. Race discrimination is the situation where people from a certain race are not taken keenly and are ignored. In business organizations even in organizations that involve CS and IT-related prophesies they should ensure that people from all races are treated equally and equal opportunities are given to all the individuals at any one time so that they can prevent themselves from falling into the wrong hands of the law (Shinder, 2005).

Individuals in an organization may be harassed due to their religion. Religion stands for the faith that a person stands with and the kind of God they worship. Religions exist in very many kinds that range from Christianity, Hinduism, Islamic, Buddhism, idol worship to devil worship. Individuals who worship a certain religion tend to think that their religion is the correct one and that the other religion are not following the right doctrines, for example, in some countries many people have been killed because they have a faith in Christianity or other forms of worship which has led to very many deaths. Religion should not be practiced in an organization as every employee should be given the opportunity to practice their religion as the laws of every country state that there is a right to religion. Religion discrimination can lead to people getting arrested and therefore every employer has to ensure that no one interferes with the religion of any individual and the employees are given time off when they need to go and worship and follow their religion. Even in CS and IT professions the same applies to them.

9.3. DISCRIMINATION

Discrimination is the case where an individual is seen less worthy than other individuals because of their condition physically mostly. The complaints of discrimination are a major problem on the rise in the current generation such that very many people are passing a complaint about this issue. Discrimination mainly exists in an organization in the election of the leaders in giving out promotions or when giving out workloads to different individuals in the organization. For one to avoid getting discriminated they have to be in close connection with the people in power and also some have gone to the extent of bribing those in power so that they cannot get discriminated (Shinder, 2005).

Individuals in an organization may get discriminated because of their gender. In many organizations the female gender is discriminated since the leaders believe that ladies should not be in power above the male gender. In the olden day's ladies were supposed to remain at home and care for the families but since the change in constitution it states that even the female gender has a right to be employed and to have access to power. Despite this you will still find that most of the people who are in power are the male gender. Gender discrimination is mainly being dealt with in any organization by the laws the country sets like there should be a gender balance in any organization.

Discrimination also arises due to difference in nationality or tribes. In most cases people tend to favor someone of their own so it may be very difficult to acquire employment from a person of a different tribe from you as they will overly check to see where your rots are. This situation is being dealt with by reducing the cases where one gets favors because of his tribe or nationality and not his qualifications by the laws different countries set. In the last few years, many people have traveled out of their countries and have been given jobs elsewhere in other countries easily. This has also applied to CS and IT-related professions where no matter the person's tribes or roots they are still given the opportunity to work in different companies. Failure to follow this law can land most individuals in a situation of the employers getting arrested and fined and therefore to prevent such occurrences, the individuals aim at ensuring that there is no discrimination in any organization (Shinder, 2005).

Lastly, an individual may be discriminated because of their physical condition, for example, people with disabilities exist everywhere in the world and this individuals may fail to get employment since the employers may see them as incompetent to the job such that they may think that they may not be able to work appropriately but the new laws states and explains that disability is not inability and therefore they aim to ensure that even the disabled get job opportunities and they have also set laws on this account that states a certain percentage of disabled individuals that should be employed in any organization.

In these professions, there are some discrimination that individuals face in these field of work. Discrimination is where by an individual is denied an opportunity or is disregarded among other employees. Discrimination can occur in various ways for instance when it comes to employment. There are various types of discrimination in the workplace which include age, religious, sex, race, and ethnicity among others. Discrimination is one among the personnel issues that individuals face while in the workplace in the field of CS and information technology (IT) (Shinder, 2005).

9.3.1. Employment Discrimination

Employment discrimination is very common. This is where an individual is denied an opportunity to work for a given organization due to various reasons. For instance, in CS professions, this line of work was said to be make dominated as a majority of the individuals that carried out CS were males. This denied several individuals more so women to venture into such lines of work. This in its own way has led to discrimination when it comes to women being employed in such professions. This brings about discrimination through gender. This made it hard for women to enter into such fields. There is a form of stigma that was created so that women would not enter into such fields. It was then referred to as a male profession. This so much affected the employment rate of women in such professions. When it comes to job interviews, most of the employers will automatically consider male candidates even though female candidates may be equally skilled. This posed a challenge for women to enter into such fields of work (Skillspanorama, 2016).

Apart from gender discrimination, there is also age discrimination. In majority of the workplaces today that are based on technology, a majority of the individuals that are employed there are the youth. This is because the youth are said to be more technological and greatly embrace the use of technology in the workplace so if they are employed to work in IT professions, they will be able to do their best. This kind of though greatly disadvantage the old folks who want to venture into CS and IT professions.

You may find that any technology profession that requires creativity and innovation is mostly given to the young individuals. For the elder ones, most of the professions that they are employed to work in mostly entails them teaching on such professions more so in CS. In IT most of the teachers that teach it in universities of higher learning are young individuals. Generally, this means that a majority of the elder people are greatly disadvantaged when it comes to employment in such fields of work. This brings about the employment discrimination in terms of age as the older people are the ones who are greatly disadvantaged.

In countries that experience a lot of corruption, there is a great possibility that a majority of people will not get employment even though they are well qualified for the job. This is because there are frequent cases where people are denied employment because of their ethnic background. You may find that because the owner of an organization us of a given ethnicity, he or she may choose to employ individuals from his or her own ethnic background. This denies other individuals an opportunity to gain employment in the profession they are well trained and equipped to undertake (Shinder, 2005).

On the issue of corruption, the individuals may gain employment in unjust ways. Some of them bribe employers so that they can get to have the job opportunity and for others since they are related to a certain employer, they can easily get the job opportunity. This is unfair more so to individuals who are qualified to get such employment opportunities. This has been experienced in a majority of workplaces even those related to CS and technology. This creates a form of discrimination to the individuals who end up being denied the employment opportunity.

CS professions tend to be very demanding. For instance, teaching may require an individual to be on the premises of the learning institution early and end up leaving late depending on the work load. Due to this, a majority of women have been denied employment opportunities. This mostly applies for pregnant women. Majority of employers don't want to deal with the hustle of looking for other candidates to fill in for the woman when she goes for a maternity break. This is the reason why many employers choose not to employ pregnant women not only in IT and CS professions but in other fields of work. This brings about the pregnancy-based discrimination in the workplace (Shinder, 2005).

9.3.2. Payment Discrimination

The payment in the workplace is usually the salary that is given to the employees. In CS and technology professions like other professions, there have been some discrimination when it comes to the salary given to the employees. The most common in this has been the gender discrimination. The most common has been where by the males in most of the professions are given more salary compared to the women. Even though the male and female may have had the same level of skills and qualifications, a majority of them were paid less than the men (Shinder, 2005).

This also applied when giving the employees promotions. In most cases the men would be given more of the promotions compared to the women. The promotions would be being terms of a raise in the salary or a bigger office within the workplace. The age discrimination would also apply to the paying of the salary. In most cases, the older employees are paid more than the younger employees. For some organizations, the employees are paid according to their age groups. This is among the reasons why youngest people choose to venture into private practice rather than being employed under another individual.

9.4. HOSTILE WORKING ENVIRONMENT

Hostile working environment has also been among the issues that the individuals in the CS and IT profession encounter. For an employee to have a good performance and good work ethic, they need an environment that will allow them to do so. For the IT professions, it is mostly the older employees who have experienced the hostile working environment. The fact that a majority of the people working in this sector are young people, it will pose quite a challenge to them as they will have to work more in order to keep up with the other employees (Shinder, 2005).

For a majority of them the hostility comes from their colleagues. The young employees in the workplace have a negative stereotype against the older employees in the workplace. The deem them to not be able to adapt to efficiently using technology because they are older. For most of them, they are not involved in the creative process or you may find that a majority of them are not involved in the company projects. This negative attitude creates a hostile environment for them so that their performance is not as high as what they would have wanted to put out there.

Hostile working environment may also be in the form of gender discrimination. This is mostly experienced by women more so in the CS professions. For instance, the women doing engineering courses in the field of CS are most likely to experience discrimination. The discrimination they encounter is mostly from their male colleagues. For some they get teased by their colleagues for doing a "man's job." This may not create a very good working ng environment to them as they will be uncomfortable and therefore their performance will also reduce. Women who are strong hearted are the ones who get to survive in such working conditions (Shinder, 2005).

9.5. POOR WORKING CONDITIONS

Poor working conditions is among the challenges that most individuals face in the workplace. This also applies for professions in CS and IT. Poor working conditions may be due to lack of and hardware architecture, there are some equipment that is needed in order to create the type of wares needed. If such equipment is lacking and the employees are still required to meet the job demand by the end of the day, then they have been given a poor working condition.

This is one among the challenges that most of the employees' experience more so in upcoming working institutions. This will limit their work performance as well as deliverance and in the long run it may affect the workplace. In the third world countries, for professions like teaching CS and IT to students may be a challenge. For one, there is a lot of lack of equipment to facilitate the teaching and learning process. This is also a form of poor working conditions (Shinder, 2005).

9.6. LACK OF EQUIPMENT

The lack of equipment is mostly linked to the teaching profession in the teaching and learning process. For instance, the teacher will be required to make adequate use of a computer in order to clearly illustrate something. For instance, a subject like programming, will require the teacher and the students to have computers for them to easily acquire programming skills. In most learning institutions, learning tools such as computers are a limited resource. Therefore, the teacher is limited on how to conduct the lesson. The lack of resources ends up frustrating the teacher. This therefore places the teacher in a poor working condition. He or she may be forced to look into other ways of conducting the lesson so that in the long run the students end up getting the required skills (Shinder, 2005).

Not only in the teaching profession but also in other professions as well. As illustrated above, it may be in the field of computer engineering or any other.

9.7. LACK OF A STABLE POWER SUPPLY

Lack of a stable power supply is also among the challenges that individuals face in the working environment. Most of the professions in CS and technology deal with the use of tools that require electricity in order for them to work. Some of the individuals in this field of work are faced with the challenge of poor power supply. This creates a major challenge for them as they will not be able to complete tasked work within the time allocated. This will also lead to the pilling of the workload such that they will have huge loads of work to cover and it might be stressful for the individuals.

For those individuals in private practice, they have the task of identify a location where they can easily access the customers as well as ensuring that they have a stable power supply. This leads to most of them setting up their businesses in the cities which will be much more expensive for them.

9.8. OUT-DATED TECHNOLOGY

For the recent graduates in CS and IT courses, they are trained using the recent technology that is available in the market. This is to enable them work in the most technological work environment. For some of them, they are employed into various organizations. The challenge is that for some of these organizations, they still rely on the use of outdated technology. For instance, if one is employed as a programmer but the computers that are available are very outdated such that they cannot accommodate the recent programming languages such as Java.

This poses a challenge for the individual if they want to carry out programming tasks using such devices. Another example includes software and hardware engineering. If the technical equipment becomes obsolete very quickly, then the individual may not be able to produce an equipment that will be compatible with the current technology state. This is also a good illustration of a poor working environment (Shinder, 2005).

The disadvantage of a poor working environment is that it reduces the employee's performance in the workplace. Also, the quality of product produced will not be good.

9.9. UNEMPLOYMENT

Unemployment is among the challenges that most individuals are facing in the various professions CS and IT included. Even though some of these individuals have the necessary required requirements, there are still high cases of people lacking job opportunities. For the younger individuals, this may be attributed to the fact that most employers are not comfortable employing the because recent studies show that most of the younger employees are most likely to quit their jobs after two or three years of working in order to look for better employment opportunities. Since employers don't want to go through the process of hiring individuals all over again, they opt not to hire them.

This has greatly contributed to the large numbers of youth who have qualifications but cannot secure good job opportunities. Some of these individuals opt to look for employment in other countries. The disadvantage is that there is no certainty that they will be able to secure the job opportunities in those countries. Most of them have been left to tarmac for jobs for some number of months or years for them to get the job opportunities. Though some CS professions have a high demand such as teaching, still for the other professions it may be a real hustle getting a job (Shinder, 2005).

Majority of the individuals with skills in IT and CS have opted to start their own businesses and firms in order to get a source of income. The major challenge is that for them to start such businesses, they need to have capital in order for them to start the businesses. The capital may be large sums of money which may be difficult for them to acquire so they are forced to look for loans from different individuals. This is also why many individuals cannot get employment.

9.10. CYBER CRIME

Cybercrime mostly affects individuals in the IT profession. Some individuals are responsible for creating content or images as a part of their profession. They are the ones who are more susceptive to this crime. You may find that an individual has developed content to be sold in the internet. Another individual with hacking skills uses their skills and gets access to this content, steals it and poses it to be their own work. Not only developed content, also programs and applications that have not yet been licensed under copy write.

The individual may introduce a virus to the owner's program and crash it only for them to develop a similar program and sell it. Cybercrime has been a great challenge for a majority of individuals in the workforce. This makes all the hard work and time placed into the content or program they developed to be a waste. Majority of them have been forced to look for ways to ensure the safety of the content and programs they developed. It has involved the purchasing antivirus programs as well as other cyber-crime protection packages in the software that they use.

9.11. INTERPERSONAL ISSUES

Interpersonal issues refer to challenges that individuals may encounter when relating to other individuals. It refers to the conflict that is experienced by individuals while in the workplace. Interpersonal issues are experienced by individuals in various professions, CS and technology included. There are various interpersonal issues experienced in such workplaces. There are various types of interpersonal conflict experienced in the workplace. An example is the man versus self-conflict. This is a scenario where an individual is experiencing conflict within themselves. This may be due to the individual having a hard time deciding or the laxity that the individual has and he or she may not have been happy with it (Skillspanorama, 2016).

The other type of conflict is the man versus man. This is in the scenario where by two or more individuals are in conflict with each other. They will tend to disagree with each other on various things. In the CS and IT professions, this is a risk because the employees are required to work with each other in order to come up with new ideas and innovations. This is a challenge in the workplace as the work environment will not be as suitable for them.

The other type of conflict is the man versus society. This is where the society does not agree with the employees. This may be viewed in the sense that the society refuses to purchase the products or services offered by the professional in this line of work. This type of conflict majorly affects the business as the individuals will not be able to sell their goods and services and in the long run, they may not be able to obtain a source of income. The conflict may be due to the inability of the individuals in the workplace to understand the needs of the society.

There is also a conflict that consists of man vs machine. This is more so in IT-related professions but to some extent it affects the CS related professions. Here is where man is in conflict with the type of machines that are being used. For instance, a programmer using a computer that uses outdated technology. The programmer may end up being in conflict with the computer as it will limit some the materials and tools that have been provided by the computer to be used in the process of programming.

The programmer may opt to use a better computer that avails the latest technology used in the current trends. It may also be in the form of man versus nature. This is applied to things in nature such as electricity. If there is a problem with electricity or the power supply, then the individuals in the workplace will be in conflict with nature because nature will be failing them. This the reason why business owners sensitize on location before they set up their businesses. These are among the interpersonal issues or conflicts that are experienced in the workplace (Skillspanorama, 2016).

9.12. THEFT

Theft is a major personnel problem because it gives the employees lack of peace of mind as they worry about the safety of their property. Many individuals may face to work appropriately if they have to worry about their things getting stolen. Many workers leave their jobs because of the poor state that is in their work place when their belongings start getting lost. Its normally the work of other employers that they steal the belongings of their colloquies and it is mostly an inside job in most organizations.

Theft has been reduced in most organization by measures that the organizations have taken. Among this measure is the organizations have inserted CCTV cameras in their organizations. CCTV cameras are cameras that are inserted in buildings that record all the activities that take place in the organization. This has helped many organizations to reduce theft because most people who steal will be afraid to steal for fear of getting caught. It will also enable individuals to trace their goods and items in case they get lost as they can review the recordings and capture the thief of their properties. CCTV cameras have also enabled individuals to get the confidence to work in an organization since they will have less fear of theft and loss of their things and items. They are most often input in the door entrances of buildings.

Another way to increase the security of an organization is employing people who guard the organizations mostly at night or even during the day. Most organizations have watchmen who stay up all night looking after the organizations to after the organizations and to raise alarm in case of any thieves trying to break in the organization. Also, during the day there are guards who prevent unauthorized individuals from entering the organization and ensure those who enter legally. This has enabled orderliness in the organization and has reduced theft in any of the organizations. Security against theft has also been enhanced by inserting alarms that go on when a certain property is being stolen or when thieves try to break into the business organization. By these alarms going on it makes the guards aware and also surrounding community and therefore they can take the necessary action to arrest the thieves before they get away. It has also instilled fear in the thieves and therefore theft has decreased significantly (Skillspanorama, 2016).

By reducing theft in any organization, it has helped to ensure the safety and security of any organization. It has also led to a decrease in blame in the organizations.

9.13. COMMUNICATION BARRIERS

Poor communication is experienced in the IT and CS professions. Communication is a very crucial element as it allows the transfer of information from one individual to another. It facilitates the sharing of concepts and ideas among individuals. It is a major obstacle to ensuring the success of a business. There are several factors that contribute to the poor communication in such professions. The poor communication leads to the downward performance of the various CS and IT professions.

The following are some of the factors contributing to poor communication in the various IT and CS workplaces.

9.14. LACK OF CONFIDENCE

Lack of confidence is mostly found amongst the young individuals joining the workforce. The lack of confidence is a major contributor to poor communication. You may find out that an individual may have an idea but due to the lack of confidence they may choose not to share the idea. If they choose to share it then they will not be able to effectively explain the idea they had. They will be so nervous till the fact that they will not be able to compose themselves and choose the right words that will effectively illustrate the idea they had hence poor communication. This is mostly experienced among the young employees as they have not had much experience in the workplace.

9.15. STEREOTYPES

Stereotyping over the years has become the major contributor to the poor communication among individuals. Stereotyping occurs in various ways. In the IT-related professions, the major stereotype is against the older employees. They are negatively stereotyped to be outdated. This implies that they cannot be able to use technology effectively and it may be challenging for them to adapt to the latest advancements in technology. This makes it hard for them if they want to share an idea or concept on something related to technology as it will be deemed irrelevant.

It may also occur that the project manager may choose to only involve the younger employees in the creative process. This will create a communication barrier between the employees. Stereotyping affects the communication process in that the younger employees negatively stereotype the older employees. This will also lead to them developing a negative attitude towards the older employees. This will lead to the younger employees not listening to the older employees and this creates a communication barrier.

9.16. LACK OF CLARITY

This also contributes to poor communication. For a task to be carried out effectively, the communication needs to have high levels of accuracy so that the right task is done. Lack of clarity means that some of the crucial details in the information may be omitted. The lack of clarity may be due to the channel of communication that was used. For instance, if information was given to a certain individual and they were to share it to others, the individual may not have captured all the important details. The information may end up being distorted leading to poor communication.

9.17. LANGUAGE BARRIER

This mostly applies to workplaces that have employed individuals from different walks of life which is taking place in most of the organizations. For such individuals, depending on the type of country they come from they speak different languages. When they are put under one organization then there will be major problems in the communication process. The pronunciation of words may be different and some words may have different meanings. This may cause lack of clarity in the information being passed on and therefore causing poor communication.

9.18. STAFF ATTITUDES

Staff attitudes refers to how the staff or employees view the work environment. It also entails the beliefs of the staff towards the profession and the work environment. Attitude affects everything we do. It will determine who we do things and how we will perform certain tasks in the work environment. Negative attitude is among the issues that are encountered in the CS and IT workplaces. For instance, since most of the CS professions are male dominated, the women in such fields of work may have a negative approach towards the work environment. They may view the profession to be difficult as most of the individuals in the workplace are male counter parts.

Things such as negative attitude towards the employers may affect the work environment. If the employees and the employers are not at good terms then there will be a lot of challenges in the workplace. As the employees will have a negative attitude towards the employer, they will not give them any important information on things that will require urgent attention. These are some of the negative attitudes in the workplace. They contribute to the poor performance in the workplace by the employees.

9.19. DISHONESTY

This vice affects many professions and has caused the downfall of many individuals. Dishonesty manifests itself in different ways. It may be informed of poor management which leads to the misappropriation of funds in the workplace. It may also present itself in the case where the employees are dishonest to the employer.

Take the case where an employee is required to come up with a program or application that is original in nature. Since the employee does not want to do most of the dirty work, he or she may decide to copy another program or application that is not theirs. Some purchase these programs from other individuals at a cheaper price.

This will be dishonesty from the employee as he or she is required to come up with their own idea to present before the employer. This has led to the frequent cases of organizations being sued for stealing ideas from other individuals. Dishonesty may also occur in the case whereby an employer promises to give the employees a raise or time to retreat but they know that they cannot fulfil such promises. The various forms of dishonesty negatively affect the different professions.

9.20. POOR WORK ETHIC

For an individual to survive in the job industry or in their profession, they need to have a good work ethic. This is a challenge that has been faced by most employers and employees in the various professions. Work ethics refers to how an individual will behave in the work environment and also how they handle themselves in the workplace. It is the sense of drive and go-getting attitude that an individual has. Good work ethic is an essential requirement for a successful business. It is a key tool that helps an individual get a chance in the employment industry and they can also be Refereed by their employers.

However, many employees struggle with the issue if good work ethic is among many employees in the CS and IT profession. This more so applies for the young employees. Many of them have poor work ethic. For them, it about covering the amount of work that was intended for the day. They will not work extra hours so as to reduce the work load. Some individuals leave the offices even before the work hours are hours done. Others choose to report late for work or may show up late without even apologizing to their employers for arriving late.

It devastating that some of the employers choose to give their employees their own workloads for them to do it for them. This is because a majority of them have poor work ethic. Work ethic also affect the aspect of time management. Most of the workplaces have the challenge of their employees spending most of their time on social media. This means that time meant for work is used in social media platforms therefore the workload keeps on piling for the workers and this later on stresses them out (Shinder, 2005).

9.21. POOR WORK STRATEGIES

The work strategies help to ensure that there is smooth criminal running in the work place. This is in terms of division of labor and teamwork in the business. Most professions, CS and IT inclusive are faced with the challenge of poor work strategies. You find that there is uneven distribution of labor so some employees end up being over worked while others are okay with their work loads. For those who are over worked, they end up being stressed and this reduces their performance in the work place.

Teamwork is a major factor in and the CS and IT professions. It is applied in the process of creating games and programs. There are companies that have a challenge when it comes to creating of teams to take on various projects. This reduces the quality of the products that will be produced which would have been much better if a group of individuals who can work well together are assembled to work on the projects. It is there for advisable for the managers to carefully choose the business strategy that will be employed to ensure success of the business.

9.22. VIOLENCE

Violence in an organization is the state where the workers and the employers are in constant argument and disagreement between each other. Violence leads to the down fall of many organizations since it brings about disunity as people are putting most of their focus on hurting each other rather than understanding one another. An extreme case of violence leads to the workers engaging in physical fights with one another and they can result in damaging many organizational equipment. It is an uncouth behavior that is a major personnel problem that may be faced in an organization or a business enterprise.

Violence is a personnel problem in an organization that may also affect individuals who are taking up CS and IT oppressional courses because it does not affect an individual but it affects all the workers at large. It mainly comes about when one individual is favored on the expense of the others in most organizations. You may find in an organization a certain individual gain favor from the employer such that they are given simpler duties than the others and most promotions are given to them despite the fact that there are still other individuals in the same organization who are more qualified than them. This creates jealousy to boom and it may lead to violence as each individual wants full rights and they may also feel diminished.

Violence breeds hatred leading to individuals lacking peace of mind when they are carrying out their duties. It hinders work progress when the victims of violence engage in a fight or start throwing tantrums. Violence also distracts the other employers from carrying on with their duties in the appropriate way (Shinder, 2005).

Since it is a personnel problem, many organizations have taken the issue with a lot of concern such that any individuals who are caught in this situation can be thoroughly charged or punished or they can even lose their jobs. The government has also chipped in by setting rules and laws that ensure the equableness and fairness of every working person in a company and they warn employers against favoring a certain individual and this has brought rise to the settling of this problem.

Business organizations also have set team buildings that the workers of the organizations have a day off together that they carry out activities that are fun and eat together so that they can know each other better and they can relate in the appropriate manner together and this has promoted a lot of peace and understanding within the organizations. Also, the employers work together to ensure that they provide adequate favors to each employee and they treat each person with equality and fairness and this has assisted to reduce violence in the organization. It is therefore a major regulatory policy in almost all business organization every employee must avoid violence at any cost (Shinder, 2005).

9.23. POOR WAGES

Poor wages are the situation where employees are paid a very little amount than the amount of work they are performing. It is a very great disappointment to do a lot of work and you are given a very little amount of pay that does not fit the amount of work you have performed.

Many individuals get discouraged and makes them to quit in search of greener pastures where they will be given a better pay than the ones they are receiving. Many individuals in CS and information technology related professionals face this personnel problem because many employers tend to think that the work the perform is very little and hence, they are paid very little amount of money whereas they perform a lot of work which is not seen easily. This may discourage a lot of students from taking up the course for the fear of getting low wages.

Low wages may also arise a result of corruption in the business such that the people who should pay the employees squander the money and they end up paying the employees a very small amount of money since they have used it for their own benefit.

The government has sort to make a change in this sector by stating a fixed range of money that such professions must pay at any one time Also some organizations that fight for the right of the workers have been created such that incase the employers do not pay the employees in the right way; the employees can complain to these organizations and they can take the necessary action that is required.

The employees also organize strikes and boycotts where they campaign for their rights and they refuse to go to work until their salaries are increased with immediate effect (Shinder, 2005).

9.24. WORK OVERLOAD

Work overload is when the people who are employed are given a lot of work to perform in a short period of time. Some employers are ruthless and they do not keep in mind that a person's body gets exhausted and it needs rest from time to time. They give their employees a lot of work to perform and they require it done in a short period of time and it should be done perfectly. This is a personnel problem in CS and IT-related professions when these individuals are given a lot of duties to perform in a short period of time.

The outcome of work overload is always negative and it mostly affects the outcome and the results of the work that was being done. Most of the times the work done is always of poor quality and it is not fit as it should be because the individuals make a rush when performing the task such that they do not pay close attention on ensuring that the work is correctly and perfectly done but they pay attention on ensuring that they complete the job on time and meet the deadlines at the required time.

9.25. POOR MANAGEMENT

The organization management is the major key to ensure that the business runs smoothly. If the management of an organization fails it spells doom that the whole organization is crumbling. In the organization they have to maintain good relations between the managers so that they can ensure the stability of the organization. Poor management affects the employees because it determines the kind of leadership skills that is given to the employees and therefore it is a major personnel problem that needs to be avoided at any cost possible.

When there is poor management in an organization it is detected by the availability of corruption in the organization such that the money invested instead of being used in the company for the benefit of the company the people in the lead use it for their own benefits and hence the company ends up to experiencing very minimal profits than it should. It is also seen by the overworking of the employees and poor communication between the managers and the employees.

When the management does not communicate in the correct way it may mislead the employees causing them to perform a lot of errors and this may lead to the downfall of an organization. It is therefore the duty of any business organization to ensure that they have managers who can be trusted and who perform their work in the way that is transparent and that is correct. They can do this by voting in managers who are trustworthy and taking time to scan and inspect the behavior of the individuals who are given power before they are handed over this power. Poor managers can also be sucked if their work is seen to be fishy and new trustworthy ones employed (Shinder, 2005).

9.26. INSUFFICIENT NUMBER OF SKILLED PERSONNEL

When there is insufficient number of skilled personnel in an organization, the amount of work needed to be done will be a lot a therefore the employees who are available will be overworked. There is also a case where the employees are enough though they are not skilled enough and the outcome of this us that the work done will be of poor quality and the business organization will not earn a lot of profit or can make losses too. Employers who interview people ensure that the individuals who they offer the job be are skilled so as to prevent this condition.

The advantage of having the sufficient amount of skilled personnel in a CS and IT is that the work that should be done will be done more faster than before. The quality of the work will also be improved because when the individuals work together, they can share knowledge and they can come up with new ways that can enable them to perform the work in a better way that will bring forth better outcomes than before. It is therefore necessary that the employees in any business organization to be properly and perfectly skilled at his job.

9.27. ADVANTAGES OF DEALING WITH PERSONNEL ISSUES

The organization cannot fall into the wrong hands of the law: When a business organization aims to ensure that it deals with all the personnel issues in their organization, they can prevent themselves from getting caught and detained for not following the rules that are set by the government. For example, if an employer harasses an employee sexually, they are normally detained for they have gone against the rule that states that they should not harass anyone sexually and they are therefore answerable to the court of law but if they avoid this then they will avoid getting detained too. Other organizations have been shut down for good by the government because they fail to obey the rules and policies set by the organizations.

By organizations dealing with personnel issues it also means that they deal with them in such a way that it does not affect other companies or it does not affect the society at large. They must use ways that are correct according to the government and they should not break any rules in the process of finding the required solutions to their problems.

Communication is enabled: Communication is the passing of information from one person to another such that the individual receiving the information receive the required information that was being passed initially. When a business organization is facing a personnel problem then communication may be hindered by this as they will result to the work output having a lot of errors that could be avoided easily before. Communication is therefore a key factor in any organization and any factor that may hinder it should be corrected with an immediate effect.

Some personnel issues such as violence may hinder communication process because people have negative feelings towards each other and they may fail to communicate with one other.

Teamwork is promoted: By solving personnel issues, it brings about the promotion of teamwork. Teamwork is the ability of employees and employers in an organization to work together peacefully towards a common goal. Most of the personnel problem bring about a fall in the teamwork that was build and it makes the relationship of the workers to go down hence many people stop focusing on the aim of attaining the company's goals but they start focusing on how they will solve the problems they are facing.

Many company managers work together to ensure that teamwork is maintained by holding events like the team building as stated above and the advantage of this is evident even from the results that come through. They therefore take time to ensure that the personnel problems are solved fast so as to ensure that the company still has teamwork between the employees and employers. Some have even created a forum that the employees can discuss any problem they may face so as to minimize the probability of them having a fall in the teamwork sector.

Employee performance is improved: The performance of an individual is the outcome and the results of the work that an individual performs. Most individuals aim at ensuring that they give out the best as the best is expected from them from the employees. If an individual faces personnel problem, they may fail to accomplish their goal of ensuring that they achieve the required standards that is needed from them by the employers. They therefore need to speak out so that these problems can be solved for them before it brings rise to negative results. When personnel problems are solved it enables the individuals to work in more favorable conditions that enable them to ensure that they face very minimum opposition from accomplishing their aims. It therefore leads to an improvement in the employee's performance and it leads to the general improvement of the company's performance (Skillspanorama, 2016).

Relationships between workers and their leaders is improved: Relationship between employers and employees should be improved because it ensures the work place has a favored environment for study. Leaders should ensure that they maintain a good relationship with their workers so that they can give out directions appropriately so that when they give out instructions, they can be Sure their instructions are received appropriate.

Also, the employed individuals must ensure that they maintain good relations with the employers so that when they perform their duties they can be upraised in a nice way and they can also receive promotions.

Outputs and Profits are increased: Increasing the outputs of a company and boosting its profits is the major goal of any business enterprise. When a company experiences constant loses it can lead to the closure of the company and therefore each company aims at ensuring that it makes profits constantly there are personnel issues then it can affect the organization negatively and therefore it can lead to the company experiencing losses but if they solve these problems on time then they can avoid losses and they can therefore experience profits.

In conclusion, CS and related courses also just like any other courses experience personnel problems which when dealt with can lead to an improvement in the work output of the individuals and many other advantages may arise. It is therefore of great importance that they maintain all the necessary conditions to ensure that they avoid personnel problems.

CHAPTER

10

Mentoring, Coaching, and Counseling of IT Professionals

CONTENTS

10.1. INTRODUCTION

IT mentors are experts who create opportunities through knowledge transfer to professionals in the computing field. By forming and building upon certain fundamental skill sets like programming, project presentation, and entrepreneurism, mentors provide people with the tools and resources they require to become impactful, self-starting successes in the tech world.

Figure 10.1. Coaching is useful in helping IT professionals identify their personal strengths.

Source: https://www.teachingprofessor.com/for-those-who-teach/faculty-mentoring-faculty-relationships-that-work/.

Typically, most of them are technical professionals operating in the computer industry. They may come from various fields such as app development, biotechnology, cybersecurity, artificial intelligence (AI) and computer-science research, though it is crucial that they must have some background working in tech industry as well. University professors can also fall under the category of mentors.Apart from offering classes, mentors should be able to respond to learners remotely through platforms like Skype, email, and even phone calls. Time commitment is also of the essence. During training, mentors are matched with groups or individuals depending on what they reveal as their main skills or fields of expertise, including what the participants need their mentor to assist them with.

10.2. MENTORS IN COMPUTER SCIENCE AND IT PROFESSIONS

Mentors empower learners with hands-on-skills by providing them with real life experience they require to thrive in the modern tech jobs. Through various programs, they impart vital skills that the professionals need to remain competitive in the technology sector including; web development, industry approved certification, IT programming, business strategy and public speaking.Many stakeholders in the IT sector are mindful of the perpetual skills shortage, plus the need for finding ways of addressing it effectually. Among the options that companies may consider is executing a mentoring program. Whereas some people may already be considering themselves as mentors to others, it's crucial that this experience is designed based on best-practice models to guarantee that both the instructor and mentee enjoy the most benefits. Generally, it's simple, and constructive, to dialogue with other people in business and share material and advice, however a realistic mentoring program must include the setting of objectives and holding every party accountable (Pask, Roger, Joy, and Barrie, 2007).

Professional growth in the IT sector is necessary both to fill the skills gap, as well as ensuring the field continues to progress and advance. Across all businesses, mentoring has regularly been a popular method for staff development. Bigger companies typically provide extra formal mentoring programs compared to smaller organizations, however most successful entrepreneurs will agree that getting a mentor or personally being the mentor is a prized tool in individual development.

The value can further be heightened in an age when people's professions are less straight and structured. Nowadays, people don't necessarily enter companies through graduate courses and pursuing a clear track through the business. Rather, individuals are entering the business world at all levels, plus taking personal responsibility in regards to their own growth.

Providing a structured mentorship program is extremely important for the industry. The more activities exist to expand and become more proficient, the quicker it will be for the company to grow and offer jobs. It may feel odd to contact someone and then request them to turn into a mentor, besides not everybody wants to become one. Plus, it can be hard to know exactly what constitutes of a great mentor; discovering the right mentor will depend on various factors which aren't always clear (Pask, Roger, Joy, and Barrie, 2007).

Some organizations have established a pilot mentoring course to make the procedure easier. Originally available to 50 individuals on a test basis, programs such as CompTIA mentoring program, can help link mentors and mentees. This program may also offer a blueprint for the mentor/mentee relationship which includes goal-establishment and accountability. Likewise, mentors can gain substantial benefits from partaking in a mentorship. Assisting someone to build their career, offering a listening ear, ensuring they're on track in regards to their objectives, and challenging their reasoning may be very rewarding. Apart from having the joy of watching their mentee thrive and succeed, mentors may also end up improving their own reasoning and learning new material.

For business, increased mentorship relationships are probably to mean companies gain access to superior talent and may offer enhanced career prospects. Keeping people involved in the IT industry can help minimize skills shortage, besides it intensifies the sector's exposure to fresh ideas. As for mentees the advantages are obvious. With an industry champion available who can assist in providing new perspectives and guidance, as well as acting as the sounding board, this can be a priceless resource. Computing is a fast-paced field, therefore it's important to have a supporter who can assist in shaping the individual's development (Pask, Roger, Joy, and Barrie, 2007).

10.2.1. Mentorship for Women Professionals

Figure 10.2. Female mentors can make women professionals feel valued in the company.

Sources: https://www.smartcompany.com.au/people-human-resources/leadership/mk-female-mentors-foster-greater-sense-of-belonging-in-engineering-students-research/.

Mentoring can go quite a long way especially for female professionals who want to be recognized for their work rather than gender. Additionally, many IT professionals wish the number of female coworkers was higher than it is currently. Unfortunately, this leads to women feeling invisible, for instance, at the conferences, while contending with the vicious culture of criticism and dominance displayed by the opposite gender (Westergaard, 2016).

There are points in time where a female IT expert professional may think they don't want to continue anymore, or it's hard and not enjoyable. They may not even like the interactions which are being made at the workplace, nor the environment anymore. However, a mentor of the same gender can act as an example, showing the female IT professionals that they too can do it. And that they can pursue computing if they indeed like this field.

Research shows that females are generally more self-critical. For instance, if you interview two professionals who are doing similar work, the male coworker may say, 'I'm managing well,' while the female coworker may claim, 'I'm struggling.'

Therefore, there is need to motivate the females who are doing well at work so that they can perform even better. There are women who may be deliberating if it's actually the ideal thing for them to pursue a career in computing, particularly if they're coming from a minority group that's underrepresented in IT, where they may look around and not see many faces like theirs.

Many women say that it can sometimes be risky to think a lot about gender issues at work, the moment they do it begins to feel like they're receiving special treatment, rather than recognition they deserve from the genuine accomplishments at work. Though at the same instance, there are variations in how people should be mentored and inspired. The method of mentorship used in one setting or company may not necessarily work in another environment and vice versa, since each business has its own unique culture and practices (Westergaard, 2016).

Without having good mentors at the authoritative level of an IT company, saying to women things like, 'You deserve this kind of experience; or you need to apply for this project because you're competent enough,' then women may find it difficult to push on with their careers since they need a strong mentorship voice to propel them to the next phase in their success journey.

10.2.2. Gender Disparity in It

Global concerns around gender difference in computing fields have gained significant momentum with the emergence of the computer-age. They have motivated various public policy discussions regarding gender equality, since computer applications have exerted heightened influence in society. The gender dialogue has helped to enhance information technology (IT) innovations, while minimizing the effects of sexism (Pask, Roger, Joy, and Barrie, 2007).

During the initial days of computer technology, women were properly represented in the sector. They often operated as "human computers," doing complex calculations and contributing in large projects. For instance, it is widely believed that the woman who coordinated the Apollo moon landing from earth was a woman.

Females also contributed greatly on ballistics calculations as well as cryptography, but despite these endeavors they were still paid less compared to their male counterparts. The main reason why women were contributing as programmers and calculation computers was since "they anticipated programming to be some low skill clerical work," while the tougher work which included formation of the firmware, male engineers were the ones who worked on. Fast-forward to the current age, programming has become an even bigger thing where both male and female professionals are present.

By the 60s, even though programming was still hyped as a decent field for ladies to delve into, various shifts were starting to occur that would assist in pushing females out of the discipline. Men who were into programming began to make the discipline more "prestigious," building professional groups, and introducing education requirements and other measures to discourage the hiring of women in this sector (Pask, Roger, Joy, and Barrie, 2007).

For instance, hiring tools were established whereby answers were collectively shared among male group members and clubs. Yet another strategy for pushing ladies out of the sector was the use of personality tests, which naturally favored individuals who weren't good at working with others, and slanted towards male applicants mostly. Once these trends were engrained into the sector, they continued perpetuating themselves into the current day. Some computing programs, like that offered in Princeton during the mid-60s wouldn't even register females into their program.

A study, done by SWIFT (Supporting Women in IT), asked more than 7,000 participants questions regarding their career choices. This survey found that women compared to males possess lower interest levels and apparent capacity in computing fields. This study (including others) offers a solid foundation for a progressive correlation between both interest levels and apparent ability with occupation choice.

Furthermore, a project launched in Edinburgh, Scotland, dubbed "Stratagems of Inclusivity: Gender and Information Society" or (SIGIS) launched its findings depending on research done in 48 different case studies throughout Europe. The findings emphasize on recruiting and retention procedures for females already involved in the sector. These techniques vary from using advertisement campaigns, role models and allocation of quotas, so as to make IT look more gender impartial (Pask, Roger, Joy, and Barrie, 2007).

Research shows that Malaysia possesses a much more equivalent split that differs around the half-way point. A career in the computing sector also suggests a safe job environment. Robust belief by the past generation that computer would be a thriving sector with many career opportunities caused caregivers to encourage their kids to take an IT career, despite the gender.

For India, a rising number of women currently are studying and choosing professions in technical sectors. The ratio of female engineers successfully graduating from colleges like IIT Bombay developed from 1.8% in 1972 to 8% in 2005. Furthermore, Arab women comprised of 59% of scholars enrolled in computing disciplines in 2014 at state-run universities found in Saudi Arabia. Eastern Europe women, particularly in Romania and Bulgaria, have considerably high rates of taking programming and technology subjects. Nevertheless, women still remain under-represented in computer fields.

10.2.3. Workforce Statistics

Women's representation in computers and IT workforce has been dropping from a high of 38% during mid-80s. As from 1993 to 1999, records showed that the ratio of women in computer/information disciplines (counting those with a bachelor's qualification or higher in a computer-related field) decreased from 33.1% to 29.6%, whereas the absolute figures rose from 170,500 up to 185,000.

Figures from the Labor Statistics Bureau in 2006 showed that women consist of 27-29% of the IT workforce. Even more, a 2013 report from National Public Radio revealed that around 20% of American computer programmers are women. However, in open source systems, only 10% of programmers are female. A gender-diverse workforce is more probable to create products which meet individuals' requirements. When females are underrepresented, it means that technical decisions are founded on men's experiences, sentiments, and judgment, causing male-slanted bias (Howley and Trube, 2014).

Additionally, evaluations of research targeting gender-diverse IT teams show that gender-distributed groups are more productive, creative, and capable of remaining on schedule plus within budget, in comparison to homogenous teams, whereas other research review indicate that the outcomes are mixed, with various other studies indicating no result, non-corresponding results or even adverse results of gender variety on team activity.

Studies done by McKinsey and Company revealed that businesses with females in top level administration were more financially stable. In comparison, review of a sample of various major American firms showed minimal effect of adding women on financial productivity, these varied outcomes give no definite evidence concerning the advantages of diversity. Publications further reveal that lack of proper participation of women in computing exempting them from the "modern economy," which requires sophisticated IT abilities in exchange for top salary positions (HowleyandTrube, 2014).

10.2.4. Insights into Choosing Mentors

Mentors are useful because, apart from providing knowledge in their computer field, they also have links with business professionals besides, most significantly, they're keen to share the information and contacts they know. Individuals who mentor are most probable to have passed through mentors at some stage themselves, who assisted them to understand the computer industry better, refine their strengths or polish skills.

The mentor and mentee relationship is mostly symbiotic. It's key to have in mind that this works as a dual-way relationship. Even though you're seeking to benefit personally from the mentor, still you're also helping the mentor in one way or another. Though many at times the mentee looks like they're getting the greater part of the agreement, the individual performing the mentoring derives something from it, too.

They get to directly impact other people's lives for the better. Through helping another individual to succeed, the mentors contribute in creating a promising future for everyone, thus gaining the satisfaction of realizing that they have made a big difference in somebody's life. With that mentioned, mentees must also do whatever they can to assist their mentors. Case in point, a younger mentee might be more skilled in forming a digital brand or becoming a social influencer. Skills which they can share with their mentors to empower them as well (Westergaard, 2016).

10.2.5. Qualities to Check in Mentors

The attributes that contribute to a great mentor basically are those which describe a good leader. These include: being understanding and knowledgeable, a great listener and amicable. Additionally, the mentor that you choose must have some passion for teaching/ coaching. Note that it's not every leader or instructor who's good in mentoring, however all commendable mentors identify the best ways of training and inspiring, without any sort of criticism, plus are always supportive. In choosing a mentor, search for those qualities, plus observe the individual for a while to see whether these qualities stand up.

10.2.6. How Mentors Can Build Your IT Career

Getting a mentor is crucial no matter your age or status. Everybody needs a person from outside who can share insights and experiences for helping their career. Mentors can assist you to see the 'larger picture."

According to some scholars, the best way to enjoy what life has to offer and be fruitful is to constantly learn. The objective is "learning the correct things at the appropriate time," which can best be achieved through a mentor. Nevertheless, having a mentor is not a one-size for everyone situation. Though it's great if you can find just one person who provides everything you need career-wise, most people in IT have in fact two or more mentors serving different purposes.

For instance, you may get a mentor for handling technology questions, where you may inquire from them what kinds of technologies are trending and another mentor who's a specialist with management matters.

Another example could include an IT expert who has participated in computer infrastructure for many years, but needs to get into development. Getting a mentor with solid programming skills may offer insight concerning what programming techniques the business is investing in, or certifications and courses that you must take in order to become relevant to the firm's needs.It's very important to get a mentor who's in the IT field. Getting a mentor within this sort of environment permits you to check where your company is heading, plus then you may start to develop your skills and experience in the fields they'll most require you in the next few years.

Getting a senior individual in your business mentor you may help to open new doors, whether it's gaining insight into what kind of training shall be most favorable to you, or the mundane items such as dealing with problematic clients or traders, or even presenting your skills whenever a fresh job opening comes up. A good number of promotions in the IT field are as a direct result of mentoring.

10.2.7. Identifying a Mentor

Identifying a mentor isn't an activity that is to be handled lightly. A decent mentor can provide advice on a long-term basis, meaning choosing the wrong person can really waste your time. The individual not only needs to have the expertise and skills for propelling their career forward, though you also must have some good chemistry with the person.

Being a mentee, you need to objectively assess your skills and accept constructive criticism coming from your mentor. Also, delve into your strategic-thinking skills and examine your career goals. It is important to understand your strengths and weakness to determine where a mentor may provide the greatest help. Before seeking a mentor, determine what your goals are from the association including the aspects that you wish to cover (such as job search, confidence building, and skills development.)

Having that understanding, weigh your abilities and weaknesses against the business's goals. This can give you a great idea of the merits you are searching for in the mentor. Let us say your business makes majority of its sales through salespeople, though the firm wants to create a more robust online marketplace in order to develop a fresh revenue stream. Getting a mentor who sincerely understands online marketing and optimization can help place you in a quick lane to responsibilities which take you somewhere you didn't even expect.

10.2.8. Where to Find Mentors

The initial place to begin is your company's HR department. Determine if it has some formal or informal mentorship program and allow a representative to know that you're interested. Besides, there are other venues to look at. Generally, the areas you can discover mentors have enhanced greatly following the creation of social media. With that mentioned, the tested 'look around you' networking with associates and colleagues is equally a great technique.

If your business doesn't have any mentoring policy in place, but you still have the wish to contribute as a change agent, then simply visit your HR department and tell them that you want to assist in setting up the plan. The most unfortunate outcome that can occur is them replying no.

The other option is using networking sites to identify people in your region who practice the job that you are seeking. Social media websites, such as LinkedIn or Facebook's Branchout, have been identified as great places to get mentors and groups having similar interests within your region. Most times, just identifying or asking the right individual is all that is required.

10.2.9. Get Things Rolling

Once you have been introduced plus getting ready to see your new mentor. Keep in mind that it is a professional relationship involving a business advisor, rather than a friendship arrangement. Thus, it must to be handled as such. Always be on time, keep in mind some specific questions, put some personal objects aside and perform your best in keeping the meeting straightforward. How regularly you meet, what to discussion and how to stay in touch must all be deliberated and agreed upon with your mentor. They will be different based on the established goals and scheduling plans. In some instances, there will be periods when a short-term objective is looming plus you should meet more often. Irrespective, you must establish a specific schedule and be flexible.

Gaining and working together with a mentor may seem like a formidable task, nonetheless you must start somewhere. Check around and identify what assets are accessible to you. You don't need to go too far. Though even if you achieve so, most IT experts who've had mentors recognize that the mileage really was worth it. Sometimes you may go somewhere that you didn't anticipate in the first place.

10.3. COACHING IN COMPUTER SCIENCE AND IT PROFESSIONS

Figure 10.3.IT coaching can be provided to anyone regardless of their age or gender.

Source: https://bataviapubliclibrary.org/computerclasses/.

Statistics show that Big Data will grow 800% over the coming decade. With the ongoing exit of boomers from business, there is heightened need for IT directors to coach teams to handle a quickly changing technology landscape. They also need to implement strategies which shall exceed customer expectations.

Computer professionals are often faced with bigger demands for rapid replies. They should understand how to register clients and users, who different from themselves, don't recognize the technology which they're using (Pask, Roger, Joy, and Barrie, 2007).

Besides, they must register IT teams in handling major IT change projects, while developing ways of coordinating major projects which have various interdependencies and need collaboration and coordination. In today's digital environment, IT coaching is an ability that can hasten the professional development as well as career achievement of a person.

10.3.1. Relevant Coaching Skills to Help Mentors Move IT Programs and Teams Forward

Mastering enrollment: Learn how to successfully engage your team so that they comprehend the true worth of a project. Most IT experts are happy when they don't need to actively talk with clients. Coaching your teammates to engage other people shall make their work a lot simpler. Here, engagement means being in a position to interact and connect with others, and then aligning on what's required as well as inquiry into really understanding what other people want. Finally, it involves to be in a position to positively share how they'll help the users or clients' expectations, plus what action shall be taken.

Talk so individuals can listen: Always learn to listen as well as speak the dialect of your clients, so that they can develop more interest in hearing whatever you need to say. Some people really don't have listening skills – they can't wait to speak or share their perspective. But when we listen intently, then we can react back to others in methods that create trust and healthy working relationships. Furthermore, coaching team mates these valued listening skills can greatly minimize the emotional stress which is tied to various IT matters.

Consider style flexing techniques: There are various different personality types, cultures, and generations functioning together in the modern IT environment. Invest some time to learn various styles and coach the teams to practice applying their style to achieve and match those of other members. Whenever we can communicate through our preferred choice of connecting and thinking, then productivity also improves due to increased understanding and relationship.

Welcome conflict: Coach IT teams so that they can be able to willing have tough conversations, so as to address conflicts. When individuals are coached how to settle conflict successfully, then there's less conflict at the workplace. Handling conflict means that they should be willing to set aside their "side" of a situation, besides be willing to consider alternative perspectives. Groups should be coached how to consider ways of reconciling, and achieving alignment plus be open to checking new options and viewpoints.

Seek accountability of all results: IT experts deal in digital information and rarely see grey zones. Coaching teams to check all outcomes from a point of neutrality will help them in discovering additional choices and options, so as to avoid problems going into the future. This needs time to relax and check before advancing forward. IT careers have high demand on both time and resources. Nevertheless, through coaching your team so that they can take time to pause and check what worked as well as what didn't work on a particular project, they shall be better enabled for the future.Steadily moving onward in your career can be a challenge plus the IT sector is especially daunting. Due to its many aspects, you must be continuously learning and advancing – though it doesn't leave sufficient time for career development. If you feel as if something's amiss in your computer career, then you're not alone. Roughly 70% of workers aren't engaged or motivated by their work, based on a 2013 study by Gallup's State of the U.S. Workplace Report. Though there are some IT professionals who would be happy to simply wade through the day, others are ready to wrestle with problems to advance to the next phase in their career.

It doesn't matter whether you're attempting to switch over to another position, seeking to be hired or only thinking about lasting improvement, a good career coach can assist you to discover what you're best at and areas that need improvement.

10.3.2. What It Requires to Become a Computer Leader

Figure 10.4. A mentor showing employees how to solve computer problems.

Source: https://johnmattone.com/how-to-measure-business-coaching-success/.

The basis of IT leadership lies in delivery; indeed, it's table stakes towards becoming a trailblazer in any organization. The next phase is advancing from just delivering what's asked, to comprehending both the client as well as problem statement, in order to deliver what's desirable. Besides, you must be able to inspire and deliver results through other individuals—whether they are colleagues or not. Ultimately, you improve on strategy, both comprehending where your company is headed and straightening your IT strategy, or influencing corporate strategy.

That's quite something to accomplish, however you don't need to go at it by yourself. If indeed you intend to progress to the higher levels of IT, then the truth is that creating a strategic blueprint for your career development is essential for lasting success and applicability—it's where a professional career coach gets in (Pask, Roger, Joy, and Barrie, 2007).

Many IT experts are technologists. There is great need for computer experts to be business-minded, effective communicators as well as strategic in planning. IT experts can't hide behind the anonymity of technology, since the consumerization aspect of IT, flexibility, and open cloud has empowered companies to go around computing if necessary in order to achieve certain objectives.

10.3.3. The Work of Career Coaches

Career coaches aren't necessarily meant to help you land a new job. In fact, a good coach mostly holds up a mirror where you can watch yourself and your circumstance with fresh clarity. Career coaching concentrates on your skilled growth and development. Basically, it allows you to expand your insight of established goals, objectives, gifts, weaknesses, aspirations, and obstacles.

This may include getting a different work internally or outside the firm. It may comprise refining your performance in the current state. It might also focus on reshaping how you watch your situation to improve your fulfillment or minimize on stress. One of the recurrent themes in IT is that nobody knows your career better than you do. But not everyone believes this is true (Pask, Roger, Joy, and Barrie, 2007).

Only a few individuals know their careers or actually have some idea regarding what they've done which is most crucial– plus most valuable – in order to be employers. Seeking advice with the appropriate career coach may help a customer clarify those achievements, and gain practical confidence in presentation before an interview panel.

Additionally, good career coaches can help somebody in any sector or profession, whether it is IT or any other related disciplines. Typically, a career coach with personal experience within your chosen field can assist you much faster, as compared to one who lacks experience. Up to that level, the coach may bring sector-specific aspects and instances into the conversation for purposes of illustrating matters and opportunities, likewise they can allow you to check your situation more candidly and faster (Pask, Roger, Joy, and Barrie, 2007).

10.3.4. Difference between It Career Coaches and Other Mentors

You might think you already got a mentor so what's the reason for getting a career coach, also? The coach normally comes from an external space and even worked with individuals at all career levels. However, there may still be some overlap.

Majority of mentors are highly-experienced professionals who provide advice to the less-practiced professionals regarding how to handle circumstances with which they don't have a lot of experience. Coaches, alternatively, concentrate more on enabling self-discovery and issue-solving. Practically, most effectual mentors do coaching on the side while coaches with strong industry experience may also perform some mentoring.

According to IT experts, the ages, duties, positions, objectives, and wishes of each professional is as varied as the persons themselves. Therefore, objectives often vary from one individual to the next depending on exactly what they wish to achieve, plus their range of experience and knowledge.

10.3.5. Advantages of Hiring a Coach

Transparency: The most significant thing coaching delivers is clarity – touching on past achievements and future goals. Failure to have clarity concerning where you've been, or where you're heading and where you intend to be is a typical matter with many career seekers not only persons in the technology sector. Working with a respectable career coach shall help to expedite a wider viewpoint about your situation, including the best ways to respond towards certain situations. They need to work alongside you to reveal that clarity, establish goals and identify or take advantage of fresh opportunities (Westergaard, 2016).

Mentees will quickly learn to become strategic in their computer career vs. taking a tactical approach. For instance, how both present and future roles can lead to solutions which constructively affect profits and efficiencies, navigating, and understanding the political realm of business, or ways of approaching a job search or interview for a computer position.

This kind of clarity may help mentees to discover what really motivates them. Including helping them to uncover a professional path they hadn't considered beforehand. You will know what subjects motivate you, so as to always put them in mind. Case in point, it's simple to assume a HR role since it's "the logical thing," but you must ensure that it's equally a great fit for you. Human resource doesn't need to be your only route to success, there are other paths that can lead you to corporate success as well (Westergaard, 2016).

Self-confidence: Sufficient amounts of confidence will help you shine out during interviews for taking up a fresh role. Understanding what you've done – realizing what you've actually achieved – makes the interview procedure a different matter. Being able to plainly articulate one's accomplishments, actual value, instantly puts a job-seeker apart. Especially when an IT professional wants to advance over to higher ranks within the company.

Achieving goals quicker and more constantly: The one mutual benefit that IT specialists who hire a coach attain is that their objectives and goals are reached more quickly, plus more frequently compared to those that don't. Mentees become better at managing their teams, engaging with peers, customer engagement and other job related tasks. Additionally, coaching is useful for handling personal matters that affect computer professionals, such as work life balance, stress, and relationships.

Privacy: Another major difference between mentors and career coaches is that mentors operate within the same firm you do, plus will offer input to your supervisor/or HR department concerning your career development. Contrarily, coaching agreements specifically create a "silence policy" while assuring you total confidentiality on your part and the coach. Confidentiality is absolutely crucial for IT coaches, they take protecting their clients' matters very seriously.

10.3.6. Access to Modern Tools and Procedures for Improving Job Performance

It's sometimes difficult to improve your computer skills without knowing where to start. A career coach can work alongside you to reveal your gifts and weaknesses, while also help you develop a plan for bridging the skills gap, and, tap into your strengths. Furthermore, coaches can act as accountability partners, working together with the client to create and abide by the commitments made.

10.3.7. Finding a Computer Career Coach

When looking for an IT coach try consulting together with some few experts to identify the one who you feel you've developed the best rapport with. They must be able to show that they got in place an organized process for expertly learning about you, the situation you're in and overall goals. Some questions that may help include: asking the coach for some short synopsis about their experience, whether they're credentialed and total number of clients that they've worked with

Word-of-mouth and references are effective ways of locating reliable career coaches. Preferably, ask friends and coworkers, industry leaders and specialists about their opinion. Oftentimes, your individual HR business can also direct you to resources. Furthermore, you can search social media sites like LinkedIn and industry journals for writings by career coaches, plus keep up with them towards making presentations at business conferences.

Equally important is fostering a positive relationship/chemistry between the coach and trainees. The most crucial part of any coaching activity is connection. Therefore, it's vital to discuss for around 20 to 30 minutes, so as to find out if indeed there's a connection with the. If absent, just consider moving on. Yet another ideal way to go is finding established career coaches who online, through social media or blogging, and following their content. Upon finding a specific blogger who resounds with you, consider reaching out to them (Westergaard, 2016).

10.3.8. Digital Career Coaching

Professionals, such as those in tech, continuously look for methods of improving their resumes and enhancing their skill sets. Because of tech talent deficiency and skills gap, many tech professionals don't have enough room to develop, despite having enough reasons for doing so. There are various ways to improve technical skills, though online boot-camps aren't as useful when addressing lack of proper soft skills, or charting a career path. This is a void which online career coaches seek to fulfill.

Digital career coaches can offer one-on-one assistance to an expert seeking for work, or enhancing their present standing. Online coaching can occur through nearly any method apart from in-person meetings, comprising of email and smartphone. The procedure can aid with various professional topics, such as career development, leadership development and team alignment.

In comparison to live career coaching, digital coaching allows the IT professional to operate in their individual space. Communicating over the phone rather than individually can lessen anxiety, promoting more open exchanges between the professional and coach. Indeed, there are options for talking through webcam to coaches, or even peers in the computing field. Some career coaches claim that they are able to get more direct with customers in a digital setting, which can be a good thing, allowing the individual getting the coaching to think about the conversation while deepening the learning as well.

10.3.9. Is Coaching Necessary for Tech Pros?

Tech experts will need a coach way more than experts from other fields due to how fast-moving the sector is. Coaches can competently use assessment metrics to detect gifts and weaknesses that a person has, both in regards to personality and knowledge sets.

They could also help professionals understand how a particular skill may be utilized in different ways, or even when searching for a new computer job (Westergaard, 2016).

Tech players may require the additional support from coaches in order to develop effective plans on their goals and skill sets. Generally, individuals from the technology industry focus more on hard skills, instead of focusing on soft skills which are presently in high demand. When a company has determined that they have enough hard-techy skills, what makes an employee to stand out past that requirement is soft skills which can be acquired through coaching.

Digital career coaching can help enhance soft skills, currently growing in popularity among computer companies. Nearly two-thirds of HR officials have withheld technology job offers coming from otherwise competent candidates since they lack necessary soft skills, a particular report found. Oftentimes, technical specialists are introverts who must acquire extravert skills, so as to be fruitful in the workplace.

Similarly, career coaching can be very helpful in steering through workplace culture, including the challenges which emerge with it. It may also assist with other types of personal development, such as building up a career path. Getting a career coach may also assist unemployed specialists get hired. Roughly 80% of individuals who pass through coaching programs perform better at work, they also get job opportunities and promotions 60% quicker than the nationwide average.

Their organizations also enjoy success with regards to productivity and earning potential (Westergaard, 2016).

For digital career coaches, there are certain factors that you must consider before making the decision to hire them. IT professionals must look for coaches with sufficient industry knowhow, including professional accreditations and coaching experience.

Ideally, the best computer coaches must have some blend of tactical instruction – they should lead learners towards a discovery journey—such as asking them 'what do you imagine you'll gain if you pursue that path?' Getting somebody you trust and who has enough experience to assist you in improving is crucial.

Preferably, search for areas which match professionals with coaches depending on compatibility levels. The goal is creating a trusted advisory relationship, which may take time to create, however getting a solid working relationship and handling principles such as confidentially can also make a huge difference.

10.3.10. Types of Coaches

First, an IT coach may be well worth any money that you spend depending on how you use their services. The idea is getting the best coach and being ready to perform the required work. As it's often said, any plan without effort or execution is merely a dream. The initial step is discovering the ideal coach based on their specific area of operation. While all kinds of coaches can offer great value, the idea is getting a coach who can fulfill your needs. Generally, career coaching can be categorized into two classes, which include tactical and strategic. But there are others as well who can be approached.

- Tactical coaches: They focus on the mechanics that involve helping their customers find new openings. Tactical coaches can help you refine your resume, discover job openings, learn new interviewing techniques, broaden your perspective of probable career directions plus other similar duties. In effect, their particular role is helping people find new prospects or opportunities.
- Strategic coaches: These primarily focus on offering long-term career counsel. They regularly work with individuals who are presently employed in IT, but would want help and guidance regarding how to steer their careers forward, possibly over several years.
- Executive coaches: They provide career counsel to their clients, though have the wider role of assisting their customers to make better business decisions, steer through corporate politics, and overcoming job-related challenges tied to their present job role.
- Life coaches: They are same as executive coaches, but the main difference is rather than helping you to steer your career, they assist you to navigate through your life generally, which might include career-based matters or otherwise.

All the coaching forms previously mentioned work directly with the clients, plus are paid and considerably simple to find since, like other experts, they mostly market their services. Moreover, your objective must be finding a coach that you have rapport with, provides quality advice, or is working within your budget.

Just like most professions, the fee range for IT coaches varies considerably based on the population they serve, coaching field, time put in and achievements as a practiced coach, including other individual and professional matters. Take note that, same as in many professional services, cost doesn't always directly relate to quality (Westergaard, 2016).

10.3.11. Points to Remember About Career Coaching

Figure 10.5. Group coaching fosters teamwork and collaboration among staff.

Source: https://www.shutterstock.com/fr/video/clip-1027633976-african-american-mentor-leader-coach-teaching-team.

The job market is rough for individuals without work, including those with jobs but working jobs they are not happy with. To put it into perspective, based on the most recent unemployment data, around 11.8 million individuals in the US are unemployed. Besides, there are probably millions more with gigs which they would leave (Pask, Roger, Joy, and Barrie, 2007).

Luckily, for those in the computer field, there is a significant number of experts out there that can help to make your search much easier. These specialists have mastered the art and skill of career counseling. As such, a career coach will help prepare you to successfully compete against the millions of other similar job seekers in computing disciplines. Whether it's landing a new position or advancing to greater levels.

To understand career coaching, it must be viewed in two angles which are the coaching itself and counseling. The objective is supporting individuals in making more informed decisions concerning their career development, as well as trajectory, including providing various tools which they can apply. These tools include polished résumés, LinkedIn profiles, and presentations to achieve their desired career goals.

Even though not every career coach has clinical training, descriptions of the field—including the work—can still vary among the traditionally trained coaches. Generally, "coaching" seems to focus on a solution-oriented system, which comprises working with customers to determine what concrete measures they can take towards achieving profession objectives (Pask, Roger, Joy, and Barrie, 2007).

"Counseling," nevertheless, is more process determined—you determine whether there are certain behavioral, emotional, and psychological matters that might be inhibiting an individual's desired career goals. Though the fundamental benefit of IT career coaching is helping people to review their professional circumstances with a higher degree of honesty, empathy, care, and curiosity. Furthermore, there's the popular concept that you just have to attend one career-coaching program and your job issues shall be resolved. It in fact takes around 8 to 10hrs of comprehensive counseling for the average client to start internalizing the primary benefits of coaching.

Largely, clients can anticipate to achieve career confidence, inspiration, encouragement, and insight through coaching. They must also feel like the coaching activity gives them the chance to relax somewhat. Career advancement or job search can cause a fair ratio of anxiety, vulnerability, and fear in persons. It's the duty of a computer coach to work with customers to unpack those emotions, in order to better comprehend how these factors could be keeping them fixed in their respective careers.

Additionally, there are various assessments which career coaches can apply to help consumers, like personality tests, accomplishment exercises and interest inventories which identify what individuals are most proud about in their profession, including job-description analyses which can identify the type of work and jobsites which are the most ideal for a person (Pask, Roger, Joy, and Barrie, 2007).

Some coaches also encourage constructive feedback coming from friends and family. Clients can be encouraged to circulate certain questions to colleagues or loved ones, plus have the replies instantly directed to the coach, so that they can prepare a report that the client can review—and potentially contemplate.

Many experts believe that IT career coaching may be useful at any point of the individual's professional path, constructive career coaching during the early college years or directly post-college may put persons on more concrete footing—not only with a nicely prepared résumé and convenient career path, instead also with the mindset which helps them to comprehend that the job path of today isn't as straight as it may have been during previous generations.

There are various career frustrations which computer professionals go through, but this shouldn't come as a surprise to anyone. Sentiments like "I hate the job, but don't see what else is there to do!" are quite common in the IT field. However, what may be quite surprising to some people is that there are also some lines such as "I've got no idea on what to do with my computer skills," or "I need assistance pinpointing what precisely I want to pursue—and ways of getting there.

Job-search anxiety is equally something that coaches frequently encounter, which may also come from professionals who want to switch over to a new company or sector of IT. Besides, there has been an ever-rising population of clients who express issues with using various social media sites, particularly LinkedIn, as aiding towards their career objectives. With help from a coach, you can beat these unnecessary anxieties and set yourself up on the trajectory towards success. Within just a few days of working alongside the coach, you will gain relevant skills in the computer industry to get a coveted job or progress your career in another way (Pask, Roger, Joy, and Barrie, 2007).

Organizational culture and worker attitude bear a significant impact on an individual's sense of career satisfaction. In fact, some experts believe organizational culture forms the single greater factor for career growth in the 21st century. For instance, Google, and Zappos are all companies which are proactive in nurturing a positive, calm, non-hierarchical, and largely enjoyable job environment. These businesses encourage workers to perform things that are beyond the typical work description, whether this is volunteering, or just creating an improved work-life balance. These factors are sure to develop an individual's sense of job satisfaction, just provided they're in the correct job to start with.

Moreover, somebody who is open to fresh ideas, ready to walk out of their comfort zone and encouraged to pursue the work which constitutes the job-search, as well as job-change process. In addition, a decent client allows their coach to act as a partner for the entire process. Furthermore, it is actually vital since there are multiple complex steps along the journey, whether it's a rough job market, or even lengthy career change. As such, clients must reach out for assistance and get help as is necessary—right from the coach as well as everybody else within their personal and professional networks—so as to succeed.

10.3.12. Factors That Can Diminish the Effectiveness of Career Coaching

There are various factors which can reduce the value of the computer career-coaching process, right from its onset up to the finish, such as extreme anxiety, low self-confidence, depression, fear, and overall resistance to change.

Sometimes, even recognizing the intensity of depression that a person is going through may be hard, especially for those working in IT fields since they often interact more with computers as compared to people. For such people, coaches typically recommended seeking medical assistance from a mental health practitioner, and within a short period they will be indeed motivated to concentrate on their respective careers.

Apart from those factors, some people are no longer performing the work because they engage in an exhaustive job search or are no longer motivated. For instance, a professional can still sabotage the process through failure.

Such a person may apply for the ideal job but fail to follow up only to see the opportunity may disappear. For career coaches, nothing compares to getting clients to gradually notice that there's real hope for the situation they're facing, especially after having begun their career growth process, only to be left feeling dejected and hopeless.

However, with the proper guidance, there are cases where people in IT have gone from feelings or disenchantment to better prospects in their career and job opportunities—even indifferent and unmotivated to improve their conditions—to feeling newly inspired and encouraged to advance forward with fresh ideas. In case you were to choose a "Golden Rule" for your career satisfaction, then what shall it be?

If you are doing something that you indeed enjoy, then it shouldn't feel as if it is work. Preferably, you must feel some sense of conformity around your job and personal values. Basically, it's only in the arena of overlap—which might or might not align to your perception of role in the globe—that a real sense of career satisfaction or fulfillment gets possible. If indeed you want a profession that brings about fulfillment, then matching your work with personal values is crucial. In case you already get fulfillment from the IT job that you hold, then the work is certainly an extension of personal values which you already have.

10.4. COUNSELING IN COMPUTER SCIENCE AND IT PROFESSIONS

10.4.1. What Does It Involve?

Career counseling refers to job-based kinds of counseling. It combines providing advice on certain topics of expertise such as IT, using counseling techniques which support clients in reaching complex decisions or facing tough situations. Career counseling mostly focuses on how individuals manage their lifestyles and everyday work. It comprises of career exploration, managing career changes, lifetime career development, plus handling other career-related matters. There's no fixed description of career counseling globally, mostly because of conceptual, cultural as well as linguistic differences. Nevertheless, the term 'IT career counseling' usually refers to professional intercession that's performed either individually or in a manage group.

There's also substantial deviation in the terminology which is used universally to define this activity. Apart from the linguistic disparity between American English (counseling) and UK English (counseling), still there are various other alternate phrases which are in joint use. They include: guidance counseling, career guidance, personal guidance and career consulting among others (Westergaard, 2016).

It typically leads to commentators combining multiple terms, such as, career counseling and guidance for inclusivity. Nevertheless, care must be practiced when shifting from one vocabulary to another since each phrase has its unique history and cultural implication.

Current empirical research corroborates the efficacy of career counseling. Practiced career counselors can help IT individuals with career-related problems. With their experience in career development as well as labor markets, they may put an individual's qualifications, experience, gifts, and shortcomings in a wide perspective while also factoring their preferred salary, individual hobbies and interests, geographical site, job market as well as academic possibilities (Westergaard, 2016).

Through professional counseling as well as teaching skills, career counselors can moreover support individuals in gaining more understanding of what actually matters for them individually, how to plan their IT professions independently, or assist them in making difficult decisions and scaling through conditions of crisis.

Lastly, career counselors are typically capable of assisting their clients to find suitable jobs, solving conflicts with their supervisors, or getting support from other useful services. It's because of these different advantages of IT career counseling that in some countries companies publicly fund guidance solutions. For instance, the EU realizes that career counseling and guidance are useful instrument for effectively combating social exclusion, as well as improving citizens' employability.

10.4.2. What the Future Portends

Scholars expect that by 2020, everybody shall be chatting with — and not just via — their computers. The importance for computer counselors, he mentions, is that computers shall be equipped with software allowing the machines to reply to their owners' questions.

Rather than live counselors being the first option for individuals with mental problems, career, relationship, and other issues, in the near future scholars believe that individuals will be able to ask personal avatar "counselors" on their workstations for feedback and counsel. The personal digital counselor shall be stocked with useful information, therefore offering constructive and useful advice. In case the artificial counselor determines that the individual has an issue beyond the scale of assistance that the computer provides, it may recommend that the individual sees an actual counselor (Westergaard, 2016).

From the bare look, that prediction seems disturbing, like advancing technology may potentially make counseling as a profession obsolete. Still, experts contend that virtual counselors will become vital to the profession since there just won't be sufficient human counselors to sustain the rising demand, meanwhile as the world turns to become more complicated and everyday life gets filled with progressively challenging issues and decisions. Many individuals will require help in making solid decisions concerning their lives. As such, the role of counseling shall become considerably important (Westergaard, 2016).

10.4.3. Who Requires Career Counseling?

Figure 10.6. Career counseling can help IT professionals discover their potential.

Source: https://bohatala. com/career-counseling/.

Career counseling is appropriate to nearly everyone in IT. You don't need to be in a learning institution to consult with a career counselor. You may be a college freshman, or somebody who intends to make variations in their selected career. What's evident is that the sooner you use career counseling services, it would be much simpler to achieve whatever you want to achieve.

Furthermore, you don't have to be in a situation whereby you don't have any clue on where you'd wish to take your life to career speaking. An IT career counselor may also be valuable for resolving conflicts, or turning around unconstructive situations like your inability to register onto a course that you applied for (Westergaard, 2016).

Basically, a career counselor works as another ear. It's somebody who listen to you, but isn't tied to you neither your family. Though they won't attempt to force you into following their footsteps. There's nothing more overbearing than being somewhat unsure about your next educational or career steps, just for one to be pressurized by peers to take up a course which they aren't interested in. By working with an IT career counselor you'll discover more about your actual strengths and interests. Additionally, working with a counselor can help you make the appropriate choice and pick a field that matches your skills and experience levels.

When properly harnessed, career counseling outcomes can determine your future. Career coaching has the ability to modify your life outlook and capacity to succeed. Career development is considered to be a lifelong process that never stops throughout your professional life. Factors, such as personal preferences, skills, background, and life circumstances can all affect the career choices of someone who wants to pursue computers as a lifelong discipline.

Turning to counselors for advice isn't something you to be ashamed about. It is an invaluable step in your career growth. By making the bold move to consult with a counselor, you are seeking not only assistance to step out of some tricky situation, but also guidance on ways to take your career to a much higher level. Always remember that IT career development is substantially more than simply deciding on the particular field which you wish to follow on (Westergaard, 2016).

References

1. Aimee, H.,& Mary, B. T., (2014). Mentoring for the Professions: Orienting Toward the Future (p. 399). Cape Town: IAP.
2. Berzai, L., (2019). Ethical Problems in Computing. Retrieved from comptia.org: https://www.comptia.org/blog/ethical-problems-in-computing (accessed on 19 March 2020).
3. Boothby, W. H., (2018). New Technologies and the Law in War and Peace (pp.16–43). New York: Cambridge University Press.
4. Bott, F., (2005). Professional Issues in Information Technology (pp. 1–75). London: BCS, The Chartered Institute.
5. Bradley, G., (2017). The Good ICT Society: From Theory to Actions (pp. 1–101). London: Taylor & Francis.
6. Butterfield, J., (2016). Illustrated Course Guides: Professionalism – Soft Skills for a Digital Workplace, 2e (pp. 1–73).Massachusetts: Cengage Learning.
7. Byrne, E.F.,& Joseph C. P., (2012). Technological Transformation: Contextual and Conceptual Implications (pp. 16–81).Berlin: Springer Science & Business Media.
8. Freedman, J., (2011). Careers in Computer Science and Programming

(pp. 5–74). New York: The Rosen Publishing Group, Inc,.

9. Goldberg, J., (2002). Great Jobs for Computer Science Majors 2nd Edn. (p. 224). New York: McGraw Hill Professional,.
10. Haftor, D., (2010). Information and Communication Technologies, Society and Human Beings: Theory and Framework (Festschrift in honor of Gunilla Bradley): Theory and Framework (Festschrift in honor of Gunilla Bradley) (pp. 1–71). Pennsylvania: Idea Group Inc (IGI).
11. Irma Becerra-Fernandez,& Rajiv, S., (2014). Knowledge Management: Systems and Processes (pp. 3–15). London: Routledge.
12. Jaschik, S., (2018). Furor on Claim Women's Choices Create Gender Gap in Comp Sci. Retrieved from inside highered: https://www.insidehighered.com/news/2018/06/25/lecturers-explanation-gender-gap-computer-science-it-reflect-womens-choices (accessed on 19 March 2020).
13. John, W.,& Richard, L., (2013). Professionalism in the Information and Communication Technology Industry (pp. 5–95). Canberra: ANU E Press.
14. Ehrlinger, J., Plant, E. A., Hartwig, M. K., Vossen, J. J., Columb, C. J., & Brewer, L. E. (2018). Do gender differences in perceived prototypical computer scientists and engineers contribute to gender gaps in computer science and engineering?. Sex roles, 78(1-2), 40-51.
15. Kizza, J. M., (2007). Ethical and Social Issues in the Information Age (pp. 19–64).Berlin: Springer Science & Business Media.
16. Maier, R., (2007). Knowledge Management Systems: Information and Communication Technologies for Knowledge Management (pp. 18–114).Berlin: Springer Science & Business Media.
17. Maria, C.,& Sarah, T., (2018). Gender and STEM: Understanding Segregation in Science, Technology, Engineering and Mathematics (p. 284). Basel, Switzerland: MDPI.
18. Niver, H. M., (2015). Careers for Tech Girls in Computer Science (pp. 9–60). New York: The Rosen Publishing Group, Inc.
19. Nonaka, I., (2005). Knowledge Management: Critical Perspectives on Business and Management, (Volume 3, pp. 42–79).London: Taylor & Francis.
20. O'Regan, G., (2018). World of Computing: A Primer Companion for

the Digital Age (pp. 1–75). Berlin: Springer.

21. Pask, Roger, Joy, & Barrie. (2007). Mentoring-Coaching: A Guide For Education Professionals: A Handbook for Education Professionals (p. 261). London: McGraw-Hill Education (UK).
22. Patrick, V. Z., Adrian, E., & Adrian, S., (2013). Regulating Technology: International Harmonization and Local Realities (pp. 1–99). London: Routledge.
23. Penny, D., Simon, J., & Barry, G. B., (2008). Ethical, Legal and Professional Issues in Computing (pp. 1–79). London: Cengage Learning EMEA.
24. Proenza, F. J., (2015). Public Access ICT Across Cultures: Diversifying Participation in the Network Society (pp. 1–9). Massachusetts: MIT Press.
25. Reins, L., (2019). Regulating New Technologies in Uncertain Times (pp. 3–104). Berlin: Springer.
26. Shinder, D., (2005). Ethical Issues for IT Security Professionals. Retrieved from Computer World: https://www.computerworld.com/article/2557944/ethical-issues-for-it-security-professionals.html (accessed on 19 March 2020).
27. Skillspanorama, (2016). ICT Professionals: Skills Opportunities and Challenges (2016). Retrieved from Skillspanorama: https://skillspanorama.cedefop.europa.eu/en/analytical_highlights/ict-professionals-skills-opportunities-and-challenges-2016 (accessed on 19 March 2020).
28. Sreekumar, T. T., (2011). ICTs and Development in India: Perspectives on the Rural Network Society (pp. 33–86).London: Anthem Press.
29. Stephen, G. N., & Ariela, S., (2012). The Impact of Emerging Technologies on Computer Science and Operations Research (pp. 1–85).Berlin: Springer Science & Business Media.
30. Trauth & Eileen M., (2006). Encyclopedia of Gender and Information Technology (pp. 1–50).Pennsylvania: Idea Group Inc (IGI).
31. Wallace, D. P., (2007). Knowledge Management: Historical and Cross-Disciplinary Themes (pp. 1–93). London: Libraries Unlimited.
32. Waltraud, E.,& Ilona, H., (2014). Gender in Science and Technology: Interdisciplinary Approaches (pp. 20–109). London: Transcript Verlag.
33. Westergaard, J., (2016). An Introduction to Helping Skills: Counselling,

Coaching and Mentoring (pp. 1–87). London: SAGE.

34. WetFeet, (2009). Careers in Information Technology (p.80). San Francisco: Wetfeet, Inc.

INDEX

J

K

L

M

N

O

P